D1001049

DUQUESNE UNIVERSITY
The Gumberg Library
Gift of

Dr. Wallace S. Watson
Emeritus Professor of English
Dean, College of Liberal Arts
and Sciences (1985-1990)

The Crisis of Political Modernism

D. N. RODOWICK

The Crisis of
Political Modernism

Criticism and Ideology in
Contemporary Film Theory

University of Illinois Press
Urbana and Chicago

For Edward Brian Lowry

Publication of this work was supported in part by a grant from the Andrew W. Mellon Foundation.

© 1988 by the Board of Trustees of the University of Illinois
Manufactured in the United States of America
C 5 4 3 2 1

This book is printed on acid-free paper.

Library of Congress Cataloging-in-Publication Data

Rodowick, David Norman.
    The crisis of political modernism.

    1. Film criticism. I. Title.
PN1995.R618   1988   791.43'01'5   88-4735
ISBN 0-252-01533-9 (alk. paper)

Contents

Acknowledgments

Acknowledgments always attest that a book is never the product of one author. And this book has benefited especially from the contributions of many friends and colleagues.

There is little doubt that this work would never have been begun or completed without the advice and encouragement of Laura Mulvey and Peter Wollen. Their suggestions and ideas informed this research from the very first and I deeply appreciate their spirit of critical debate and friendly discussion. Others who made important contributions include Peter Gidal, Simon Blanchard (former national organizer of the IFA), Ed Buscombe at the British Film Institute, Carole Meyer (formerly with the BFI Production Board), and Joan Whitehead and Nicky North at BFI Education. Steve Ungar made timely bibliographic suggestions concerning the history of *Tel Quel* and contemporary French thought.

Numerous readers made valuable contributions and suggestions including Dudley Andrew, David Bordwell, E. Ann Kaplan, Constance Penley, Tom Lewis, Michael McGee, and Franklin Miller. Others who freely shared their work and ideas, and otherwise lent a much needed helping hand, were Don Crafton, Alan Trachtenberg, Colin MacCabe, Kristin Thompson, Miriam Hansen, Annette Kuhn, Elissa Marder, Tom Levin, Tom Keenan, Jennifer Wicke, John Guillory, Anne Higonnet, Janet King, Patty White, Jean Edmunds, and Matthew Affron. Claudia Gorbman deserves a special thanks for taking time out from her own work to carefully read and edit a large portion of the manuscript. Tom Pepper and Mary Quaintance also provided invaluable editorial help.

An early version of Chapter One appeared in *Iris* and of Chapter Two in *Millennium Film Journal.* I thank those editors for their helpful suggestions and for their permission to reuse this material.

There are three people who have played special roles not only in the completion of this book, but also in my life and work.

Barbara Klinger was a constant source of support, energy, and encouragement during the accomplishment of this project. I doubt seriously whether it would ever have been completed without the sustenance of her wit and intelligence.

My friendship with Dana Polan dates from my first glimmerings and ideas on the question of political modernism in film. Since that time he has so unselfishly shared his ideas, and devoted so much time and energy to reading and discussing my work, that his influence and advice permeate every page of this book.

Finally, at the time I was finishing this book the academic film community suffered the loss of one of its most brilliant members—Ed Lowry. Ed has never ceased to be one of the most profound influences on my life and work, for it was through his friendship that I learned both love of film and, as importantly, the commitment to teach film politically. I therefore dedicate this book to his memory.

ONE

The Discourse of Political Modernism

She says, "Yes, I was talking to Joan Braderman about the subject in signifying practice, and she brought up the idea that everything is fiction except theory.
—Yvonne Rainer, "Looking myself in the mouth. . ."[1]

In a 1972 essay on Jean-Luc Godard's *Vent d'est* (1970), Peter Wollen coined the term *counter-cinema* to describe the emergence of a number of independently produced films characterized by a militant hostility to commercial, narrative cinema as well as a commitment to radical politics and formal experimentation.[2] Otherwise known in France as *films tableaux noirs*, or blackboard films, the objective of counter-cinema was to engage an admittedly limited audience with theoretical problems concerning the social function of representation and the potential role of film in political struggle.

Although in the past twenty years the term *counter-cinema* has lost its currency, the question of the necessary engagement of film practice with theory, on the one hand, and with formal innovations characteristic of modernism on the other, is still a living issue. Sylvia Harvey succinctly describes this tendency in contemporary film theory by naming it "political modernism."[3] As a theme dominating the recent history of Anglo-American film theory, political modernism is the expression of a desire to combine semiotic and ideological analysis with the

development of an avant-garde aesthetic practice dedicated to
the production of radical social effects. Although this term has
been mobilized to describe the work of a variety of independent filmmakers in Europe and America (including Yvonne
Rainer, Peter Wollen and Laura Mulvey, Jean-Marie Straub
and Danielle Huillet, Sally Potter, Chantal Akerman, Peter
Gidal, and many others), my discussion of political modernism
refers neither to a film style, movement, nor even a "theory"
properly speaking, but rather a logic or order of discourse
common to both film theorists and filmmakers since 1968.

My recourse to a concept like political modernism follows
the arguments of Mary Kelly with respect to the history of
modernism in postwar art movements. In her essay "Re-viewing Modernist Criticism," Kelly suggests that the historical and
social intelligibility of the concept of "modernism," which is
appropriate to a theory of art as well as to the art objects
themselves, is only possible if considered as a discursive field.[4]
Far from simply describing the aesthetic codes pertinent to a
style or movement in art, the discourse of modernism is considered instead as "produced at the level of the statement, by
the specific practices of art criticism, by the art activities implicated in the critic/author's formulations and by the institutions which disseminate and disperse [these] formulations. . . . [The] reading of artistic texts is always in some sense
subjected to the determining conditions of these practices,
crucially those of criticism" (RMC 41-42).

Critical and theoretical practices are not only crucial to the
reception of aesthetic works, they are also fundamental to their
intelligibility as "knowledges," conscious or not, that underwrite the conception and execution of aesthetic work as well
its reception and interpretation. As early as 1921, Roman Jakobson suggested as much in his essay "On Realism in Art."[5]
Jakobson argues that aesthetic codes are historically variable
social facts whose intelligibility relies not only on the formal
principles of aesthetic practice, but also on the theoretical and
critical conventions by which these codes are understood and
disseminated as norms of meaning, interpretation, and use. It
is a question, then, of *critical institutions* whose conventions
of interpretation and comprehension (whether formulated or

unformulated) may be canonized and subject to the same
"laws" of historical evolution and influence as aesthetic codes,
although they can develop unevenly with respect to one another.

In sum, the aesthetic text, whether it is a question of Jackson
Pollock's *Cathedral* (1947) or Wollen and Mulvey's *Penthesilea*
(1974), must be understood as being "informed by discursive
operations at the level of its conception, production, and reception in a way which is neither prior to, nor derived from,
but coincident with, language" (RMC 49). Understanding the
historical emergence of a discourse on political modernism is
therefore primarily a question of critical work on film theory.
Although the "theory" in question has not been formulated in
either a systematic or noncontradictory fashion, it may nonetheless be documented in journal articles, books, artists' statements, catalogs, and so forth, as well as analyzed as a network
of themes that construct definite objects, problems, questions,
definitions, and so forth within a determinate logic.

In the editorial introduction to an issue of *October* dedicated
to "The New Talkies," the themes characteristic of the discourse of political modernism are given exemplary expression:

> The texts presented here issue from the entrance of cinema into
> the academy. They proceed from the radical critique of rep-
> resentation, through methods of textual analysis and deconstruc-
> tion at work within the disciplines of psychoanalysis and semi-
> otics, towards the analysis of the impact of the recent resurgence
> of *text* within film practice, *specifically in its claim for a critical,
> discursive function within cinema itself.* The period in which we
> locate the development of this practice is the past decade, al-
> though its origins are seen to derive from issues, events, and
> methodological options that form during the 1960s.[6]

The editors continue their discussion by outlining a series of
issues that have governed their current editorial policy.

1. "The convergence of European and American film practice upon the critical, discursive function." This statement implicitly refers to Peter Wollen's rewriting of the history of
modernism in film according to the idea of the "two avant-
gardes." In this influential essay, Wollen asserts that there are
two basic tendencies that characterize the history of the po-

litical aesthetics of avant-garde film. The first is the painterly
tradition of North American experimental film, which defines
as "modern" art taking as its object its own materials of expression. The second is a European "narrative" tradition that from
Eisenstein to Godard is concerned with problematizing cinematic illusionism by exploiting, through various montage strategies, the heterogeneity of the semiotic channels available to
film. Moreover, Wollen notes the possible emergence of a third
trend that combines the reflexivity of the former with the intertextuality of the latter. Godard's films between 1968 and
1972 exemplify this possibility for Wollen and inspired his
aesthetic collaborations with Laura Mulvey.[7] This third avant-
garde is, in fact, what the editors of *October* call "The New
Talkies."

    2. "The manner in which film practice thereby claims a the-
oretical function." In a 1974 interview in *Screen*, Peter Wollen
argues that political aesthetics must distinguish between three
levels of film practice—agitational, propagandistic, and theoretical. Each of these levels is conceived as achieving different
purposes for different audiences: "Agitation is for a specific
conjuncture and for a specific limited audience. Propaganda
is aimed at a mass and presents a general kind of political line
and broad ideas, and the theoretical film again is for a limited
audience and a specific conjuncture but a theoretical conjuncture rather than an immediately political one."[8]

    According to the discourse of political modernism, what are
the terms of film practice's engagement with theory? On one
hand, this engagement is posed as the explicit or implicit appropriation of theory through verbal or written citation. Wollen notes this strategy in "The Two Avant-Gardes" and explores its use in his own films with Laura Mulvey. On the other,
Wollen describes the relation between film theory and practice
in terms of a "kinship of problematic" where the literary theories of the journal *Tel Quel* inform the objectives, logic, and
aesthetic strategies of his and Mulvey's films. But more importantly, in the discourse of political modernism the history
of avant-garde or experimental film is thought to be allied *a
fortiori* to problems of film theory. In this manner, Annette
Michelson and others have argued that modernist aesthetic

strategies have an expressly epistemological objective. Often referred to as the "critique of illusionism," the aim of modernist film practice is considered to be a refutation of the transparency of conventional film technique through the full exploration of the material properties of cinematic expression.[9]

3. "The social and political determinants of such developments and the question of the spectator/audience." Clearly, the objective of any politically oriented aesthetic theory or practice is the transformation of its presumed audience. The constant emphasis of the politically motivated avant-garde art movements in the twentieth century, especially those allied with Marxist thought, has been the necessity of redefining the relations that the spectator is assumed to hold with cultural artifacts in their transmission of the beliefs and values dominant in capitalist societies.

However, in the discourse of political modernism there is a decisive reorientation of the problem of the viewer and the ideological function of art through the disciplines of semiology and psychoanalysis, especially Jacques Lacan's rereading of Freud. In the sixties and seventies, this triangulation of Marxism, semiology, and psychoanalysis was accomplished by Philippe Sollers, Julia Kristeva, Roland Barthes and other writers associated with the French journal *Tel Quel* whose ideas were introduced to Anglo-American film theory primarily through the work of Stephen Heath and the British journal *Screen*. As Colin MacCabe recently notes, "Marxism's abiding problem has always been to explain the way in which capitalist relations reproduce themselves in non-coercive ways. Throughout the seventies there were many who felt that the key to such an understanding lay in an analysis of culture which would not simply read it off as an effect of the economic base but would understand its ability to reproduce subjectivities, a reproduction finally determined by the economic relations but the mechanisms of which had to be comprehended in their own right."[10]

Unlike the linguistic and formalist emphasis of the early phase of structuralism, from this point of view the principal focus of criticism is no longer the simple description of the system of the aesthetic text, but rather an analysis of the subjective re-

lations produced by aesthetic language. Of primary importance to this project were Julia Kristeva's analyses of avant-
garde literature and her attempts to establish a "science of
signifying practices." To analyze cinema as a signifying practice would include specifying in a film's particular forms of
material organization "the semiotic logic of sociality in which
the (speaking, historical) subject is embedded."[11] What is politically at stake for the modernist text here is how the status
of the subject-spectator may be problematized through modernism's particular forms of semiotic organization, or rather,
through its strategic form of disorganization, and how relations
of aesthetic pleasure and cognition might be redefined.

4. "The relation of formal innovation to the discursive project." This is the principal issue held over from the main tenets
of modernism in the arts by discussions of the avant-garde in
contemporary film theory. Formal innovation is considered
necessary to the "epistemological" problem of modernism because it links the problem of subjectivity to the semiotic forms
of the avant-garde text. For example, in his editorial introduction to *Afterimage* 5, Peter Sainsbury argues that the necessity of formal innovation is motivated by the belief "that
creative work in the arts, and particularly in film, might be a
process of re-inventing and re-constructing modes of representation and perception—conditions of consciousness—which
are systematically denied within the terms of the current socio-
political and cultural reality."[12] Although fully congruent with
the views of Clement Greenberg, I argue in subsequent pages
that the sense of statements such as this one have been fully
renegotiated within a theoretical framework more typical of
the work represented by the journal *Tel Quel*.

5. "The emergence of feminist film theory and practice and
their consequences for the discursive project." It is true, and
crucially so, that the emergence of feminism in the 1970s has
in part determined not only the political priorities of the current avant-garde, but also the *theoretical* priorities. Feminism's
stake in questions of representation and sexual difference, as
well as its interest in the conceptual tools of psychoanalysis
and semiology, are crucial determinations in the discourse of

political modernism's conceptions of how aesthetic languages could challenge patriarchal ideologies.

What I have outlined here is the discourse that political modernism presents *of* itself. However, there is reason to inquire of a discourse that represents itself as "theoretical," whether this is a theory, properly speaking, or the simple presentation of the elements of a theory, or what Althusser would call a "problematic."

According to Louis Althusser, a problematic is a structure that organizes discourse in a specific and complex configuration of concepts, questions, and definitions. It defines the problems assumed by the discourse as well as the range of their possible solutions. Although these problems may not be formulated in a systematic or continuous fashion, they nonetheless define both the limits and the continuity of "knowledges" produced. The structure of a given problematic therefore determines what is visible and eloquent within the purview of the discourse it produces and what must be silenced or rendered invisible in order to maintain the continuity and self-identity of its conceptual system (although it need not do so self-consciously). In this manner, a historically given theory "can only pose problems on the terrain and within the horizon of a definite theoretical structure, its problematic, which constitutes its absolute and definite condition of possibility, and hence the absolute determination of *the forms in which all problems must be posed. . . .*"[13] Moreover, if this structure is not necessarily present to itself in the theoretical discourse under consideration, that of political modernism, then the task of criticism is to reveal it through a symptomatic reading. The themes produced by the discourse of political modernism must be considered in another light. Rather than simply taking the discourse of political modernism at its word, the epistemological stakes unconsciously subtending the logic of this discourse and the history of its forms must now be considered.

If the *discourse* of political modernism has a specificity that can be described, it lies neither on the surface of its characteristic statements nor in their common point of reference. Rather, I am interested in the specific forms of conceptual organization that order the regularity of these statements while determining their epistemological value. In short, according to terminology introduced by Michel Foucault, my aim is to define the formation of political modernism as a specific "discursive practice."[14] According to Foucault, a discursive practice conditions the possibility of an institutionalized corpus of knowledge and determines the grounds for its intelligibility. It regulates the order and dispersion of discourse by engendering a specific grouping of objects, organization of concepts, positions of address, and kinds of rhetorical strategies. As such, the formation described presents a finite but not necessarily quantifiable field of *enoncés*. Often translated as "utterance" or "statement," an *enoncé* may indeed correspond to what I have already called "themes." An *enoncé*, however, is restricted neither to the field of speech acts nor by linguistic definition. When speaking of "discourse," Foucault refers equally to philosophical, juridical, literary, and even banal administrative writing, as well as maps, schemata, diagrams, mathematical formulas, and paintings.

The *enoncés* characteristic of a discursive practice are not quantifiable because in principle they may be produced and dispersed endlessly, but only on the basis of an epistemological finitude; in other words, and as experience demonstrates, one can speak endlessly and know or say very little. According to Foucault discursive practices are analyzed by establishing their conditions of "rarefaction." That they are prolix or prodigious matters little, for a discursive practice can be described in its uniqueness only if one is able "to determine the specific rules in accordance with which its objects, statements, concepts, and theoretical options have been formed: if there really is a unity, it does not lie in the visible, horizontal coherence of the elements formed; it resides, well anterior to their formation, in the system that makes possible and governs that formation" (AK 72). Or more simply put: "A discursive formation will be individualized if one can define the system of formation of the different strategies that are deployed in it; in other words, if one can show how they all derive (in spite of their sometimes extreme diversity, and in spite of their dispersion in time) from the same set of relations" (AK 68). The discursive formation is not a "structure," however, nor is it a privileged field of propositions or a generative system to which a field of thought can be reduced. Rather, Foucault describes it as a "collateral space"—a manner of correlating themes, concepts, definitions, questions, and rhetorical strategies that sets their conditions of emergence as such and circumscribes them as a particular, and historically specific, theoretical horizon. A discursive practice serves as a conceptual limit, not only with respect to the possibility of certain kinds of statements, but also as an "epistemic imperative" that establishes conditions of knowing prior to any cognitive subject.[15]

What I have referred to as the principle themes of political modernism, then, are not independent propositions or concepts, but rather "enunciative strategies"—ways of constituting and distributing concepts while permuting them within a finite epistemological space. Similarly, the discourse of political modernism is not a product of, nor can it be located wholly within or attributed to, a given book, essay, manifesto, author, or theoretical or aesthetic *oeuvre*. In its uniqueness as a formation of discourse, political modernism can only be defined by the following procedure:

> One stands back in relation to this manifest set of concepts; and one tries to determine according to what schemata . . . the statements may be linked to one another in a type of discourse; one tries in this way to discover how the recurrent elements of statements can reappear, disassociate, recompose, gain in extension or determination, be taken up into new logical structures, acquire, on the other hand, new semantic contents, and constitute partial organizations among themselves. These schemata make it possible to describe—not the laws of the internal construction of concepts, not their progressive and individual genesis in the mind of man—but their anonymous dispersion through texts, books, and *oeuvres*. (AK 60)

Every *enoncé* derives its identity and its epistemological status from its positioning in this collateral space as a field of association and correlation. "Every statement is specified in this way: there is no statement in general, no free, neutral, independent statement; but a statement always belongs to a series or a whole, always plays a role among other statements, deriving support from them and distinguishing itself from them: it is always part of a network of statements, in which it has a role, however minimal it may be, to play" (AK 99).

Therefore, in order to describe fully the discourse of political modernism in contemporary film theory, the elaboration of its principal themes is not in itself sufficient. An account must also be given of the intertextual context in which political modernism emerged as well as of the series of relations or schemata that enabled this context to be formulated and to produce and disperse statements. Here again the *October* editorial charts a specific path for analysis by acknowledging the historical filiation of contemporary film theory with the emergence of "structuralism" and "poststructuralism" in the sixties and seventies. More specifically, what emerges is a disciplinary web marked by the association of several "new" conceptual systems; namely, literary semiology, Lacanian psychoanalysis, deconstructive philosophy, and so forth. Concomitant with the appearance of these systems of thought was the critique and reformulation of a specific object—the *sign*—understood not as a transparency or as a representation identical to itself and its referent, but as a form of resistance, inherently inadequate to its own uses, that placed the experience of the epistemological subject under suspicion.[16] Clearly, the formulation of contemporary film theory is governed to a significant extent by its assimilation of elements from this intertextual space, especially in a manner mediated and systematized by *Tel Quel*'s *théorie d'ensemble*—a particular triangulation of textual semiotics, psychoanalysis, and Althusserian Marxism that so strongly influenced the editorial positions of *Screen* and other Anglo-American film theory publications.

The appearance of this interdisciplinary space has now been mapped more or less adequately in several studies.[17] For the moment, it suffices to note that the possibility of academic film theory in its current forms was conditioned by the theoretical agendas, rhetorical strategies, and conceptual schemata already established in this particular discursive space. And in order to comprehend the specificity of the discourse of political modernism in film theory, its themes have to be elaborated and analyzed with respect to these relational schemata.

Before beginning, however, two points must be emphasized. First, although I describe these schemata in the form of the statements and logical oppositions characteristic of the discourse of political modernism in both literary and film theory, they are not reducible to elements of a propositional logic. If one were asked to construct a theory of the avant-garde text, there might be a temptation to call these elements hypotheses; however, they are only rarely articulated in a systematic fashion, remaining, for the most part, unformulated assumptions in the discourse of the political modernism. In my analysis, I consider them to be methodological conveniences that function, according to the "laws of rarefaction," to designate relational structures subtending the formation of statements. In the *Grundrisse*, Marx describes a "relation" not as an object, thing, or concept, but as a locus or a network wherein an object or a concept is constituted by or in its relationship to other determinations or sets of determinations. Similarly, each schema that I outline describes not a hypothesis, but an element or series of elements combining and recombining in dynamic and not necessarily self-conscious constellations.

Nor can these schemata be described as constituting a discursive "system." This is my second point. The relation between academic film theory and the intertextual and institutional context from which it emerges is not one of continuity, influence, derivation, or any other metaphor of paternity. Rather, it is a question of transactional and often contradictory sets of relations of selection, exclusion, limitation, and appropriation. In describing the discourse of political modernism within this transactional space, what appears is not the system of a theory, but rather a "regularity" in the organization of concepts, assumptions, and propositions that is ordered by a definable series of oppositions. To look for regularities in the production of discourse one would not merely describe the repetition, reiteration, or reoccurrence of themes, objects, problems, and concepts, although this may be a beginning. In repetition, regularity recognizes the display of a curve that is the limit of all that can be said, understood, or considered true within a given field of discourse. This does not mean that once one has discovered the forms of conceptual organization formulating a field of discourse, and one understands the principles of rarefaction, consolidation, and unification that hold it together, that it is then possible to know and say everything or to consider the field closed off or finished. For discourse is equally productive of contradiction, nonsense, and nonrecognition—one cannot step outside of it in order to comprehend its internal configurations. This notion of regularity, to which I often refer, understands the logic of political modernism not as a constitutive theoretical unity, but as evidence of the discontinuous activity of discourse. It interrogates the different manifestations of political modernism, whether under the guise of an *oeuvre* or individual text, or author or institution.

The most fundamental theme of political modernism can be stated as follows: *the possibility of a radical, political text is conditioned by the necessity of an avant-garde representational strategy;* or more precisely, strategies emphasizing the material nature of language or cinematic presentation, especially in the form of an auto-critique. This is the precise meaning that the editors of *October* give to their formulation of a "critical, discursive function" in the cinema. Here *discursive* means a reflexive concentration on the forms and materials specific to cinematic expression; *critical* defines the "epistemological" project of modernist cinema as the full exploration of its means of representation and its "deconstruction" of normative, representational codes.

The intelligibility of this statement ultimately derives from a single, broad opposition—that of *modernism versus realism.* The history of twentieth-century debates on aesthetics founded on this opposition—the argument between Bertolt Brecht and Georg Lukács in the thirties is the best known—has been characterized by a competition between two types of textual form. Moreover, these forms are thought to be mutually exclusive according to epistemological criteria. On one hand, there is the declarative or "realist" text that assumes a normative status in its presumed transmission of " 'knowledge' to a reader whose position is stabilized through a discourse which is to varying degrees invisible."[18] The interrogative or modernist text, on the other hand, disturbs the unity and self-presence of the reader by discouraging identification and by drawing attention to the work of its own textual processes.

This division of aesthetic work into two broad, mutually exclusive genres of discourse is by no means self-evident and the genealogy of its logic is complex. However, the derivation of the discourse of political modernism is productively traced from the debate in postwar France over the theory of writing or *écriture* as a form of political action, inaugurated by the publication of Jean-Paul Sartre's *Qu'est-ce que la littérature?* (Paris: Gallimard). Published in 1947, Sartre's book demanded that the writers communicate the possibility of human freedom according to an existential ethics of political and literary action. In his opening chapter, "Qu'est-ce que l'écriture?," Sartre distinguishes between *langage*, as the collective inventory or means given to all writers to achieve the ends of communication, and *style*, which as the index of the author's freedom in language designates how one renders what one wishes to express. Since in Sartre's assessment prose is by nature bound to language and thus the responsibility of communication, Susan Sontag notes that "Sartre's inquiry into the nature of literature is throughout governed by this ethical conception of the writer's vocation, as is his relatively pejorative treatment of the 'crisis in language which broke out at the beginning of this century,' which he characterizes as a situation favoring the production of private, obscurantist literary art works confined to an 'audience of specialists.' "[19] The political obligation of writing, whose ethos is clarity and "form following function," motivates Sartre's condemnation of the French literary avant-garde of the turn of the century.

Roland Barthes responded to these arguments in a series of essays published in *Combat* in 1947, which were later turned into his first book *Le degré zéro de l'écriture*. As opposed to Sartre, Barthes was interested in restoring to *écriture* a sense of form and the politics of form such that the "crisis in language" of the literary avant-garde acquired a positive, even revolutionary value. Locating his philosophical base in Maurice Blanchot and Gaston Bachelard, Barthes gravitated toward the avant-garde of his day, championing Alain Robbe-Grillet and Bertolt Brecht through his critical essays of the 1950s and eventually defining a trajectory basic to the nascent theoretical position of *Tel Quel* in the early '60s.

Like Sartre, Barthes develops his argument through a tripartite distinction between *langue, style,* and *écriture. Langue* represents the historical dimension of literary action. Belonging to the entire linguistic community, it describes not only the possibility of the sociality of discourse, it also defines and delimits the inventory of means available to literary creation. Like *langue, style* also functions not as choice but as an inventory for the writer. But as opposed to the sociality of *langue, style* is an archive of creative resources that is profoundly individual, biographical, and ahistorical. In fact, Barthes describes *style* as the "biology" of the writer or his network of obsessions. Where *langue* and *style* are represented by Barthes as "objects" or "structures," *écriture* is defined as a process. Between the sociality of language and the individuality of style, *écriture* defines both the activity of literature as a function of conscious choice and selection and the ensemble of formal features constituting the work of literature.

Although Barthes understands the political nature of *écriture* as an *ethical* category, reflecting his engagement with existentialist positions, he nonetheless articulates this problem as one of aesthetic form. Barthes proposes a distinction between myth and history (prefiguring his use of those terms in *Mythologies*) as the opposition of "classical" to "bourgeois" *langue* whose epochs are divided by the Revolution of 1848. In the classical period before 1848, literature exists as a given; or, in Phil Rosen's description, it is for Barthes a mythical *donnée* that is totalized as a reflection of bourgeois social hegemony and inseparable from it.[20] After the revolution, however, the category of literature itself comes into question as the universality of bourgeois social domination is undermined and therefore literature is required to acknowledge its historical being. Lacking a definite and indisputable social function, identity, or value, literature is dispersed into a variety of modes of writing which, in the tradition of Paul Valéry and Stéphane Mallarmé, come increasingly to take not the world but literature and writing themselves as the object of their activity. This acknowledgment of the historical and representational character of social and ideological categories leads Barthes to name *écriture* as the "last episode of a Passion of writing, which recounts stage by stage the disintegration of bourgeois consciousness" (WDZ 5). Susan Sontag's gloss provides this account of Barthes' argument: "As literature abolishes 'more and more its condition as a bourgeois myth,' *écriture* pushes aside language and style, absorbing 'the whole identity of a literary work. . . .' As modern literature is the history of alienated 'writing' or personal utterance, literature aims inexorably at its own self-transcendence—at the abolition of literature" ("Preface," xxi).

In its historical dimension, *écriture* increasingly adopts a formal character that aims both at semiotic reduction, "writing degree zero," and the defamiliarization of literary stylistics—for example, the elimination of mimesis, foregrounding and dispersion of point of view, deanthropomorphization of narrative and emphasis on markers of narrative activity—common to the work of James Joyce, Gertrude Stein, Samuel Beckett, William Burroughs, and others.

Within a discourse on literary stylistics, the notion of *écriture* delimits the fundamental problem governing the emergence of political modernism. In Stephen Heath's description, Barthes claims for "writing degree zero," "an 'epistemological break' which recasts the whole nature of literary practice in terms of an activity of language, making it no longer a simple discursive line at the service of a fixed logic of 'the True' or 'the Real'. . . ."[21] No longer capable of adequately "representing the world," in Barthes's scenario writing in the modernist era turns inward on itself, ceaselessly reflecting on its forms and rhetorical purposes.

With the advent of *Tel Quel* in 1960 under the editorship of Philippe Sollers, the emergence of *écriture* as the name of a contemporary, avant-garde literary practice tended to dissolve the ethical and existential dimension of "writing" in favor of the formal and theoretical conceptualization characteristic of the discourse of political modernism. In the critical and rhetorical strategies of *Tel Quel* writers such as Barthes, Sollers, and Jean-Louis Baudry, the concept of *écriture* was presented not as a transparent representation or as the recovery of a fundamental meaning resolvable to an identity of any kind, but as a production or process where writing and reading were understood as moments of equal value.

In the rhetorical uses of the *Tel Quel* group, *écriture* referred to at least three different though interrelated concepts: a practice of avant-garde fiction, a theory of the sociality of language, and a philosophical concept specified in the work of Jacques Derrida. Moreover, among the theorists of the *Tel Quel* group, the concept of *écriture* tended to eliminate as much as possible the boundary between aesthetic and theoretical work. "Writing," Barthes asserted, "is in its widest sense a theory. It has its theoretical dimension and conversely, no theory can refuse *écriture* if it is to resist being mobilized by a pure *écrivance*, that is, a purely instrumental use of language. . . . Theory, if it is conceived precisely as a permanent auto-critique, must unceasingly dissolve that signified or meaning which is always prepared to reify itself under the name of "Science." And it is in this way that theory articulates itself . . . within *écriture* as the rule of the signifier.[22]

By the time of the Colloque de Cerisy in 1963, *Tel Quel* had defined its editorial project as the development of a theory of *écriture* that emerged equally from the textual practices of criticism and avant-garde fiction.[23] Throughout the sixties *Tel Quel* engendered a new division within the concept of *écriture*, or what Jean-Louis Baudry called its two axes: "its concrete practice—fiction—and the theoretical formulation of that practice."[24] On this basis, the second principal theme of political modernism can be described: *that modernist writing is intrinsically a theoretical activity.* Consequently, a second binary division opened in the discourse of political modernism defining the formal activity of the modernist text as a *theoretical practice* opposing the *ideological practice* of realist forms.

This presumed theoretical function of modernist work, as conceived in opposition to the ideological values of realist work, is described succinctly in Stephen Heath's study of the *nouveau roman*. Moreover, Heath's adaptation of an Althusserian terminology to describe this opposition (theoretical versus ideological practice) tells much about the Anglo-American reception of *Tel Quel* thought and the development of the discourse of political modernism in film theory.[25] Heath argues that modernism's critique of realism must be understood as challenging realism as a particular mode of aesthetic cognition coextensive with the general ideology proffered by the triumph of capitalism in the nineteenth century. Criticizing the literary system he calls the "Balzacian text," Heath claims that the appearance of literary realism is linked to a nineteenth-century conception of science as an immanently perfectible instrumentality that is both neutral and objective in its description and comprehension of "nature": "Language, in fact, is taken-for-granted in Balzac's project, which therefore defines itself firmly in what might be called, after Husserl, the *natural attitude* towards reality. . . . Language is thought as being self-effacing in the process of the presentation of things, in the reproduction of society. . . . It is here that the fact of the 'perfection' of Balzac's writing may be understood; not source of the real, but instrument of its representation, its limits are the limits of the real itself" (NR 18).

To the extent that both literature and science adopt mimetic systems of representation, understood as coextensive with the world and dissolving themselves into the informed gaze of the reader, Heath considers them as equivalent to the empiricist epistemology criticized by Althusser as the foundation of ideological knowing.[26] By effacing its means of literary presentation, the realist style is assumed to function ideologically since it allows received meanings and forms of meaning to circulate unchallenged and unchecked in society as a "natural" visibility or pure perception.

Alternatively, what Heath calls the "practice of writing" is described as an exploration of and a challenge to the processes of signification through which meaning circulated within society. By concentrating on the difference of aesthetic representation as a form or system with its own intrinsic "laws," Heath argues that modernist writing enables an understanding of the "real" as being produced in language, or as given in the forms of intelligibility permitted by a given society. Within these terms, he defends *Tel Quel*'s theory of political modernism where *écriture* is deemed to have an intrinsically theoretical and antiideological function. Sollers himself justifies the

theoretical status of writing according to the philosophy of
Derrida. In Sollers's reading, Derrida's deconstruction of a
metaphysics founded on *parole*—the voice as signifier of self-
identical Being or the unity of thought and word—relies on
the demonstration of what speech must exclude as the price
of its rationality, and which always threatens to disassemble
it; that is, *écriture* understood as fiction, the irrational, deceit,
in short, the nonidentity of sign and thing. On this basis, Sollers
argues that the category of the literary is used to marginalize
the potential forms of knowledge available through aesthetic
discourse by characterizing them as simply fictive or imaginary. Similarly, the notion of *écriture* as formulated in *Tel Quel*
represents the effort to comprehend the "epistemological
break" achieved in philosophy by Karl Marx, Friedrich
Nietzsche, and Sigmund Freud, and in literature by Lautréamont, Stéphane Mallarmé, James Joyce, and Raymond Roussel.
For Sollers, the concept of *écriture* thus represents the development of an epistemology hostile to empiricism that ex-
pands the limits of aesthetic and theoretical discourse.

Derrida's philosophy in this period can be characterized as
proposing a general theory (grammatology) that takes writing
as its object, deconstruction as its activity or "method," and
whose aim is a critique of the history of metaphysics as presence. The concept of "presence" may be understood as having
three basic senses with respect to Derrida's philosophical project. First is the concept of Being as the self-authenticating
presence of Truth and Reason in metaphysics. A second meaning derives from linguistics and the philosophy of language in
the concept of *parole*—alternatively "speech" or "voice"—
which guarantees in the presence of the speaker the veracity
of an utterance as the identity between thought and word (*logos*). Yet a third sense is that given to presence by empirical
science as the "natural" intelligibility of objects whose potential meanings need only to be intuited or perceived. This has
the effect of extending the relation of identity from thought
to word to thing and back again. Derrida himself suggests this
interpretation in a gloss on Aristotle's *De interpretatione* in *Of
Grammatology:*

If, for Aristotle, for example, "spoken words . . . are the symbols of mental experience . . . and written words are the symbols of spoken words" . . . it is because the voice, producer of *the first symbols*, has a relationship of essential and immediate proximity with the mind. Producer of the first signifier, it is not just a simple signifier among others. It signifies "mental experiences" which themselves reflect or mirror things by natural resemblance. Between being and mind, things and feelings, there would be a relationship of translation or natural signification; between mind and logos, a relationship of conventional symbolization.[27]

In Aristotle, Derrida defines the logocentrism of Western metaphysics in the relation of *parole* or speech to Being. Derrida's notion of logocentrism is equivalent in one sense to Heath's reading of the "natural attitude" in realist fiction—the reduction or effacement of the materiality of language in its conveyance of things. However, by defining the spoken word as the signifier of presence, truth, and authentic being, logocentrism becomes the principal object of Derrida's critique of the Western metaphysical tradition. Here speech is considered as the "good" writing of Plato's *Phaedrus*: the support of a voice fully present to itself, its signifier, and its referent; in sum, self-identical Being. In Derrida's view, this position can only be asserted through an opposition where *écriture* is already conceived as danger or threat: writing divides the "natural" bond between thought and voice, word and thing, and is thus represented in philosophy as fiction, articulate deception, sophistry, or narcosis. For Derrida, classical philosophy thus divides the problem of representation into two routes: on the one hand, metaphor as a detour from truth that necessitates a return to the author as the center and source of fiction or the authentification of its meaning; and on the other, mimesis as repetition or the being-present of the referent through the effacement of the signifier since writing betrays speech and must not be understood as displacing it. According to Derrida, the opposition *parole/écriture* subtends all representation, aesthetic or philosophical, as the paradigm for a series of axiomatic oppositions that constitute the episteme of Western metaphysics—*phonē/graphē*, being/nonbeing, interiority/exteriority, thing/sign, essence/appearance, signified/signifier, truth/

lie, presence/absence, and so on. Moreover, this system distributes its oppositional terms in an hierarchical series that
prioritizes the first terms while suppressing the second or defining them as supplemental or ancillary.

According to Derrida, writing is also systematically degraded
in Saussurian linguistics, which relies on the the indestructible
unity of sign, system, and subject. And if there is a distinct
division between "structuralism" and "poststructuralism," it
is marked by the critique of Derrida, Kristeva, and others on
the linguistic foundation of these unities. In both cases, the
voice functions as the sign of truth, presence, and authentic
being, while writing is either rendered as a radical alterity or
as secondary, destructive, and deceptive with respect to speech.
In Christopher Norris's summary, the object of "grammatology" is to reverse this proposition in order to demonstrate

> that writing is in fact the *precondition* of language and must be
> conceived as prior to speech. This involves showing, to begin
> with, that the concept of writing cannot be reduced to its normal
> (i.e. graphic or inscriptional) sense. As Derrida deploys it, the
> term is closely related to that element of signifying *difference*
> which Saussure thought essential to the workings of language.
> Writing, for Derrida, is the "free play" or element of undecid-
> ability within every system of communication. . . . [It] is the
> endless displacement of meaning which both governs language
> and places it forever beyond the reach of a stable, self-authen-
> ticating knowledge. In this sense, oral language already belongs
> to a "generalised writing," the effects of which are everywhere
> disguised by the illusory "metaphysics of presence." Language
> is always inscribed in a network of relays and differential 'traces'
> which can never be grasped by the individual speaker.[28]

Here yet another sense of the term *écriture* is suggested.
For as the sublimated precondition of all language, the radical
other of speech, writing also exceeds and has the power to
deconstruct the episteme of Western metaphysics. For Derrida, then, deconstruction names a critical activity that consists
in rewriting key moments of philosophical or literary texts to
demonstrate that what they exclude, in the effort to foreclose
meaning in a "transcendental signified," is in fact internal and
necessary to the organization of their textual systems. In this

manner, the activity of deconstruction relies on operational-
izing the function of difference in a given text as the sublimated
condition of its writing. The force of deconstruction as critical
reading relies on the isolation of moments of aporia or irrec-
oncilable paradox or contradiction in the text. Then one demonstrates that these moments function simultaneously as an
authorizing center for the textual system (guaranteeing its stability and coherence by restricting semiotic productivity and
the play of contradiction through either the sublimation or
displacement of difference) and as a potentiality for the disruption and collapse of the system. Therefore, deconstruction
encompasses "writing" as a structure of investigation that acknowledges all that is incriminated in the opposition *parole/
écriture*: the absence of the author or speaking subject; displacement of the centering force of the referent or signified;
interpretability or interminable analysis; and deployment of a
space and time that is not identical to itself.

   In the late sixties, Sollers's debt to Derrida was enormous
(even though his adaptation of Derrida for a theory of avant-
garde practice caused profound philosophical irregularities),
and with the simultaneous publication in 1967 of *La voix et le
phénomène, L'écriture et la différence*, and *De la grammatologie*, Derrida's influence as the philosophical underwriter of
Tel Quel had become incalculable. What a certain reading of
Derrida enabled in this context was an understanding of "deconstruction" both in its specific sense, as a "method" transforming philosophical and literary discourses as the object of
a philosophical critique, and in its general sense as the name
of an avant-garde aesthetic practice informed by theory. Among
the contributors to *Tel Quel*, Philippe Sollers and Jean-Louis
Baudry were the best representatives of a tendency to mobilize
Derrida's work in defense of the theoretical activity of aesthetic work as based on the following principle: *in its dismantling of the codes of realist fiction, the theoretical work of the
text of écriture is to be understood as an activity of deconstruction.* This proposition opens a third major opposition in the
discourse of the political modernism, *code versus deconstruction*, where the former designates the ensemble of formal fea-

tures characteristic of the realist text in their ideological functioning, and the latter signifies the reflexive designation and
negation or criticism of those codes as strategically accomplished by the formal structure of the modernist text. Thus
Heath characterizes the *nouveau roman* as an "anti-novel" in
its systematic targeting and deconstruction of the conventions
of the "Balzacian text." The aesthetic work described in the
discourse of political modernism is similarly portrayed as a
productive negativity or as the "anti-body" of the realist text.

However, it is essential to understand that Sollers's conception of deconstruction as a modernist aesthetic practice (which
reappears in contemporary film theory under a variety of
names) was already significantly displacing Derrida's original
theorization. For Derrida, *écriture* described the general condition of intelligibility in language as a structure of difference.
In philosophical texts governed by metaphysical concepts, such
a notion has been globally repressed while it is generally acknowledged or set into play in texts of the literary avant-gardes.
Derrida never claimed at this point that his philosophy had a
specifically political dimension in either theory or practice,
except as a theory of reading. Under the editorship of Philippe
Sollers, however, *Tel Quel* attempted to negotiate for Derrida's
conception of *écriture* a basic affinity with Marxism-Leninism
and dialectical materialism. In Sollers's essay "Niveaux se-
mantiques d'un texte moderne," this effort was implicitly
understood in the division between "writing" and writing, the
former defining, in the situation of the modernist text, a materiality of signification repressed in the latter.[29]

In "Un pas sur la lune," an essay written originally as the
preface for a Latin American edition of *Of Grammatology*,
Sollers describes what he believes to be the fundamental importance of Derrida for an aesthetic practice allied to dialectical materialism.[30] The most important issue here is Sollers's
specification of prose, narrative, and expressive writing as an
ideological norm of representation whose universal acceptance
has been guaranteed by the domination of *parole* in the logocentric epoch. He thus effects a particular displacement in
the *parole/écriture* opposition that marshals the activity of deconstruction as a theory of political action for the avant-garde

text, and aligns it with a now familiar series of terms: *realism/ modernism, ideological/theoretical practice*, and finally, *idealism/materialism*.

The basic elements comprising this theory of aesthetic deconstruction are easy to formulate though they often yield difficult conclusions. They are concisely, if not cogently, articulated in Jean-Louis Baudry's important essay "Écriture/ fiction/idéologie."[31] A brief discussion of these elements is useful because "Writing/Fiction/Ideology" appeared in translation in an issue of *Afterimage* that was widely cited as an important discussion of questions of political modernism in contemporary film theory. In this respect, Baudry's essay provides an interesting vantage point from which to observe the transactions taking place between French literary theory and Anglo-American film theory. Baudry also provides a digested theory of the text of political modernism as well as a defense of its deconstructive activity as theoretical practice. Moreover, in a neighboring essay in *Afterimage*, Noel Burch and Jorge Dana argue explicitly for an extension of these ideas into film theory as a defense of the counterideological capacity of modernist films. (I discuss their arguments at length in Chapter Four.) Thus, an understanding of this difficult essay proves useful in understanding how the rhetorical strategies of a literary, political modernism are deployed in film theory.

Baudry's arguments concerning the text of *écriture* as a form of political modernism may be described as five basis themes.

1. *The text of écriture is defined through its antithetical or negative relation with narrative.* Both Sollers and Baudry name "fiction" as the specific field of action of writing. They emphasize that the work of deconstruction will best take place in the realm of aesthetic activity where narrative codes may both be cited and dismantled. In this manner,both Sollers and Baudry mobilize the code/deconstruction opposition in relation to that of *parole/écriture*. In "Writing/Fiction/Ideology," Baudry specifies the special relation that the text of *écriture* holds with narrative: to deconstruct those codes of expressivity where one recognizes the repression of the signifier and the "hypostasizing transcendentalization" of the signified. Moreover, this is understood as work specifically at the level of

ideology since " 'literature' provides an especially fertile ground for ideology to the extent that, involving as it does work at the level of *langue*, literature brings into play the system of language (which must obviously remain unconscious) in which everyone is led to represent himself" (WFI 24). In sum, what narrative works upon or transforms as its raw material are those codes of expressivity that derive from practical communication; in other words, "speech" conceived with the full force of the philosophical critique that Derrida has brought against the concept.

2. *The text of écriture is nonrepresentational and nonexpressive.* This premise derives from a definition of realism as an ideology of conventional narrative form. In this conception, the aim of the realist text is to attain a maximum state of legibility or readability where its language is thought to be coextensive with the world that is its object. To the extent that this language is transparent or instrumental, the "readable" work respects and reiterates the received forms of social intelligibility as an unconscious and unchallenged process in which social norms are consumed, learned, and reproduced.

If ideology is defined as a double movement—the production and reproduction of given forms of social intelligibility through norms of reading and writing as well as the effacement of the material conditions of that intelligibility—then one form of political action available to aesthetic work is to restore consciousness of this process. Modernist writing is required to interrupt the legibility of the text and to emphasize a sense of the materiality of its language and structure. In *Logiques*, Sollers argues for an understanding of the illegibility or "unreadability" of the avant-garde text as a form of resistance—the mark of noncomplicity with the modes of expression of the socially given "real." Here Sollers describes what he calls a provisional myth of language as the perpetual oscillation between two unrealizable extremes: total illegibility or opacity and complete transparency. (In Chapter Five, these ideas will be deployed in a different way in the theory of antinarrative offered by Peter Gidal.) If the ideal of novelistic or realist expression is to define meaning as a language identical with the world and Being (the intuition of a "reading consciousness" of the meaning intended by a "creating consciousness"), then the ideal of *écriture* is to deflect meaning—to deploy itself as *nonsavoir* or an infinitely deferred or displaced meaning. Thus *écriture* confronts readers with their desire to possess knowledge "through" a text or to ascribe meaning or intelligibility to it in an unproblematic fashion. In Baudry's summary,

> Unreadability thus becomes the crux of reading, the obstacle it must overcome, the resistant surface against which the inert force of ideology batters, thereby revealing itself; in other words, it becomes what must not, cannot, be read by a society fragmented amongst its individual members. We should make clear at this point that unreadability cannot be made manifest through the discursive mode, implying as this does a comprehensive code universally accessible; it must necessarily be situated in a text-in-fiction; in other words, precisely in a text which brings into play everything that "general writing" deals with unconsciously. (WFI 31)

3. *The text of écriture is based on the elaboration of a formal system that intensifies perception of the materiality of signification as the "dialectical" reversal or negation of codes of expressivity or narration.* Again it is Sollers who gainsays Derrida's philosophy as providing, in its reversal of the system of priorities governing the relation of *parole* to *écriture,* a dialectic and a materialism: "LA PENSEE DE LA TRACE SERAIT FONDALEMENT MATERIALISTE" ("Un pas sur la lune," 17). The sublimation of the trace, which founds the epoch of logocentrism, is designated by Sollers as an idealism. And Derrida, having determined the time of the trace as preceding that of logos, and as a history so far proscribed by the pretended universality of the phonological era, figures prominently in the restoration of *écriture* to materialist philosophy. Moreover, for Sollers this reversal of conceptual priorities is dialectical and as such has a definite epistemological impact.

A similar understanding of materialism in textual practice is crucial for Baudry since, in his description, ideological domination depends on an illusion of universality that does not recognize "that historically situated 'works' rest upon a formal system which is analysable, relative, and thereby liable to be replaced by others" (WFI 23). For Baudry formalism is an explicit precondition for the theoretical activity of *écriture*. The formal work of *ecriture* is to systematically foreground the devices of fictional writing, and ground them in their specific and material textual existence while eschewing any representational or expressive characteristics external to that existence. The movement of aesthetic deconstruction, if it is to disable the work of ideology, consists of a radical reduction. This entails the production of a purely formal space that functions to displace any textual feature that defers consciousness or perception of the specific, material character of the signifier. In this manner, Baudry develops his notion of *écriture* according to its antithetical relation with expressive or narrative devices including linear causality, teleological or ends-directed structure, psychological attributions of narrative voice or point of view, and diegetic reference. In later chapters, there will be ample opportunity to unpack and criticize this forceful equation of form or structure with materialism.

4. *With the elimination of conventional narrative form and causality, the work of écriture produces its textual space in the form of process-oriented, serial, or permutational structures.* Similar to the definition of pictorial modernism as the fragmentation, reduction, or leveling of perspectival space, Baudry calls for a notion of textuality generated in the form of a grid or hieroglyph. Adopting a term from linguistics, Baudry explicitly defines hieroglyphic space as *determinative*; that is, as a signifier added to another signifier in a manner that reduces phonological ambiguity by intensifying the material, written character of the sign. The work of enunciation in the text of *écriture* is thus produced as a "redoubling" or "reinscription." In other words, *écriture* is based on a fundamental textual reflexivity or autodesignation of code whose aim is "to make the text appear as text, writing as writing and to denounce . . . all expressive reading which strains toward a signified . . . (WFI 26). Having lost its supports and, as Derrida says, no longer being subject to, dependent on and second to the Logos, writing ceases to be an instrument of representation, becoming instead the locus of an action which cannot be termed representation since nothing external is represented in it" (WFI 29). Similarly, as Peter Wollen insists later, this form of writing

requires a reading that is less an act of "translation" between sender and receiver than a productive decipherment on the part of the reader.

5. *The relations constituting the formal space of the text of écriture also determine the forms of its possible readings.* In other words, the formal possibilities of *écriture* describe not only an intrinsic condition of textual meaning, but also the process of meaning construction through which the text of *écriture* engages its prospective reader.

According to Baudry, the construction of meaning by the reader can no longer be construed as a passive reception of the text. If the metaphysical relation between *écriture* and *parole* is reversed, and if the world and the condition of its intelligibility become contingent on language or symbolic representation, then the world itself can only be considered as textual. Understanding in the world then becomes a profoundly semiotic process—a project of productive decipherment where signs are designated and reconstituted in ever renewable forms of intelligibility. In a metaphor taken from Freud, Baudry describes the act of interpretation as secondary elaboration in the dream-work: a text adding itself onto another text ad infinitum. The notion of intelligibility becomes a continuous process of reinscription—of texts working upon other texts, doubling and reconstituting them. However, this is not a cumulative process; it is in no way resolvable to a state of plenitude in which the world would finally become coextensive with the signs that comprehend it. Instead, in Baudry's description the world is displayed across a surface of textual materiality and dimensionality and therefore knowledge of the world (decipherment) and communication of that knowledge (writing/reading) are only consignable to an activity of textual reinscription, redoubling, and reconstitution.

For Baudry, the hierarchization of writing and reading is thus subject to the same deconstruction as that of *écriture/parole.* They must now be considered as nonidentical yet mutually determining activities bound by their intertextual relation: "[The] decision to read reveals a writing, a mark already made, a text already proffered, an inscription. An inscription which becomes readable only when redoubled by an act of

writing which offers it to be read. Reading is shown therefore
to be an act of writing just as writing is revealed as an act of
reading—reading and writing being merely simultaneous moments in a single process of production" (WFI 25). Thus the
text of *écriture* presents a movement or play of signification in
which the production of sense involves the mutual activity of
writer and reader. In Sollers's metaphor, writer and reader
have become coactors in the scenography of the text.

In sum, for Baudry and Sollers *écriture* describes a textual
fiction that, without narrating, poses theoretically the problem
of narration. Acting reflexively on the structure and mechanisms of textual production, it aims to negate or reverse those
forms of enunciation that compel us "to accept utterances
without questioning their enunciation, and to consume products without questioning their production" (WFI 35).

Baudry and Sollers's discussion of the forms of reading proper
to the deconstructive capacity of avant-garde texts presents
the most forceful assertion of political modernism: that the
political activity of the modernist text derives not only from
its critique of ideology, but more importantly from *modernism's reconsideration of the subject it addresses*. The emphases
on formal experimentation and the nonrepresentational capacity of art, the equation of deconstruction with negation, the
identification of reflexive forms with an epistemological or theoretical value, and the insistence on the *work* required by the
reader as the restoration of a perception of form or materiality
denied him or her by the presence and plenitude of narrative,
are all oriented toward a desired transformation of subjectivity
in which art and literature could play a decisive role. Or in
D. I. Grossvogel's account, "if political effort and speculative
theory can be justified only to the extent that they are *necessary* steps to *actual* change, the touchstone that determines
the value of any speculation is the spectator."[32]

This emphasis grew in importance through the efforts of a
number of theorists to construct a materialist theory of the
subject by correlating, on the one hand, the work of Louis
Althusser in Marxist philosophy and the theory of ideology,
and on the other, Jacques Lacan's revolution in psychoanalytic

theory. Elisabeth Roudinesco notes that the reception of Lacanian psychoanalysis in France was set by the context of the
Algerian war and the increasing militancy of French intellectual and student movements.[33] In this cultural situation, psychoanalysis was appealed to sometimes as a universal science
capable of explaining the unconscious functioning of societies,
and sometimes as a theory of the subject whose emphasis on
"decentering," as opposed to the adaptive ego-psychology of
American Freudianism, suggested a fragile entity capable of
transformation and assimilation to militant values. In Colin
MacCabe's summary, "Lacanian psychoanalysis, thus used by
the *Tel Quel* group, furnished a criterion of value—in so far as
the text remained open so did the subject. And it was this
subject in process, never arrested within a fixed identity, which
functioned as a new political model of subjectivity, the final
break with a bourgeois ideology understood largely as an ideology of closure and identity" (C68 9).

In this context, psychoanalysis was understood as a political
theory displacing the Sartrian concept of *engagement*, and its
humanism of the guilty conscience, with a structural and materialist science. At the same time, Lacan powerfully contributed to the critique of phenomenology on the one hand, and
the linguistic origins of structuralism on the other, undertaken
in different ways by Julia Kristeva, Roland Barthes, Michel
Foucault, and Jacques Derrida.

From the point of view of the French academy, Louis Althusser was among the first to recognize Lacan's contribution
to these debates and to encourage his support. By 1963 he
had introduced Lacan's writings to his seminars at the pres-
tigious Ecole Normale Supérieure (ENS), and after Lacan's
break with the Société Française de Psychanalyse, Althusser
assured the continuation of his seminars by giving them a home
in the ENS. Through Lacan, Althusser saw the means to liberate French Marxist thought from its sorry postwar state under the influence of the ideological constraints of Zhdanovism,
and the opportunity to advance the theory of ideology through
Lacan's transformations of the category of the subject in psychoanalysis.

These ideas permeate Althusser's writings on the problem
of ideology, especially his important essays "Freud et Lacan"
and "Idéologie et appareils idéologiques d'Etat."[34] The second
article, despite its fragmentary and tentative arguments, represents the culmination of Althusser's thought on this subject.
In "Idéologie et appareils idéologiques d'Etat," Althusser's
challenge to previous theories of ideology (from Destutt de
Tracey through Feuerbach and Marx) is systematically presented through a psychoanalytic vocabulary. Most importantly,
Althusser uses psychoanalysis to displace the problem of ideology from the context of delusion and the battle between true
and false ideas, in order to explain how and why societies
unfailingly encourage individuals, through noncoercive means,
to act against their own interests and accept a status quo that
fails to respond to those interests.

Concepts of the unconscious, the imaginary, the subject, and
of negation [dénégation] are recruited from psychoanalysis by
Althusser to describe the functioning of ideology. According
to Althusser, ideology is related to the unconscious in that it
is transhistorical. Although the functioning of ideology is certainly realized in historically specific ways, like the unconscious its general structure is universal and essential to all social
exchange, whether in a capitalist or socialist context. On this
basis, Althusser produces the following definition: "Ideology
is a 'representation' of the imaginary relation of individuals to
the real conditions of their existence" (ISA 162). The use of
the term imaginary here does not refer to a situation of delusion or knowing acquiescence to a fiction. Rather, for Althusser the function of ideology is intangible save where it is
realized in the material behaviors, actions, rituals, and practices of daily life that more often than not are perpetuated
through institutions [appareils] controlled directly or indirectly
by the State (e.g., education, communications, the legal-jur-
idical system, and even the church and the family). Moreover,
the structure of ideology is inherently "imaginary" in that it
resides in images or representations. It is in fact essentially
narrative in form complete with a pregiven mise-en-scène, del-
egated roles and actions, and conventional responses. In this
respect, the ultimate function of ideology is to produce and

perpetuate the categories of subjectivity necessary to the
smooth functioning of a society—the punctual and efficient
laborer, the regular voter, the loyal churchgoer, the willing
taxpayer and recruit of the armed services, or the dutiful par-
ent and child—and to encourage concrete individuals to adhere
to those roles.[35] Thus Althusser says that the subject is necessary to the definition of ideology such that "the category of
the subject is constitutive of all ideology only in as much as
all ideology has for its function (which defines it) of 'constituting' concrete individuals as subjects" (ISA 171).
To the extent that individuals identify with and act out these
roles and social relations that serve in the material support and
perpetuation of a given State, one can say they are subjects
of the State. What remains to be explained is how and why
these categories of subjectivity can be produced and represented as desirable in the face of unemployment, disenfran-
chisement on the basis of race, demagoguery, conscientious
objection, and an alarming divorce rate. For Althusser, the
classical subject of philosophy—defined by its self-identity, self-
consciousness, and noncontradiction—is of no use for comprehending this problem. Rather, one must turn to psychoanalytic
models of identification and the construction of subjectivity
that describe the subject as divided within itself and capable
of acting on contradictory relations of knowledge and behaviour. Here the central concept for Althusser is that of negation.
In Freud, negation [*Verneinung*] refers to the capacity of an
individual to hold mutually contradictory beliefs or to both
affirm and deny the truth of a proposition without acknowledging the presence of contradiction. Similarly, Althusser explains the "imaginariness" of the ideological relation as splitting the subject between recognition [*reconnaissance*] and
miscognition [*méconnaissance*]; that is, an individual gladly
submits to the lures of ideology because either s/he recognizes
or perceives her or himself therein, or wishes to conform to
the idealized ego presented by a given category of subjectivity.
However, this recognition only takes place at the price of a
repression of the historical origins and economic motives of
the social relations sustained in ideology. Although ideology
sustains the subject in a relation of practical knowledge [*sa-*

voir], it cannot give access to true scientific or theoretical knowing save through the agency of a symptomatic reading.

In the 1960s, the centrality of the category of the subject for the analysis and criticism of ideology was accepted widely in both French and Anglo-American cultural theory. "If one is concerned to analyse art in its social and political context," writes Colin MacCabe, "then one of the absolute necessities is to give an account of the processes of identification and disidentification, the methods by which fictions bind us into representations of both world and self" (C68 9-10). In terms of a general theory of culture, it was once again *Tel Quel* that set the context for bringing Althusser and Lacan together on the terrain of cultural criticism, while weaving the principal themes and rhetorical strategies of political modernism through the problem of the subject. Of paramount importance was the encounter between semiology and psychoanalysis, and Marxism and feminism, in the work of Julia Kristeva. Kristeva has been justly credited with shifting literary analysis from text-oriented models toward a theory of the subject in the development of "a semiotic based on the material character of the signifier and the practice of writing as a subversion of conventional codes, especially those of representation, and a 'destructuration' of the conscious . . . subject in favour of a subject fissured and split by articulation with the order of the unconscious and his or her own body."[36] It was also Kristeva who supplied the most replete models for explaining the intricate relations between processes of literary signification and the representation of subjectivity and desire, as well as understanding how these processes could either contribute to or undermine the power of a specifically oedipal and patriarchal language.

It is generally acknowledged by MacCabe and others that the work of Kristeva and *Tel Quel* was singularly responsible for the revolution in film and cultural studies that occurred in the seventies. At the same time, MacCabe has succinctly noted how the agonistic conception of textuality in the discourse of political modernism, in its adaptation for film theory, also circumscribed and eventually impeded further work on issues of ideology, identification, and subjectivity in cultural criticism. In the positions generally associated with *Screen* after 1971,

> The specificity of film was to be located in the field of vision: insofar as a film fixed the subject in a position of imaginary dominance through the security of vision then it fell immediately within bourgeois ideology, insofar as it broke that security it offered fresh possibilities. It was by drawing on psychoanalytic accounts of vision in voyeurism and fetishism that *Screen* elaborated its account and critique of the cinema. The disruption of the imaginary security of the ego by a problematising of vision was linked to Brecht's emphasis on the breaking of the identificatory processes in the theatre as the precondition for the production of political knowledge. (C68 9)

Similarly, it is easy to understand how Althusser's emphasis on ideology as an imaginary relation based on perception and specularity, as well as his suggestion that an ideological practice could be countered with the development of a theoretical practice or "truly" scientific criticism, figured prominently in the paradigm. However, MacCabe also notes that "the political weight given to writing which disrupted the stability of meaning and identity was deeply problematic. If questions of subjectivity were placed at the centre of political inquiry, the only politically valid form of art was one which broke with any fixity of meaning to inaugurate a new decentered form of being" (C68 8). It is in this manner that MacCabe depicts

> the crippling weight of normative criticism which affects any fundamental theory of identification (Marxist or psychoanalytic) when it divides works of art in relation to criteria of identity which are automatically evaluative. In *Screen* the adopting of Lacanian forms of psychoanalytic argument had effectively reintroduced criteria of value which denigrated forms of popular cinema in favour of a certain number of politically avant-garde texts: Godard, Straub, Oshima, etc. . . . As avant-garde positions were valorised, Hollywood was produced negatively: classic narrative Hollywood cinema was evaluated in terms of the constant placing of the spectator in a position of imaginary knowledge. This cinema was held to deprive the spectator of any perspective for social or political action except for privileged moments when vision was fleetingly disturbed by a pressure the text could not contain. (C68 11)

The question of the subject is no doubt decisive. Yet in the discourse of political modernism, the elaborate emphasis on the *forms* of subjectivity thought to be characteristic of certain kinds of texts, and the generic division of texts according to criteria of form (modernist or realist) and epistemology (theoretical or ideological and illusionist), threatens to displace that question with respect to any serious historical, material, or social analysis. To the extent that the discourse of political modernism has divided the question of texts and their ideological effects on the basis of a binary logic of division and exclusion, one must assume both the essential integrity and self-identity of aesthetic forms, as well as an intrinsic and intractable relation between texts and their spectators, regardless of the historical or social context of that relation. It is precisely these two issues that this book sets out to challenge by submitting the discourse of political modernism to a historical and critical analysis.

Therefore, despite the divergences, debates, conceptual struggles, arguments, and polemics that accrue between the various positions I discuss, political modernism can be understood as a precise field of discourse, a set of rhetorical strategies (the notion of the "epistemological break," the binary logic that opposes modernism to realism, materialism to idealism, theoretical to ideological practice, deconstruction to code), and a definitive network of themes. Moreover, it is my conviction that the history of contemporary film theory, and the institutional weight that film studies has attained and still carries, can only be understood in this context. Chapter by chapter I trace out this network as a conceptual space that traverses the formulations of the various critics, theories, and editorial policies that I discuss. In Chapter Two, I discuss Peter Wollen's attempts in a number of essays to rewrite the history of modernism in film through the theoretical framework of semiology in order to justify an "epistemological" film practice according to the criterion of formal reflexivity. In Chapter Three, I describe the influence of *Tel Quel* on debates in French film theory between 1968 and 1972. Of equal importance is how French film criticism drew upon Althusser's critique of empiricist epistemologies to devise a formal typology that could

decide the degrees of ideological "knowing" presented by different kinds of films. Attention is also given in this chapter to
key essays in *Cahiers du cinéma* and *Cinéthique*, as well as the
theory of deconstruction implicit in Jean-Louis Baudry's influential essay on the cinematic apparatus. Chapter Four exam-
ines Noel Burch's theories of political modernism and cinematic form, and Chapter Five assesses Peter Gidal's theory of
"structuralist/ materialist" film as antinarrative. In Chapters
Six and Seven, I discuss the attempts by Peter Wollen and
Stephen Heath to redeem narrative for a theory of political
modernism and I trace more precisely the influence of Kristeva
on *Screen*'s theories of subjectivity and signifying practice.
Chapter Eight analyzes problems of sexual difference and feminist theory in the discourse of political modernism through
the attempt to define the specificity of a feminine writing in
literature and film. The concluding chapter summarizes and
criticizes the question of the subject as its has been addressed
in the discourse of political modernism. Alternatively, I suggest
the possibility of a theory of reading where the productivity
of meaning is accounted for not only according to the formal
dynamics of the aesthetic text, but also in the intertextual relations between the text and critical practices, theory, pedagogy, and other discourses of interpretation or reception that
may negotiate the range of a given text's possible readings and
modes of consumption.

NOTES

1. Yvonne Rainer, "Looking Myself in the Mouth . . . ," *October*
17 (Summer 1981): 65.
2. Peter Wollen, "Counter Cinema: *Vent d'est*," *Afterimage* 4 (Autumn 1972): 6-17.
3. Sylvia Harvey, "Whose Brecht? Memories for the Eighties,"
Screen 23.1 (May/June 1982): 45-59.
4. Mary Kelly, "Re-viewing Modernist Criticism," *Screen* 22.3
(1981): 41-62; hereafter referred to as RMC. I am aware of the
debate in the history and theory of art that attempts to differentiate
between the terms *modernism* and *avant-garde* with respect to twentieth century art movements. Relevant discussions of this problem
can be found in Renato Poggioli's *The Theory of the Avant-Garde*,

trans. Gerald Fitzgerald (Cambridge: Harvard University Press, 1968);
Peter Bürger's *Theory of the Avant-Garde*, trans. Michael Shaw (Minneapolis: University of Minnesota Press, 1984); and Matei Calines-
cu's *Faces of Modernity* (Bloomington: Indiana University Press, 1977).
I will state here and reiterate often that I am not in the least interested in the description of art movements or even artistic practices.
Rather, my analysis is concerned with the history and criticism of a
specific formation of theoretical discourse. The terms *avant-garde*
and *modernism* are often used interchangeably in the discourse of
political modernism and perhaps a critique should be made of the
confusions that result from an inexact terminology. However, political modernism is not a theory properly speaking and I have chosen
to approach it in the "positivity" of its manifestations, which includes
analyzing the system of its irregularities, contradictions, and silences
as well as what it self-consciously defends as theoretical or critical
knowledge.

5. In Ladislav Matejka and Krystyna Pomorska, eds., *Readings in
Russian Poetics: Formalist and Structuralist Views* (Ann Arbor: Michigan Slavic Publications, 1978): 38-46.

Following Richard Wollheim, I would also insist that when attempting to describe the theory, practice, and reception of aesthetic
work, it is sufficient to "point to positive practices, conventions, or
rules, which are all explicit in the society (the artworld), even if they
are merely implicit in the mind of the actual agent (the representative
of the artworld)." See his *Art and Its Objects*, 2d ed. (Cambridge:
Cambridge University Press, 1980): 162.

6. The Editors, "The New Talkies: A Special Issue," *October* 17
(Summer 1981): 3; emphases mine. Although this editorial is signed
collectively, at the 1982 conference on "Cinema Histories, Cinema
Practices" at the University of Wisconsin-Milwaukee, Annette Michelson claimed the work as her own.

7. "The Two Avant-Gardes," *Edinburgh Magazine* 1 (1976): 83-
84. Significantly, in a later article appearing in the same year as
October 17 ("The Avant-Gardes: Europe and America," *Framework*
14 [Spring 1981]: 9-10), Wollen explains the personal motivations
behind these arguments and discusses why the "third avant-garde"
failed to materialize in the way he originally imagined. These arguments are developed at greater length in the next chapter.

8. "*Penthesilea, Queen of the Amazons*: Laura Mulvey and Peter
Wollen interviewed by Claire Johnston and Paul Willemen," *Screen*
15.3 (Autumn 1974): 131.

9. See, for example, Annette Michelson's influential essays " 'The
Man with the Movie Camera': From Magician to Epistemologist,"

Artforum (March 1972): 60-72; "Screen/Surface: The Politics of Illusionism," *Artforum* (September 1972): 58-62; and "Paul Sharits and the Critique of Illusionism" in *Projected Images* (Minneapolis: Walker Art Center, 1974): 20-25.

10. Colin MacCabe, "Class of '68: Elements of an Intellectual Autobiography 1967-81" in *Tracking the Signifier* (Minneapolis: University of Minnesota Press, 1985): 7; hereafter cited as C68. This striking analytical memoir serves as the introduction to a collection of MacCabe's essays.

11. "The System of the Speaking Subject" (Lisse: The Peter de Ridder Press, 1975): 4. Kristeva's most representative work on this problem is her magisterial *La révolution du langage poétique* (Paris: Editions du Seuil, 1974).

I should make clear that I will in no way attempt a comprehensive account of theories of subjectivity here. My only interest in this chapter is how the theory of the subject was addressed in the discourse of political modernism. For a more general discussion of theories of subjectivity in relation to the aesthetic text, see Steve Burniston and Chris Weedon's "Ideology, Subjectivity and the Artistic Text," *Working Papers in Cultural Studies* 10 (1977: 203-33; and Rosalind Coward and John Ellis's *Language and Materialism* (London: Routledge and Kegan Paul, 1977). A useful summation specific to film studies is Paul Willemen's "Notes on Subjectivity," *Screen* 19.1 (Spring 1978): 41-69.

12. Peter Sainsbury, *Afterimage* 5 (Spring 1974): 2.

13. Louis Althusser and Etienne Balibar, *Reading Capital*, trans. Ben Brewster (London: Verso, 1979): 25.

14. See, in particular, *The Archaeology of Knowledge*, trans. A. M. Sheridan Smith (New York: Harper Torchbooks, 1972); hereafter referred to as AK. I am aware that Foucault's emphasis on the "positivity" of discourse might undercut an effort to mobilize his theories through the agency of a symptomatic reading. Moreover, the difficult relation of influence and debate between the historical methods of Althusser and Foucault are too complex to deal with adequately here. As my argument develops, I hope to demonstrate the affinities between these two philosophers as well as the adequacy of my appropriation of them for the type of theoretical readings I propose.

15. Referring to Foucault, Frank Kirkland states that "An epistemic imperative is neither a form of knowledge nor a cognitive duty for the knowing subject. Rather it is what Foucault calls a '*law of rarefaction*' which governs and institutes the *specific* deployment of what is said and what is known in an epoch. That is to say, it screens

and permits specific statements to form to the exclusion of others."
Frank Kirkland, "The Discursive Policy of Modernism," Symposium
on Modernism in Art, Literature, and Philosophy, University of Okla-
homa at Norman, 15 April 1981.

16. See, for example, Phil Rosen's "The Politics of the Sign in Film
Theory," October 17 (Summer 1981): 5-21; cited hereafter as PSF.

17. For example: Fredric Jameson's The Prison House of Language
(Princeton: Princeton University Press, 1972); Robert Scholes's
Structuralism in Literature (New Haven: Yale University Press, 1974);
Jonathan Culler's Structuralist Poetics (Ithaca: Cornell University
Press, 1975); Frank Lentricchia's After the New Criticism (Chicago:
University of Chicago Press, 1980); and Terry Eagleton's Literary
Theory (Minneapolis: University of Minnesota Press, 1983). These
historical glosses should in no way be considered as some constitutive
unity. To the extent that they describe the history of the assimilation
of "French" theory in an Anglo-American context, it is a discontinuous history of debate, conflict, and contradiction representing not
so much the reception as the formulation of a specific theoretical
space.

18. These distinctions are attributed to Emile Benveniste as described by Catherine Belsey in her Critical Practice (London and
New York: Methuen, 1980): 91.

19. Preface to Roland Barthes's Writing Degree Zero (Boston: Beacon Press, 1970), trans. Annette Lavers and Colin Smith, xv. Barthes's
Writing Degree Zero will be cited as WDZ.

20. PSF 14-17. Rosen also justifiably criticizes Barthes's argument
for its reflectionism characteristic of "standard" Marxism.

21. The Nouveau Roman: A Study in the Practice of Writing (Philadelphia: Temple University Press, 1972): 210; hereafter cited as
NR.

22. Cited in French in NR 202. The translation is mine.

23. In 1967, Sollers reflected on the importance of the Cerisy
colloquium: "In the wake of this conference . . . our emphasis was
no longer simply a formal research on fiction, rather we elaborated
a critical space that no longer distinguished between levels—critical,
poetic, novelistic—of text. At the same moment, our research specified how literary discourses inserted themselves in the political;
today we are simultaneously elaborating a theory of écriture and a
theory of literary action, where the latter finds itself entirely transformed from the beginning." "Tel Quel aujourd'hui," France Nouvelle 1128 (31 mai 1967): 21; my translation.

A complete history of Tel Quel thought would be too extensive to
treat here. For two excellent accounts, see Leon S. Roudiez' "Twelve

Points from *Tel Quel*," *L'Esprit Créateur* XIV.4 (Winter 1974): 291-303, and Stephen Heath's chapter on Sollers's in *The Nouveau Roman*: 179-242. I am especially indebted to Heath's account. Another interesting account is presented in Elisabeth Roudinesco's *Histoire de la psychanalyse en France*, 2 (Paris: Editions du Seuil, 1986), especially 530-50 passim.

24. "Writing, Fiction, Ideology," *Afterimage* 5 (Spring 1974): 23 [hereafter referred to as WFI], trans. Diana Matias from "Ecriture/fiction/idéologie" in *Théorie d'ensemble*, ed. Philippe Sollers (Paris: Editions du Seuil, 1968), 127-47.

25. Heath, of course, was not only one of the best known apologists for *Tel Quel*, he was also an editor of *Screen* in the early seventies. An excellent, short history of *Screen*'s editorial policies in the context of French thought is provided in MacCabe's "Class of '68."

26. See for example the essays collected in *For Marx*, trans. Ben Brewster (London: Verso, 1977). I discuss the assimilation of Althusser's philosophy to the discourse of political modernism more thoroughly in Chapter Three.

27. Trans. with a preface by Gayatri Chakravorty Spivak (Baltimore: Johns Hopkins University Press, 1976): 11.

28. Christopher Norris, *Deconstruction: Theory and Practice* (New York: Methuen, 1982): 28-29.

29. In this essay, Sollers describes his version of the competing senses of the terms of writing in the following manner: "—first, and here the word is employed without quotation marks, is writing in the current sense: that which is effectively written or the phonetic writing used in our culture which corresponds to a representation of speech [*parole*]. . . .

"—secondly, and the word is now written in quotation marks, by 'writing' one designates the effect of an opening of language, its articulation, its scansion, is overdetermination, its *spacing* (Derrida), in such a way that there always appears an archiwriting [*pré-écriture*] within writing, a trace anterior to the distinction signifier/signified, a graphic retention of sound within speech at the same time as an organic inscription which thinks, simultaneously, its mark and its effacement. . . ." (My translation from Philippe Sollers's, ed., *Théorie d'ensemble*: 318).

30. *Tel Quel* 39 (automne 1969): 3-12. This project may also be identified, to a greater or lesser extent, in "Programme," *Tel Quel* 31 (automne 1967) which also served as Sollers's introduction to his study of "limit-texts," *Logiques* (Paris: Editions du Seuil, 1968), in "Division de l'ensemble," his introduction to *Théorie d'ensemble*, in

Sur le matérialisme (Paris: Editions du Seuil, 1974), and many other texts.

31. *Tel Quel* 31 (automne 1967): 15-30, reprinted in *Théorie d'ensemble* and translated by Diana Matias in *Afterimage* 5 (Spring 1974): 22-39.

32. D. I. Grossvogel, "Reappropriating the Political Film," *Diacritics* 5.2 (Summer 1975): 48.

33. See her *Histoire de la psychanalyse en France, 2*, especially 381-414. Roudinesco draws an interesting portrait of the Ecole Normale Supérieure as an institutional context structuring the relation between the formation of educational and political ideologies and the philosophical training of a whole generation of militant intellectuals in France.

34. The former originally appeared in *La Nouvelle Critique* 161-62 (décembre-janvier 1964-65), and the latter in *La Pensée* (juin 1970); both were subsequently anthologized in *Positions* (Paris: Editions Sociales, 1976). Both trans. Ben Brewster in *Lenin and Philosophy* (New York and London: Monthly Review Press, 1971). The essay on "Ideology and Ideological State Apparatuses" will be cited as ISA.

35. A personal example is closest to hand. Growing up in Texas in the late fifties and early sixties, a typical (secular) schoolday was marked by the following rituals. After the 8:00 A.M. bell, the day invariably began with the recital of the Pledge of Allegiance, a short prayer, and a moral thought for the day, all led by student "volunteers" over the school's public address system. The metaphorical dimension of "public address" would be important for Althusser. For these rituals served (in fact still serve) to reproduce individual schoolchildren as "subjects" of state, religious, and moral ideologies whose only material existence is their preordained narrative format. Of course, while the content of this narrative changed daily, its structure was invariably the same and participation in it was obligatory.

Moreover, a structure of identification was central to this process of "subjection." It was the dubious privilege each morning of three of our fellow students, under the watchful eye of the principal and vice-principal, to lead these rituals and to exemplify a behavior that was to be replicated simultaneously by each and every student, themselves under the no less attentive eye of their home room teachers. Thus, ideology appears as a system of representation perpetuated under the aegis of a State institution that serves to unite individuals within pregiven and habitual categories of subjectivity—of state allegiance, religious belief, and moral example. Curiously, for Althus-

ser the question of whether these children "believed" these ideologies is not necessarily relevant. What counts is that they daily and
habitually willingly *acted* upon them, and even competed (as we did)
to be the "voluntary" leaders. In ideology, subjection to power is a
"privilege" and thus ideology structures desire in relation to power.

    36. Peter Wollen, " 'Ontology' and 'Materialism' in Film," *Screen*
17.1 (Spring 1976): 13.

TWO

Modernism and Semiology

Writing in 1972 in the British journal *Afterimage*, Peter Sainsbury editorialized "for a new cinema." The goal of this new
cinema was to achieve a break that challenged rather than
sustained film's dominant social use as a vehicle for mass ideologies. This rhetoric of the definitive aesthetic break, and of
the transformation of the artwork so as to resist rather than
perpetuate bourgeois ideology, is characteristic of the general
discourse of modernism in the arts. It is not surprising then
that the history of *Afterimage* is coincident with, and representative of, the emergence of the discourse of political modernism in Anglo-American film theory. From the appearance
of its first number in 1970—"Film and Politics"—*Afterimage*'s
project was twofold: first, to recover the history of modernism
in film and to understand the alliance of film with past and
contemporary avant-garde movements; but more importantly,
to emphasize what was understood as the inherent alliance of
modernist film practice with past and present revolutionary
movements (e.g., the Soviet Revolution of 1917, Third-World
liberation movements, the contemporary student, labor, and
feminist movements in advanced industrial countries, and so
on).[1]

Even more fundamental was the desire expressed in *Afterimage* to construct a theory that identified modernist form in
film with a critique of ideology. In this respect, Sainsbury's
editorial argument attempts to justify as coextensive practices

the aesthetic project of the New American cinema, as exemplified by Hollis Frampton's *Zorns Lemma* (1970), and the
political project of Jean-Luc Godard and Jean-Pierre Gorin's
Vent d'est (1970). According to Sainsbury, these films are exemplary in forging a relation between art and politics because
they avoid two primary idealisms: one that pursues formal experimentation as an end in itself, the other that ignores the
problem of aesthetic representation in pursuit of direct and
literal political argumentation. On a sliding scale between what
one might call in that era a politics of the signifier and a politics
of the signified, *Zorns Lemma* and *Vent d'est* mediate two extremes. What is common to them both is the attempt to produce, through reflexive representational strategies, knowledge
about the social function of aesthetic texts. They are, in Sainsbury's words "epistemological films":

> An art which has epistemological value is necessarily reflexive.
> Reflexive art is that, like cubist painting and like the cinema of
> Godard, Frampton, and an increasing number of others in Eu-
> rope and America, which contains, on one level, reference to
> nothing but itself. Just as the paintings were about perspective,
> line and form and drew the two dimensional world of canvas
> and frame into the picture itself, so the films are about the
> constituents of cinema, its history and its traditional forms, its
> use of spatial and temporal relationships and its processes of
> recording and transcription. ("Editorial," 3-4)

This equation of aesthetic reflexivity with a nonideological
capacity in the work of art has fundamental affinities with
Clement Greenberg's version of pictorial modernism. Over-
whelmed by the products of mass culture, the purpose of the
work of art is to organize itself around those values only to be
found in art: "Content is to be dissolved so completely into
form that the work of art or literature cannot be reduced in
whole or in part to anything not itself."[2] But there are also
fundamental differences. Greenberg's position is both conservative and hermetic. By insisting on the integral self-identity of the work of art and severing it from social content, the
modernist work is said to eschew a world of ideological confusion and violence, thereby preserving a tradition of artistic
quality that the proliferation of mass culture threatens to de-

vour. The "epistemological" tendency, on the other hand, is not the preservation or continuation of a tradition, but rather its negation or critique. Rather than attempting to preserve the intrinsic, formal values of art, this conception of the modernist text aims to produce knowledge about art in its relation to society. This is to be achieved by a dialectical movement where the organization of the modernist text is conceived as a formal negation—the designation and criticism of an artistic tradition against which the text must be read and interpreted.

Sainsbury's editorial does not fully articulate this position. What I wish to point out, rather, is how and in what terms his argument is structured by a desire common to his historical moment; that is, to rewrite modernism in relation to its postwar conceptualization by Greenberg and others. The history and discourses of modernism were thus marshaled in defense of the concept that a politically consequent film practice—one that would engage in an ideology critique and therefore measure itself against an epistemological standard—must necessarily incorporate avant-garde (i.e., modernist) representational strategies.

If certain aspects of Greenberg's arguments are silenced here, it is because they had already been displaced by another theoretical context defined by modernism's encounter with semiology. Historical and theoretical parallels between modernism in the arts and semiology had already been drawn by Peter Wollen in his 1972 "Conclusion" to *Signs and Meaning in the Cinema,* and were extended in his influential essay, "The Two Avant-Gardes."[3] According to Pam Cook, the fundamental importance of Wollen's thesis concerning the "two avant-gardes" was threefold: first, it brought together, if only polemically, two kinds of film practice that were previously thought incompatible—formalist and militant; second, it revealed the history of modernism in the arts and its influence on filmmakers as a body of work previously ignored by film history; and last, in Britain at least, it described points of common interest between the problems of avant-garde filmmaking and the study of ideology in contemporary film theory.[4]

Throughout the early seventies Wollen persuasively argued for the necessary alliance of modernism with a semiotic understanding of the work of art, thus laying the foundation for the principle axiom of political modernism: the equation of a reflexivity with an epistemological function in the cinema.[5] In "The Two Avant-Gardes," Wollen's principal thesis is that the uneven development of film history and theory has produced two distinct, contemporary avant-gardes. These two avant-garde movements are differentiated not only according to their institutional frameworks and financial support, but also, and most importantly for Wollen, by their aesthetic assumptions and historical and critical origins. By now the argument should be a familiar one since it is described in embryonic form in Sainsbury's editorial. One avant-garde, characterized by the films of Jean-Luc Godard, Miklós Jansco, Jean-Marie Straub and Danielle Huillet, and others, is understood as descending from a literary tradition in modernism; the other, designated by the films of the American and European Co-op movements, is understood as descending from a painterly tradition. Moreover, in Wollen's view this split is already reproduced in the film movements of the twenties: the painterly tradition, represented by the films of Fernand Léger and Dudley Murphy, Francis Picabia and René Clair, Man Ray, Viking Eggeling, Hans Richter, and others, explores pictorial values through time and light; the literary tradition, represented by the Soviet montage school, evidences the influence of futurist sound poetry, and experimental novel and theater in its exploration of problems of meaning and reference in narrative.

The historical situation of both avant-gardes, Wollen argues, originates in a crucial break in the history of representation initiated by the revolution of cubism and its influence on the literary avant-gardes:

> The innovations of Picasso, and Braque, were seen as having an implication beyond the history of painting itself. They were intuitively felt, I think, very early on, to represent a critical semiotic shift, a changed concept and practice of sign and signification, which we can now see to have been the opening-up of a space, a disjunction between signifier and signified and a change of emphasis from the problem of signified and reference, the classic problem of realism, to that of signified and signifier within the sign itself. (TAG 79)

In their fragmentation and leveling of perspectival space, and their emphasis on the materiality and constructedness of the work of art, Wollen credits the cubists with a basic semiotic intuition and nascent ideology critique. Meaning is understood here as a product of the intrinsic signifying operations of the aesthetic message as opposed to a mimetic conception that makes meaning (the signified) contingent upon the suppression of the signifier in an ever more perfect correspondence between sign and world.

In tracing the influence of this intuition, Wollen's most compelling assertion, though not clearly stated, is forcefully implied. Full comprehension of the modernist revolution was deflected since aesthetic practice developed more or less in ignorance of the theoretical revolutions, inaugurated by Ferdinand de Saussure and Sigmund Freud. This assertion appears most clearly in Wollen's critique of the theoretical assumptions subtending the historical emergence of the two avant-gardes as two primary idealisms. For example, the Soviet montage school (represented primarily by Sergei Eisenstein) is criticized for remaining preoccupied with the problem of realism (in the sense of developing ever more compelling representations of an emerging revolutionary culture) and for merely extending modernist dramaturgy by giving priority to the signified in the search for new forms for new content. Veering radically in the other direction, nonobjective art suppresses the signified altogether, forging "an art of pure signifiers detached from meaning as much as from reference" (TAG 79). Without the context of a semiology, the justification for abstraction lapses into various forms of idealism: symbolism or spiritualism (e.g., Vasily Kandinsky, who locates meaning in an *Überwelt* of pure ideas), formalism (the Bauhaus—art as pure design), and two aspects of Greenbergian modernism, art as objecthood or pure presence and abstract art as the teleological search throughout the history of art for a means of expression belonging only to art.[6]

Therefore, Wollen's objective in "The Two Avant-Gardes" is to regain the originary, "materialist" emphasis of modernism by rewriting its history through the historical development of semiology and, subsequently, to lay the critical foundation for defining a modernist, political cinema as an epistemological cinema. The philosophical groundwork for this project began in Wollen's 1972 "Conclusion" to *Signs and Meaning in the Cinema*. Wollen's principal argument here is that since 1968 the cinema has entered a transitional phase or achieved a "break" in Louis Althusser's terminology. This historical break is marked by cinema's delayed encounter with modernism since it was only in its infancy at the time of the "heroic phase" of the avant-garde (1905-17) and of the philosophical revolutions being carried through by Freud and Saussure. The material preconditions for this encounter prefigure Wollen's bifurcated history of the cinematic avant-gardes. One aspect of cinema's encounter with modernism occurs in the painterly aesthetic developed by the New American Cinema in the postwar period; the other derives from the investigation of cinematic narrative initiated by Godard and other modern European filmmakers. By finally bringing together political commitment and argumentation with a reflexive, semiological critique of the forms and materials of cinematic expression in their ideological functioning, Godard is credited with accomplishing a crucial shift in the history of modernist film. In Wollen's view, Godard's films of the post-'68 period define a synthetic third avant-garde. With this in mind, Wollen's stated task is to attempt "on a theoretical level, to try and explain what this potential break with the past involved, would involve if it were to be carried through. This raises problems about the nature of art, its place in intellectual production, the ideology and philosophy which underpin it" (SAM 158).

In Wollen's view, what are the philosophical preconditions that mark an epistemological break within the history of cinema as initiated by its encounter with modernism? One basic premise has already appeared in Wollen's discussion of cubism's "semiotic shift" as problematizing notions of realism and expressivity in representation. In like manner, Wollen's first move in "Conclusion" is to criticize linguistic philosophies that construe language simply as an instrument of communication, a position common to Roman Jakobson, Luis Prieto, and M. A. K. Halliday. In Wollen's discussion, this entails a model of linguistic acts where individuals communicate through the agency of a common code. The sender maps his or her message onto an ideational representation (signified) and a material form or signal (signifier) and transmits it through a given channel to the receiver who obtains and decodes the original message: "Clearly this model of language rests on the notion of the thinking mind or consciousness which controls the material world. Matter belongs to the realm of instrumentality; thus, the consciousness makes use of the material signal as tool. Behind every material sign is an ideal message, a kind of archisignal. In essence, this view is a humanised version of the old theological belief that the material world as a whole comprised a signal, which, when decoded, would reveal the message of the divine Logos" (SAM 159).[7]

According to Wollen, the dominance of this language model engendered a number of aesthetic theories that deemphasized the materiality of the artwork. Foremost among these theories was romanticism that cast signals as symbols "to be decoded not by applying a common code but by intuition and empathy, projection into the artist's inner world" (SAM 159). In this view, the sense of any agency of a common, historically determined and socially defined code was suppressed, rendering both artistic intention and audience response as a matter of spiritual attunement or of a sympathetic response to the work's revelation of eternal values. In critical theory, however, since romanticism denied the need for self-conscious interpretation, the classical view prevailed. Because aesthetic messages were often complex and ambiguous, classicism understood the function of criticism as clarification—maximizing the intelligibility of the message through a full and adequate decoding that could only be accomplished by expert readers. Classical criticism thus posited a content to works of art that guaranteed their intelligibility in the form of knowledge about their historical origins and of their cultural and social situations. Ultimately, in Wollen's view, this led to a variety of positivism where the work of art was "interpreted not as a body of ideas or experiences, but as the expression of the artist's racial or geographical or social situation" (SAM 160).[8] In this context, the materiality of the aesthetic message is equally supressed in the

attempt to recover the biography of the artist as the condition
of the text's meaningfulness.

For Wollen, the theoretical break of modernism must be
measured against these views—first in its discrediting of artistic
intention and aesthetic content; and second in its rejection of
a utilitarian understanding of representation. Aesthetic signification is then understood not as the expression of an artistic
consciousness, but as a determination on subjectivity. In its
earliest stages modernism made it possible for the artist to
concentrate on the material character of the work. However,
with the exception of Freud's influence on the Surrealists and
the alliance of the Russian Formalists with the Soviet avant-
garde, the philosophical background of the early modernist
movements were by and large a mixture of idealist philosophies
that hypostasized rather than discredited the intentional subject, as well as utilitarian theories of language and representation. Lacking an adequate philosophical context with which
to assess the theoretical intelligibility of this break, the modern
artist could only lapse into either a mystic naturalism (e.g., the
spiritualism of Kandinsky or the suprematism of Malevich where
the artwork is equated with a natural object, thus effacing its
status as sign), or as a tehnocratism concerned only with the
perfection of the instrumental nature of artistic materials.[9]

In "The Two Avant-Gardes," this same argument is transformed *mutatis mutandis* by Wollen's division of the cinematic
avant-gardes into literary and painterly lineages, though not
without some distortion of the positions he criticizes. Since
cinema works on more than one semiotic channel (photography, speech, music, sound effects, and graphic writing), and
uses multiple types of code, throughout its history it has in-
corporated a variety of artistic practices and theories. One
lineage develops the abstract tendency in painting, working
with pure light or color, nonfigurative design, or the expressive
deformation of conventional photographic imagery, while the
other develops the organizational principles of montage characteristic of either associational patterns found in poetry and
dream or based on analogies with musical composition. But,
according to Wollen, these two lines develop independently
of one another, one toward an idealism of the signifier or form,

the other toward an idealism of the signified or meaning. For Wollen, the aesthetic of Eisenstein is the best example of the latter, owing to his preoccupation with rehabilitating a representational dramaturgy rather than breaking with it, which is read symptomatically in his rejection of Vertov's work as "formalist jack-straws." At the other end of the scale, the painterly lineage resulted in a formalist idealism in the search for a "pure cinema" exploring the nature of cinematic process as an ontological essence.[10] Dissatisfaction with the search for kinetic solutions to pictorial problems led to an interest in specifically cinematic problems. For Wollen, this insistence on the ontological autonomy of film is simply the displacement of a painterly aesthetic (essentially Greenbergian modernism) into the realm of filmmaking: "The tendency of painting to concentrate on its own sphere of materials and signification, to be self-reflexive, has been translated into specifically cinematic terms and concerns, though . . . 'specifically cinematic' is taken to mean primarily the picture track" (TAG 80; emphasis mine).

If Wollen's intention in both the 1972 "Conclusion" and "The Two Avant-Gardes" is to rewrite the history of modernism through semiology in order to restore its sense for a materialist theory of signification and its value for ideological criticism, then this last statement contains a particularly compelling move. Having expressed his dissatisfaction with the exclusion of the problem of verbal language and narrative from the majority of avant-garde films, Wollen continues to explain that this represents the mark of "an aesthetic which was itself founded on concepts of visual form and visual problems which exclude verbal language from their field, and may be actively hostile to it. This is part of the legacy of the Renaissance which has survived the modernist break almost unchallenged, except in isolated insistences—Lissitzky, Duchamp, Picabia and, extremely important, recent conceptualist work" (TAG 80).

Taken alone this observation is interesting, but more the expression of a critical value judgment than a point of theory; placed against the background of Signs and Meaning its fundamental importance for Wollen is clear. The refusal to incorporate verbal language in aesthetic practice epitomizes a symptomatic silence with drastic implications for the theory and practice of the avant-garde—an ignorance of semiology, here understood by Wollen as a linguistics. Arguing that the cinema, more than any other art form, represents the lure of a purely instrumental language, "a means of communication in which the signals employed are themselves identical or near-identical with the world which is the object of thought," Wollen criticizes "presemiological" avant-gardes for simply transferring their object from "world" to "form" (SAM 165). They thus continue to support a fundamental idealism by presupposing an identity between sign and referent or truth and experience, rather than concentrating on the forms of intelligibility that language permits and semiology theorizes. The very iconicity of the image-track, whether or not it is used toward representational ends, becomes the ground for a profound suspicion of cinema's "inherent" resistance to language.

The rejection of verbal language by the painterly avant-gardes, then, becomes virtually equivalent to a rejection of theory. The hoped for synthesis of the two avant-gardes, however, will restore the identification of modernism and semiology as the foundation of a theoretical or epistemological cinema. Thus for Wollen the importance of semiology is that it understands the text as a material object "whose significance is determined not by a code external to it, mechanically, nor organically as a symbolic whole, *but through its own interrogation of its own code. It is only through such an interrogation, through such an interior dialogue between signal and code*, that a text can produce spaces within meaning, within the otherwise rigid straight-jacket of the message, to produce a meaning of a new kind, *generated within the text itself*' (SAM 162; emphases mine).

Here Wollen's understanding of the importance of semiology for modernism is brought fully to light. Utilitarian theories of communication dissolved the materiality of the text by deferring meaning (the operation of code) and its ultimate referent to a moment anterior to the message: the translation of thought into word, language as the expression of Being; in sum, the philosophical impulse that Jacques Derrida has criticized as the logocentrism of Western metaphysics. However, semiology restores the function of code to the structure of the message and thereby produces meaning as a form of autodesignation. The modernist aesthetic message is therefore understood as dominated by the operation of code; it is metalingual and self-referential in that meaning is not a product but a process where the act of communication ("the interior dialogue between signal and code") is reproduced within the structure of the message itself. For Wollen, this reflexive model of the aesthetic message is the only basis for proposing a theory of political modernism that accounts for an epistemological function in film.

Clearly, Godard's film practice between 1968 and 1972 is a key reference point for Wollen's theoretical statements. In particular, *Vent d'est* receives extensive treatment in both the 1972 "Conclusion" to *Signs and Meaning* and a contemporaneous essay, "Counter-Cinema: *Vent d'est*." Wollen's accounts of this film provide a succinct example of what his version of epistemological modernism concretely entails. In *Signs and Meaning*, *Vent d'est* is deemed exemplary of Wollen's desired merger of modernism and semiology. The revolutionary impact of Godard's work is understood as his interrogation of the basic premises of filmmaking and film language that have heretofore gone unquestioned by filmmakers and spectators in their acceptance of the illusionist standards of commercial, narrative cinema. By strategically organizing his films to impose difficulties in reading, in Wollen's view Godard compels the spectator to reflect on how he or she looks at films—as passive consumer or active participant—and how meaning is achieved in films. Therefore, the criterion of reflexivity renders semiological analysis and modernist aesthetic practice as functionally equivalent. Similarly, in the "Counter-cinema" essay, Wollen's definition of a semiotic reflexivity, or the production of a dialogue between signal and code interior to the message itself, becomes the linchpin of what Laura Mulvey later characterized as a "negative aesthetic." Here the reflexive structure of the text of political modernism is mapped onto a series of formal negations organized according to the opposition of modernism to realism. In this respect, the text of counter-cinema is marked by its interiorization and critical interrogation of the codes of Hollywood narrative cinema—for example, narrative transitivity (linear and teleological exposition); emotional identification with the characters and diegesis; representational transparency (masking of the means of production); a singular, unified, and homogenous diegetic space; textual closure presupposing a self-contained fiction—all of which are designed to yield a narrative pleasure aimed at pacifying the spectator.

In point of fact, Wollen's counter-cinema, which must accomplish the semiotic "deconstruction" of these elements of code, may be described in three points.

1. The text of political modernism cannot be conceived instrumentally: "it is a material object which provides conditions for the production of meaning, *within constraints it sets itself.* It is open rather than closed; multiple rather than single; productive rather than exhaustive" (SAM 163; emphasis mine). With its episodic construction, disjunct and digressive narrative development, its multiple diegetic registers, and its refusal of narrative closure, *Vent d'est* is a privileged example of Wollen's counter-cinema. Bertolt Brecht's theories of epic theater are also often invoked as a model.[11] By foregrounding its means of representation, and ceaselessly question normative codes of narration and meaning *Vent d'est* becomes an "open text" that renders meaningless any attempt at a singular or exhaustive reading. Later, Wollen adopts from Kristeva the term *intertextuality* to describe the formal structure of counter-cinema. In this respect, once the priority of reference to the "real world" has been disputed, a modernist aesthetics is free to exploit the variety of semiotic channels available to a given medium, breaking down the illusionist homogeneity and transparency of the work by opening it up to different orders and types of discourse in a play of allusion, citation, and parody. Meaning is then produced in a differential ordering of signifiers, rather than in reference to a transcendental signified in either the form of an illusion of reality or that of the monumental aspect of presemiological modernisms.

2. Once the text has been opened up centrifugally—that is, once it has become intertextual—a difficulty in reading is imposed. For Wollen, this has the effect of emphasizing the interpretive faculty of the reader. Since there is no longer a

unitary code nor a fixed meaning to which one can refer, textual semiosis takes the form of a "hesitation" in that it "deliberately suspends 'meaning', avoids any teleology or finality,
in the interest of a destruction and re-assembly, a re-combi-
nation of the order of the sign as an experiment in the dissolution of old meanings and the generation of the new ones
from the semiotic process itself" (TAG 82).[12] By imposing this
practice of reading, the modernist text also overturns the myth
of the reader as a passive, receiving consciousness. Through
its forms of autodesignation and intertexual referencing, in
Wollen's view the text actively engages the reader in the process of decoding and the production of meaning. The reader
is thus placed in the role of an active producer, rather than of
a passive consumer, who might thoughtfully entertain social
contradictions and political argumentation. And, rather than
being encouraged to identify with the text, the spectator is
"distanced" from it. He or she finds no surrogate within the
film. Instead, the spectator is addressed directly as an audience
member. For Wollen, the goal of the modernist text is no longer
simply the production of pleasure or narrative entertainment.
It equally presents the spectator with contradictions and arguments aimed at unsettling and provoking action in the audience.

    3. This practice of reading imposed by the form of the mod-
ernist text generates a subjective response that Wollen calls
"meaning effects": "just as this text, by introducing its own
decoding procedures, interrogates itself, so the reader too must
interrogate himself, puncture the bubble of his consciousness
and introduce into it the rifts, contradictions and questions
which are the problematic of the text" (SAM 163-64). Thus
Vent d'est is endorsed as a privileged example of a cinema
whose intelligibility is no longer measured against its representation of a socially and culturally recognizable reality.
Rather, cinematic meaning is produced openly through a contradictory organization of various codes and types of discourse
set into play within the text. In this manner, Wollen credits
Vent d'est with demonstrating that "the cinema cannot show
the truth, or reveal it, because the truth is not out there in
the real world, waiting to be photographed. What the cinema

can do is produce meanings and meaning can only be plotted, not in relation to some abstract yardstick or criterion of truth, but in relation to other meanings" ("Counter-Cinema," 16).

In "The Two Avant-Gardes," Godard's post-'68 films (or rather, Wollen's readings of them) achieve an even greater historical impact in Wollen's bifurcated history of modernism in the arts and film. In Wollen's view, having discovered an alternative route between an idealism of the signifier (form) and an idealism of the signified (meaning)— or between a Greenbergian pictorial reflexivity and a literary realism—Godard had returned to the point of the original epistemological break instigated by the cubist revolution in painting. Wollen compares the aesthetic impact of Godard's films to that of Picasso's *Les desmoiselles d'Avignon* (1907) in that both works present the possibility of working within a space opened up by the disjunction of signifier and signified. Godard's work is thus understood as offering a third direction in the history of the cinematic avant-gardes; i.e., what Wollen had already termed *counter-cinema*. Godard's aesthetic practice is similarly likened to an expansion of Eisenstein's dialectical montage such that formal conflict takes place not between successive signifieds, but between different codes and channels of expression. Refusing the conventional unities of film form, such as the anchoring of sound to an image, Wollen argues that Godard has rendered problematic the "natural" relationship between the five materials of expression available to film: photographic reproduction, verbal speech, inscription (writing), sound effects, and music.

> For Godard, conflict becomes not simply collision through juxtaposition, as in Eisenstein's model, but an act of negativity, a splitting apart of an apparently natural unity, a disjunction. Godard's view of bourgeois communication is one of a discourse which gains its power from its apparent naturalness, the impression of necessity which seems to bind a signifier to a signified, a sound to an image, in order to provide a convincing representation of the world. He wants not simply to represent an alternative "world" or an alternative "world-view," but to investigate the whole process of signification out of which a world-view or an ideology is constructed. (TAG 82).

When Wollen asserts that Godard's films deliberately suspend meaning, it is in order to emphasize that, by exploiting the heterogeneity of semiotic channels available to film, Godard is more concerned with a process than a product, that is, with the possibility of meaning or the construction of a variety of meanings. But more importantly, by deliberately aligning Godard's aesthetic practice with the problem of meaning construction, Wollen decisively allies these films with a form of theoretical inquiry proper to semiology itself. Having started with the question of cinema's delayed encounter with modernism in *Signs and Meaning*, "The Two Avant-Gardes" continues by examining modernism's delayed encounter with semiology as evidenced in Godard's work. Here, finally, is the point of Wollen's rewriting of the history of modernism: to restore the intelligibility of modernist aesthetics as a counter-ideological practice through the theoretical context semiology as the attempted recovery of film's theoretical or epistemological heritage. The cinema having been born as the contemporary of Picasso and Saussure, Godard's programmatic "return to zero" is nothing more or less than film's recovery of what was lost to it due to an uneven development of aesthetic and philosophical resources.

This task being accomplished, how does the "third avant-garde" define itself as a politically consequent aesthetic practice? Within the limits set by the discourse of political modernism, the key to this question resides for Wollen in the third of the three points discussed above. Being organized according to a series of negations where normative, ideological codes are targeted and "deconstructed," the immediate yield of a "semiotically reflexive" text is the production of "meaning effects" that "introduce" into the spectator's consciousness the "rifts, contradictions, and questions which are the problematic of the text." "The meaning of texts can be destructive of the codes used in other texts," writes Wollen, "which may be the codes used by the spectator or the reader, who thus finds his own habitual codes threatened, the battle opening up in his own reading. . . . A valuable work, a powerful work at least, is one which challenges codes, overthrows established ways of reading or looking, not simply to establish new ones, but to

compel an unending dialogue, not at random but productively"
(SAM 171-72).

But according to what imperative would this dialog or this
mutually determining activity between text and spectator take
place? Among Wollen's most productive and interesting emphases is that the range of meaning attributable to a given
aesthetic practice is intimately tied to the theory subtending
that practice. And it is precisely on this basis that Wollen's
own views about the possibilities of political modernism must
confront several aporias. The epistemological privilege of political modernism, whose history and theory Wollen wishes to
regain, is presented as a particular relation to semiology as the
science of speech. Wollen's insistence is not, simply speaking,
that the third avant-garde must found itself on semiotic theory;
more importantly, the text of political modernism must itself
interiorize a semiological structure.

This insistence is not as confusing or difficult as it might
initially seem. For example, Wollen's presentation of the aesthetic break inaugurated by cubism is predicated on the idea
that the structure of the artwork was *modeled on the structure
of the sign itself.* Indeed, this is the basis of Wollen's definition
of semiotic reflexivity and the epistemological privilege it en-
joys. As opposed to utilitarian theories of language, the first
premise of semiology is the nonidentity of sign and thing or
the arbitrary relation of the signifier to the thing signified such
that the text modeled on this structure must bracket out all
reference to anything but its integral, self-identity.[13] In Wollen's reading cubism's intuition of an aesthetic practice founded
on semiology is based on a rhetoric of abstraction and interiorization: "a shift of emphasis from the problem of signified
and reference" (that is, the content of the work of art as the
perfectible reproduction of a natural world already endowed
with meaning) to a reflection on the relation between signifier
and signified *within* the artwork itself (or the "interior dialogue
between signal and code"). For Wollen, cubism achieves an
epistemological break with illusionist representational practices by foregrounding and pointing to is own semiotic constructedness.

On the one hand, it is not difficult to accept at face value Wollen's assertion that the elimination of reference is one of the fundamental concepts of nonrepresentational painting, especially since this is a constant theme of modernist criticism. However, it is significant that Wollen provides no specific analyses of how cubist painting articulates the relation of signifier to signified as a problem of the internal dynamics of its form. On the other hand, Wollen's discussions of the history of modernism in relation to film practice contain numerous examples of this strategy. Even Peter Sainsbury's comments are predicated on establishing a relation between signifier and signified within the modernist text, but only according to a specific and largely unconscious equation: a politics of the "signifier" is identified with the problem of the formal organization of the image or the coding of iconic relations; the politics of the "signified" is equated with meaning in the form of political rhetoric or argumentation, in fact, a politics of speech.

Similarly, Wollen argues that the importance of Godard's films is that while they clearly engage a politics of image and form, they have also insisted on the incorporation of the discourse of Marxist political culture which, in Wollen's emphasis, is a culture of books and verbal language. Placed against Wollen's stated dissatisfaction with the refusal of language in avant-garde films, this observation presents some problems for understanding exactly what his notion of film as an epistemological or theoretical form of inquiry might be. First of all, these two essays clearly imply that the banishment of language in avant-garde films is linked to a symptomatic refusal of the forms of intelligibility that semiology brings to a modernist aesthetics. This observation would not in and of itself cause any problems if Wollen's definition of the sign were more consistent. Even though both *Signs and Meaning* and "The Two Avant-Gardes" arguably deal with the same critical issues, the former works itself out roughly within the Peircean framework outlined in its last chapter while the latter involves poststructuralist concepts within a Saussurean terminology, a project that Jacques Derrida rendered philosophically problematic almost eight years earlier in *De la grammatologie*. In this manner, the most compelling argument presented by Wollen in *Signs and*

Meaning—that the aesthetic message might reflexively designate within its structure the interrogation of its own code and
thus its condition of meaning—loses its force in translation to
the later essay. Whereas in the original argument producing
a "space" within the message meant opening an interior dialog
between signal and code, in "The Two Avant-Gardes," this
same "spacing," reproduced as a dislocation between signifier
and signified, may arguably be interpreted as a version of montage consisting of an interrogation of the image track by the
sound track.[14] This interpretation gains credibility when we
recall that Wollen's history of the two avant-gardes contrasts
an aesthetics of the signifier (that is, of the painterly and the
image) with an aesthetics of the signified (narrative or verbal
language). Extending Wollen's discussion of Godard, then, are
we to assume that an epistemological activity of counter-cinema is reducible to the incorporation of a political discourse
("a Marxist political culture . . . one of books and verbal language") as so many signifieds, verbal or written signs, to be
organized within a modernist aesthetic strategy? Or that a theoretical activity of film practice is tantamount to appropriating
the discourse of semiology in such a way that the sound track
launches a "semiotic" interrogation of the image track and its
normative forms of organization according to codes of narrative transitivity, identification, transparency, and closure? Although in his most didactic and exhortatory moments this is
certainly the case in some of Godard's Dziga-Vertov period
films, to be fair, I do not believe Wollen would wholly accept
(and not without justification) this presentation of his argument.

However, this overvaluation of speech in relation to image—
in fact, the very opposition of these terms in Wollen's writings—poses particularly acute problems. In Wollen's view, the
original sin of modernism, especially in relation to film, derives
from a theory that understands aesthetic language as identical
to, and the instrument of, a freely creative consciousness. To
Wollen's credit, his work may be understood as one of the
most powerful critiques in film theory of a view, common since
the Port Royal grammarians, that language is simply the reflection, imitation, or instrument of thought. But it is necessary

to remember how he links the criterion of reflexivity to an epistemological standard in art. Reflexivity in the text of counter-cinema, for example, is portrayed as a self-actualization of the aesthetic message in order "to produce meanings within constraints set by the message itself." These constraints are themselves telling in their extension from an activity of the text to a presumed spectatorial activity. That "internal dialogue between signal and code" or that internal scission between signifier and signified, which in Wollen's account is the product of a fundamental intertextuality, must reproduce themselves as a scission or a productive difference within the spectator's consciousness. But what enables this process to take place? How can a text that brackets out all reference to anything but its own internal constructedness open itself to an "outside" either in the form of intertextual referencing or an address to the spectator in the form of "meaning effects"? To the extent that the negative and critical function of counter-cinema bases itself on the necessity of reflexivity and the formal autonomy of the text, it must face an irresolvable contradiction in its theorization of the spectator. As Rodolphe Gasché has pointed out in another context, the association of reflexivity with a deconstructive criticism always relies on a version of negativity which, by inscribing within the text the process of its own construction, will render "visible" to the reader the suppressed elements of the textual work.[15] But is it not precisely the measure of a self-evidential representation that the discourse of political modernism set out to criticize in illusionist cinema? Rather than a difficulty in reading, which is supposed to encourage a productive and active semiosis in the spectator, is it not the case that what is asserted in place of a mimetic theory of representation is in fact a "negative" identity theory where contradictions produced "semiotically" within the modernist text are said to be reproduced as "gaps and fissures" in the spectator's consciousness? As an epistemological relation, reflexivity can only be awkwardly considered here either according to a standard that equates visibility with self-evidence in the semiotic constructedness of art, or as the doubling of a reflexive situation in the spectator whose conscious activity mirrors that of the text. As a model for an epistemological relation inscribed within the text, which thus redoubles itself as a relation inscribed within the spectator, reflexivity becomes an envisioning of the spectator as a specular reflection of the internal dynamics of the forms of the text.

Therefore, in his most polemical moments, Wollen seems to promote a purely formalist model of the modernist text as an autonomous structure that produces meaning intrinsically. In this respect, his particular insistence on the self-identity of the aesthetic text, and his formulation of the epistemological privilege of reflexivity according to a hierarchical division between image and speech perfectly reproduces the discourse of autoaffection that Derrida, for one, has criticized as exemplary of the representational theories of Western metaphysics. The process of meaning in this view can only be construed as an intimate relation between signifier and signified, voice and thought. This view is not only perfectly reproduced in Saussure's semiology, but is also characteristic of the emphasis on interiority and autodesignation in those discourses on modernism where the subject must be considered as identical with the text it confronts. The interest of the concept of intertextuality—which could account for a relation of exteriority where the meaning of a given text is produced according to its historically particular insertion with a determined discursive formation or its differential and structured relation with other texts—is mistakenly equated here with the creative use of certain textual figures, such as elements of parody, irony, citation, or autodesignation.

On the basis of this and similar contradictions, Sylvia Harvey has observed that "In one of those odd reversals of history, some of the antirealist theorists of the '70s made a mistake very similar to that of Lukács: they tended to assume that texts could be defined as 'radical' on the basis of stylistic properties alone, rather than on the basis of the tripartite relationship between textual properties, contemporary social reality and historically formed readers" ("Whose Brecht," 51). Similarly, in her book on *May '68 and Film Culture* (London: British Film Institute, 1978), Harvey describes four problems that must be confronted and criticized in the concept of "epistemological modernism":

1. The tendency to replace an interest in the *relationship* between specific means of aesthetic representation and a social reality conceived of as distinct from those means, with an exclusive concern with the means of representation. . . .
2. The tendency towards an essentialist position on the question of form, for example the argument that a particular style is essentially progressive or essentially reactionary.
3. The tendency to think through the problem of formal innovation only in terms of the internal organisation of the literary, dramatic or filmic 'text', and not in terms of the insertion of that text within a particular apparatus, within a system of consumption, distribution or exchange specific to a particular society and a particular historical moment.
4. The tendency to offer a puritanical defense of the "work" (of reading, of meaning production) which the modernist text invites the reader to perform, and an accompanying underestimation of the importance of pleasure and entertainment. (*May '68*, 69-70)

To further elaborate and explain these points, and to establish a historical understanding of their specific determinations in the discourse of political modernism—above all in the equation of reflexivity with a textual, epistemological relation—we will have to turn to critical debates in French film culture in the period after May 1968, in which the positions of Peter Wollen and other Anglo-American theorists of the early '70s were forged.

NOTES

1. Peter Sainsbury's "Editorial" appeared in *Afterimage* 4 (1972): 3-4, which brought together articles by Noel Burch, Paul Sharits, Malcolm LeGrice, an interview with Hollis Frampton, and Peter Wollen's influential "Counter-Cinema: *Vent d'est.*" *Afterimage* has systematically followed an editorial policy of publishing work that associates film theory, politics, and avant-garde cinema. Issue No. 2, for example, was dedicated to "Avant-Garde Film" and No. 3 was devoted to "Third World Cinema." *Afterimage* 5 (Spring 1974), entitled "Aesthetics/Ideology/Criticism," presented one of the first and still most substantial efforts at defining a semiotics of the avant-garde text. No. 6 (Summer 1976) was devoted to "Perspectives on English Independent Cinema"; No. 7 (Summer 1978) contained articles on

Straub/Huillet, Yvonne Rainer, Michael Snow, Godard/Miéville, and so on; Nos. 8/9 (Winter 1980-81) was a double issue exploring the relationship of "primitive" cinema to contemporary avant-garde practice; and No. 10 (Autumn 1981) resurrected texts and figures of the French Impressionist movement. Also, at about the same time that *Afterimage* began publication, another influential but short-lived journal, *Cinemantics*, appeared with similar kinds of articles and ed-itorial projects, while *Screen*, having undergone changes in editorial direction, was publishing essays and translations influenced by de-velopments in French film criticism and theory.

2. "Avant-Garde and Kitsch" in *Art and Culture* (Boston: Beacon Press, 1961): 6. Also see his "Modernist Painting" in *Arts Year Book* 4 (1961): 103-08.

3. The 1972 "Conclusion" appeared in the 3d edition to *Signs and Meaning in the Cinema* (Bloomington and London: Indiana Uni-versity Press, 1972): 155-74 (hereafter cited as SAM). "The Two Avant-Gardes" (hereafter cited as TAG) was originally published in a special issue of *Studio International* on the European cinematic avant-gardes, 190.978 (November/December 1975): 171-75, and reprinted a year later in *Edinburgh Magazine* 1 (1976): 77-84. This booklet appeared in conjunction with the 1976 Edinburgh Film Fes-tival whose special events that year included "avant-garde cinema" and "psychoanalysis and cinema." Besides Wollen's article, trans-lations and glosses were published on essays by Christian Metz and Julia Kristeva along with articles on psychoanalysis by Rosalind Cow-ard and Stephen Heath, feminist film practice by Claire Johnston, and two bibliographies, one along the axis "semiotics-Freud and La-can-film-ideology," the other on "avant-garde cinema."

4. The impact and reception of Wollen's essay is discussed in Pam Cook's "Teaching Avant-Garde Film: Notes Towards Practice," *Screen Education* 32/33 (Autumn/Winter 1979/80): 83-98; Sylvia Harvey's *Independent Cinema?* (Stafford: West Midland Arts, 1978); Phillip Drummond's "Notions of Avant-Garde Cinema" in *Film as Film* (London: Arts Council of Great Britain, 1979): 9-16; and Wollen's own update "The Avant-Gardes: Europe and America," *Framework* 14 (Spring 1981): 9-10.

Both Cook and Wollen note the cultural and historical situations that enabled the "two avant-gardes" argument to have a special impact in Britain. First would be a tradition of political cinema which, from the GPO documentaries to the Free Cinema movement, was committed to strategies of documentary and social realism, thus mar-ginalizing the efforts of the existing British avant-garde (e.g., Len

Lye, Humphrey Jennings, and Michael Powell) as "ultra-left utopi-anism." Second would be the emergence of the Independent Film-maker's Association as a viable force that presented the political necessity of discovering patterns of correspondence among rival aes-thetic factions allied under the rubric "independent cinema."

5. This is not to ignore the enormous influence of Annette Mich-elson who was among the first to explore these ideas in several in-fluential essays including " 'The Man with the Movie Camera': From Magician to Epistemologist," *Artforum* (March 1972): 60-72; "Screen/Surface: The Politics of Illusionism," *Artforum* (September 1972): 58-62; "Paul Sharits and the Critique of Illusionism" in *Projected Images* (Minneapolis: Walker Art Center, 1974); and "Film and the Radical Aspiration" in *New Forms in Film* (Montreux 1974): 9-16.

6. Victor Burgin explicitly links this aspect of Greenberg's thought with a liberal progressivism. In this view, the history of art move-ments is depicted in a problem/solution paradigm where each gen-eration of artists is understood as taking up the formal problems left uncompleted by their predecessors. Modernism is thus equated with progress since it is the culmination of a tradition, a continuous de-velopment in the history of Western art. This history is understood by Greenberg as the search for a means of formal organization coex-tensive with the flatness of the picture plane since this was the only condition that painting shared with no other art. Moreover, in Green-berg's view, the intelligibility of past masters was misconstrued if not read back through this particular context. In this manner, art history was relegated to a formalism and reduced to a set of unargued aesthetic conditions without recourse to any political, economic, or technological determinations that might have been operational. See his "Modernism in the *Work* of Art," a paper delivered at the 1976 Edinburgh avant-garde event and published in *Twentieth Century Studies* 15/16 (December 1977): 34-55.

7. The most commonly known communications model of this type is Roman Jakobson's. In his "Closing Statement: Linguistics and Po-etics," published in *Style in Language*, ed. Thomas A. Sebeok (Cam-bridge: The MIT Press, 1960), this model is described as follows: "The ADDRESSER sends a message to the ADDRESSEE. To be op-erative the message requires a CONTEXT referred to ("referent" in another, somewhat ambiguous, nomenclature), seizable by the addressee, and either verbal or capable of being verbalized; a CODE fully, or at least partially, common to the addresser and the addressee (or in other words, to the encoder and decoder of the message); and,

finally, a CONTACT, a physical channel and psychological connection between the addresser and addressee, enabling both of them to enter and stay in communication. All these factors inalienably involved in verbal communication may be schematized as follows:

CONTEXT

MESSAGE

ADDRESSER————————ADDRESSEE

CONTACT

CODE

Each of these six factors determines a different function of language" (353).

The importance of this digression, outside of clarifying Wollen's argument, is to note the difference of this model with respect to the systemic view that Wollen criticizes. In Jakobson's defense, his model not only fully describes a variety of linguistic acts by identifying the dominance of one of its aspects in the structure of a message, this model can also be understood as compatible with Wollen's own version of the aesthetic message. An aesthetic message dominated by the function of code ably corresponds to the reflexive procedures Wollen describes. I will discuss these implications later on as Wollen's uneasy assimilation of concepts from structural linguistics to poststructural criticism.

8. Wollen extended these arguments in "Some Thoughts Arising from Stanley Mitchell's Article," *Screen* 12.4 (Winter 1971/1972): 162-66.

9. This complaint is repeated in Malcolm LeGrice's history of the avant-garde *Abstract Film and Beyond* (Cambridge and London: The MIT Press, 1977).

10. Wollen extended this criticism to contemporary avant-garde movements in a later article, " 'Ontology' and 'Materialism' in Film," *Screen* 17.1 (Spring 1976): 7-23. I will return to these arguments in Chapter Six.

11. Brecht is often referred to both in *Signs and Meaning* and "The Two Avant-Gardes." And in the "Counter-Cinema" essay, Wollen's model of an alternative, antiillusionist cinema compares favorably with, and is undoubtedly conceived in reference to, Brecht's model of epic theater as outlined in his notes to *Mahagonny*, "The Modern Theatre is the Epic Theatre" in *Brecht on Theatre* (New York: Hill and Wang, 1964), trans John Willett, 33-42. However, this particular adaptation of Brecht's theories to cinema within the discourse of poltitical modernism causes certain deformations to Brecht's thought.

I will return to this problem in Chapter Six. For an interesting critique of the theoretical reception of Brecht in this period, see Sylvia Harvey's "Whose Brecht? Memories for the Eighties: A Critical Recovery," *Screen* 23.1 (May/June 1982): 45-59, as well as my own *The Political Avant-Garde: Modernism and Epistemology in Post-'68 Film Theory*, dissertation, The University of Iowa, 1983, especially 234-95.

12. Also see Stephen Heath's *The Nouveau Roman: A Study in the Practice of Writing* (Philadelphia: Temple University Press, 1972): 15-43, where similar points are argued.

13. In Chapter Six, I will describe how Wollen subsequently modulated this position to distance himself from the practice of "structural" film characteristic of the British and North American avant-gardes. I will also discuss, in a more detailed fashion, the theoretical difficulties of Wollen's resolute Saussureanism.

14. To Wollen's credit, he was to engage this problem in a more comprehensive fashion in a later essay, "The Field of Language in Film," *October* 17 (Summer 1981), 53-60. Even in this essay, though, he does not relinquish what I see as an idealization of verbal language. I will return to this argument in Chapter Six.

15. See his "Deconstruction as Criticism," *Glyph* 6 (1979): 177-215.

THREE

Ideology and Criticism

> I take the view that only when . . . the determinations of the
> apparatus (the camera) that structures reality by its inscription
> have been considered, only then could the cinema objectively
> examine its relation to ideology. . . . [Before] proceeding further
> we must first tackle one of the most pressing problems of
> cinematography in France; and that's a problem of . . . [the]
> deconstruction of the ideology produced by the camera.
> —Marcelin Pleynet, "Economical-Ideological-Formal"[1]

Peter Wollen ends the revised edition of *Signs and Meaning in the Cinema* by asserting that it is only in confrontation with Hollywood that anything new can be produced in either critical theory or aesthetic practice. A shift of emphasis characteristic of the post-1968 period is communicated by this attitude. The motivation for this shift was the desire to revolutionize film study itself—first, by introducing a Marxist aesthetics to its field of inquiry, and second by welding a theory of ideology to semiotic and formal analyses as a way of understanding cinema's potential for either perpetuating or undermining the formulation and circulation of value systems under late capitalism. Wollen's program for rewriting the history of modernism in film within the context of semiology was already characteristic of this trend. By opposing idealist aesthetic theories and illusionist cinema to a reflexive or epistemological film modernism, Wollen's theory emerged from a theme already present in the discourse of political modernism:

the desire to found a theory of ideology in a critique of the "realism" of studio films, and contrariwise, to assess as theoretical the work of filmmakers like Godard in their "semiotic" struggle with the dominant, Hollywood codes of film form. Strategies of semiotic analysis had been used to renovate genre and auteur studies of the classical cinema; now they must be mobilized to criticize the ideology of its forms and to pose alternatives to its system of representation.[2]

The emergence of this theme—where a critical theory of ideology based on a definition of realist form in the cinema is linked to a countertheory of the epistemological value of modernist forms—is productively traced to debates in French film theory. These debates began to appear in the aftermath of the student and worker revolts of summer 1968, above all in the journals *Cahiers du cinéma* and *Cinéthique*. The political shock of May '68 and the widespread reevaluation of cultural life it initiated cannot be overestimated as a historical reference point for contemporary film theory. Without question, it set the context for a programmatic shift in the editorial policy of *Cahiers du cinéma* in 1969 and *Screen* in 1971, as well as the inauguration of a host of new journals including *Cinéthique* and *Afterimage*.[3] By October 1969, *Cahiers du cinéma* began publishing work in textual semiotics and formal analysis, best represented by Raymond Bellour's essay on a fragment from *The Birds*.[4] The interest in textual semiotics derived from the idea that the kinds of "knowledges" produced by films and other aesthetic texts could no longer be reduced to their presentation of given contents or arguments; rather, equal attention had to be given to the internal dynamics of textual form. *Cahiers du cinéma* and other journals argued that a theory of ideology could no longer be relegated to the province of false ideas or false consciousness. The function of ideology had to be defined as well in the formal means of signification available to aesthetic practice. In fact, in his afterword to Bellour's essay, Jean Narboni, a *Cahiers du cinéma* editor, criticized Bellour for implicitly retaining an auteurist emphasis and for not addressing the question of ideology in the logic of signification underwriting the classical sequence in Hollywood cinema.

Narboni's critique of Bellour was based on his reading of the Marxist philosopher, Louis Althusser. And it is through *Cahiers du cinéma* and *Cinéthique's* introduction of Althusserian philosophy to film theory, in their debate concerning problems of ideological criticism and a potentially revolutionary "theoretical practice" in film, that the opposition of realism to modernism, as a function of opposing idealist to materialist epistemologies, can best be traced. That Althusser's Marxism should underwrite this debate is by no mean's self-evident. However, as Laura Mulvey notes, Althusser's critique of Hegel and of empiricist epistemologies as an "ideology of the visible" proved attractive to film theory.

> Over and over again he stressed that knowledge, far from being derived from perception, from the visual, actually demanded a refusal to see, a looking away. This made it possible to understand the ideological role of cinema not simply in content terms but as involving the spectator's way of seeing the images on the screen. . . . In this way, we can acquire the elements of a theory of ideology, drawing both on marxism and psycho-analysis, which would make it possible to envisage a counter-strategy for the cinema in which the theory of film and film-viewing as such would be important, rather than simply explicit ideological opposition to the content of the vast majority of films. Hence formal questions become politically crucial because ways of seeing are not natural and given, but bear a close relationship to ideology.[5]

Similarly, Mulvey notes that any counter-cinema conceived in opposition to the prevailing ideology would of necessity seem avant-garde since, in order to produce a different form of knowledge, it would also have to adopt a different means of formal organization.

Phil Rosen has argued that this reading of Althusser's work was also readily compatible with *Tel Quel's* theories of literary modernism.[6] For those engaged with *Tel Quel's* theories of textual practice and criticism, the attractiveness of Althusser's attempts to define a materialist theory of ideology compatible with semiology and Lacanian psychoanalysis cannot be overestimated. This particular assimilation of Althusser's thought by *Tel Quel*, which determined a number of specific problem

areas for studies of film and ideology, was instrumental in the
formation of the discourse of political modernism. Having defined a possible politics of the sign in the conjunction of modernism and semiology, and in opposition to the ideology of
realism, the major problem facing post-'68 critical theory was
the following: how can one differentiate among kinds of texts
according to the kinds of knowledges they are thought to produce? Althusser's attempts to define a scientific as opposed to
ideological knowledge within a philosophical critique of empiricism as an "ideology of the visible" seemed to provide
definite criteria for this project.

The terms of Althusser's appropriation by film theory may
be described as the attempt to redefine his critique of epistemology "semiotically" through the version of modernism
presented in the critical and aesthetic practice of writers associated with the *Tel Quel* group. The initial terms of this
appropriation, and the debate it inspired, were set out in a
series of articles in *Cahiers du Cinéma* and *Cinéthique* in the
fall and winter of 1969.[7] Both journals allied themselves closely
to *Tel Quel*, having published essays and/or interviews with
Tel Quel writers and footnoting them frequently. What is most
striking in the French critical discourse of this period is the
centrality of the concept of the *coupure epistemologique* or
"epistemological break" that was adopted from Althusser's
studies of ideology and the philosophy of science by both *Cahiers du cinéma* and *Cinéthique*. Similar to Wollen's later use
of the term, the idea of the epistemological break was instrumentalized as an aesthetic concept. However, in Althusser's
writings the concept of the break was first and foremost a
historical and *theoretical* concept. It described the revolution-
in-thought where a given "problematic" (a specific organization of concepts, problems, definitions, etc.) separates itself
from its ideological prehistory in order to constitute the conditions for scientific knowledge, or what Althusser called "theoretical practice."[8] Through its specific transformation of a
determinate raw material (ideological concepts) into a determinate product (scientific knowledge), Althusser's theoretical
practice takes its place among the other "practices" (eco-

nomic, ideological, political) that together organize the social formation.

By establishing an opposition between ideological and scientific knowing, the concept of theoretical practice was of particular interest to both *Cahiers du cinéma* and *Cinéthique* in their attempts to define a political aesthetics; and, to the extent that the former meant it to describe the desire to institute a critical theory, and the latter a theory of production, both were in near accordance with Althusser's thought. However, under the influence of *Tel Quel* notions of modernism and the avantgarde, the idea of the epistemological break was transformed into an aesthetic and formal concept. Despite their stated differences, *Cahiers du cinéma* and *Cinéthique* developed similar categorical systems for defining the possibility of a "materialist" cinema allied to revolutionary struggle, as well as that of a "scientific" critical theory through which this cinema could be conceived. Both journals were united in recognizing the necessity of a semiotic modernism that defined the materialist text in terms of formal "work on the signifier." And both supported this proposition by theorizing cinema's production of an "impression of reality" as an ideology-in-general (in Althusser's terms) peculiar to the materiality and technology of cinematic expression.

Tel Quel's influence on the debates regulating Althusser's assimilation by French and Anglo-American film theory is clearly articulated in an interview with *Tel Quel* editors Jean Thibaudeau and Marcelin Pleynet in issue No. 3 of *Cinéthique*. The very title of this interview, "Economique-Idéologique-Formel," places the question of cinema at the intersection of aesthetic practice with other social practices such as the economic and the ideological. In his comments, Pleynet criticizes *Cinéthique* for an unreflected economism that supposes that marginal films, produced and distributed outside of the mainstream of capitalist economy and sympathetic to proletarian struggle, automatically communicate revolutionary values. Pleynet refutes this view with the argument that the opposition of marginal to dominant cinema is not primarily determined by economic practice, but by ideological practice. He emphasizes that the revolutionary potential of marginal cinema de-

volves less from an economic definition (alternative or oppositional mode of production) than from its potential for "formal
research" on the material specificity of the cinematic signifier:
"If we are to reject a position of naive avant-gardism and see
the birth of a cinema whose political effectiveness is real, then
we must primarily examine the materials potentially available
to it. . . . By this I mean that before we can declare it to be
'revolutionary', we need to know in what sense the cinema
can be so (EIF 153-54).

The decisive question for Pleynet was: "which films appear
to be determined by theoretical work—work, that is, which
endeavors to consider the cinema in the manner of what Althusser calls 'differential specificity'?" (EIF 149). Two observations are required here. First, by insisting on the necessity
of defining the "differential specificity" of cinematic practice,
Pleynet was not simply promoting the autonomy of aesthetic
practice (which is actually Althusser's sense of the term), nor
was he suggesting that the cinema should advance in the direction of pictorial modernism. The recognition of cinema's
specificity as a signifying practice was motivated by the desire
to demonstrate how it had been massively determined, tech-
nically and materially, by the ideological, that is, as a practical
"code" that ensured that the representational system of mass
cinema reproduced the point of view of the classes that economically controlled the apparatus of cinema production. In
this manner, *Tel Quel* provided the necessary foundation of a
semiotic modernism capable of displacing Althusser's ideas on
the relative autonomy of the aesthetic in favor of an equation
that linked the problem of realism to the philosophical perspective of idealism. Problems of aesthetics were conflated
with problems of epistemology to give precedence to Althusser's critique of empiricism. And although Althusser and other
philosophers such as Pierre Macherey had already developed
the elements of a theory relating art and ideology, these ideas
rarely came into play in the discourse of political modernism.
Instead, the battle between realism and modernism was rendered synonymous with the philosophical struggle between
idealism and materialism. This move overdetermined an argument that understood the cinematic apparatus as producing

an idealist *vision* through which, in a negative moment, one could also locate the possibility of a nonideological knowledge in the definition of a "deconstructive" or "materialist" cinematic practice.

Pleynet's ideas on the differential specificity of the cinema—which implicitly structured both *Cahiers du cinéma*'s and *Cinéthique*'s position on the impression of reality or what Pleynet called cinema's "ideological effect"—required that any understanding of the cognitive relations imposed by the cinematic signifier be rendered within the problematic of Althusser's critique of empiricist epistemologies. In this respect, Pleynet notes the prevalence of idealist discourses about the cinema that "assume a priori the nonsignifying existence of an image-producing apparatus, as if this apparatus could be indifferently put to this or that use, for the benefit of the left or of the right" (EIF 158).[9] For Pleynet, to consider the political uses to which the camera may be put, one must first understand the ideological effect produced by the cinematographic apparatus itself, as well as the cognitive relations it imposes on the vision of the spectator in its representation of reality.

Pleynet's argument is that the evolution of the technology of photographic recording has been conditioned by the code of scientific perspective inherited from Quattrocento optics, which functioned

> to "rectify" any anomaly in perspective, so as to reproduce in its full authority the code of specular vision as it was defined by Renaissance humanism. It is interesting to note that precisely at the time when Hegel announced the end of the history of painting, at the time when painting became conscious that the scientific perspective which determines its relation to forms depends on a specific cultural structure . . . at this precise point in time we find Niepce inventing the photographic process, a process which was to reinforce the end declared by Hegel as well as produce, in mechanical fashion, the ideology of the code of perspective, its norms and its censorships. (EIF 159)

In Pleynet's view, the technique of photographic registration appears as a "scientific" technology to replace and reinforce the ideological relation between form and perception signaled by Hegel's announcement of the end of art: the erosion of neoclassicism by the nascent painterly avant-gardes which, throughout the second half of the nineteenth century systematically explored ("internally distanced" Althusser would say) the decayed ideology in which they blossomed—its pictoral forms, materials, and codes. Heir to the philosophical system underpinning Hegel's aesthetics, the camera reproduced and disseminated a particular mental and ideological structure that overdetermined the status of its representations and the spectatorial relations they allowed. Pleynet argues that the camera immediately produced a fictional structure that the spectator can master only by assuming the imaginary place of an "Absolute Subject," merging his or her gaze with the reproduction of an idealized perspectival space. Following Althusser's critique of Hegelianism, Pleynet terms this form of idealism "empiricist."

Althusser's unusual appropriation of this concept should be clarified since it crucially informs Pleynet's ideas on the kind of knowledge (or nonknowledge) that the cinematic apparatus permits, as well as the kind of "knowledge effects" its deconstruction might allow. In his writings on epistemology, Althusser opposes knowledge-as-production ("theoretical practice") and an empiricist concept of knowledge-as-vision, as competing forms for the mental appropriation of reality. According to Ben Brewster's commentary in *For Marx*, Althusser defines the concept of empiricism in its widest sense as including "all 'epistemologies' that oppose a given subject to a given object and call knowledge the abstraction by the subject of the essence of the object. Hence the knowledge of the object is part of the object itself" (*For Marx* 241).[10] Since knowledge is immanent in the object, it is accessible to direct observation; thus the abstraction of knowledge from the object only requires the operation of an informed gaze on the part of the subject. According to Althusser, this position confuses "thought-about-the-real" with the "real-itself." Two forms of theoretical idealism may be identified here. First, rather than constituting knowledge, theory is the by-product of preexisting "natural" laws. Since knowledge has an empirical existence outside of the subject, cognition is dissolved into the attenuation of a gaze. Second, since the condition of knowledge is described as a feature of the object, all meaning must derive ontogenetically. Thus "reality" is elevated metaphysically as always richer and more living than the theory that attempts to comprehend it. From the point of view of empiricism, theory is only an abstraction or approximation of the concrete, always lacking somehow both with respect to Reality and perception. Similarly, the discursive foundations of theory are instrumentalized since only a neutral conduit is required for the subject to attain knowledge of reality.

Pleynet considers the cinema's revolutionary potential to be constituted solely by the degree to which a deconstruction of this empiricist ideology produced by the camera can take place. And the possibility of this deconstruction relies upon the adequate theorization of conventional cinematic practice whose mental appropriation of reality is equatable with the idealist and empiricist epistemology it inherited from Hegelian metaphysics and the disappearance of the referent in painting.

Economic, ideological, formal: the rhetoric of the break in French film theory after 1968 must be defined along this continuum as a transaction between ideology and form. The opening gambit of this debate took place in the often cited editorial "Cinema/Ideology/Criticism," where Jean-Louis Comolli and Jean Narboni began to outline the future project of *Cahiers du Cinéma* as building a "scientific" critical theory. As opposed to *Cinéthique,* Comolli and Narboni argued that filmmakers had no hope of reorganizing the existing means of production, distribution, and exhibition. As economic and technical products of a capitalist economy, they wrote, all films are always already overdetermined as ideological products and therefore *all* films are political. Filmmakers can only intervene at the aesthetic level since they cannot work independently of this economic/technological apparatus. And in order to be effective, they have to be prepared both theoretically and practically to deal with the ideological determinations coextensive with the cinematic apparatus.

Subsequently, Comolli and Narboni argued that the task of critical theory is to explain the various kinds of relations film form may have with ideology. For the editors of *Cahiers du cinéma*, who were primarily interested in questions of critical reading, the important question was the following: "... which films ... allow the ideology a free, unhampered passage, transmit it with crystal clarity, serve as its chosen language? And which attempt to make it turn back and reflect itself, intercept it and make it visible by revealing its mechanisms, by blocking them?" (CIC 3). Two points deserve comment here. First, the rhetoric of the break is formulated within a metaphorics of vision and visibility. It establishes a continuum that either facilitates an ideological perception, or turning back on itself illuminates the work of ideological fabrication within the text of the film. In either case, knowledge is the product of a simple perception or of a self-evidence of sight. Second, the possibility of this break occurs within the work of the text itself; it is an intrinsic, formal property of given texts.

In this manner, Comolli and Narboni began to establish a theory of cinematic representation on the basis of an explicit citation of Althusser's definition of ideology.

> What the camera registers in fact is the vague, unformulated, untheorized, unthought-out world of the dominant ideology. Cinema is one of the languages through which the world communicates itself to itself. They constitute its ideology for they reproduce the world as it is experienced when filtered through the ideology. (As Althusser defines it, more precisely: "Ideologies are perceived-accepted-suffered cultural objects, which work fundamentally on men by a process they do not understand. What men express in their ideologies is not their true relation to their conditions of existence, but how they react to their conditions of existence; which presupposes a real relationship and an imaginary relationship.") So, when we set out to make a film, from the very first shot, we are encumbered by the necessity of reproducing things not as they really are but as they appear when refracted through the ideology. This includes every stage in the process of production: subject, "styles," forms, meanings, narrative traditions; all underline the general, ideological discourse. (CIC 4-5)

This "general ideological discourse" is a mode of representation that organizes real or lived experience in the form of an imaginary (unthought, unformulated) relation. At every stage in the process of film production, cinematic form and style act as a system of aesthetic constraints. Rather than reproducing the "world" spontaneously and automatically, as the ideology of realism would have the spectator believe, the cinematic apparatus always operates selectively, limiting, filtering, and transforming the images that are its raw material. The impression of reality is thus defined as an ideological effect—the apparently spontaneous creation of a believable, fictional world as an imaginary relation produced by a historically specific industrial and technological practice.

Comolli and Narboni end this paragraph by stating that "the film-maker's first task is to show up the cinema's so-called 'depiction of reality'. *If he can do so there is a chance that he will be able to disrupt or possibly even sever the connection between the cinema and its ideological function*" (CIC 5; my emphasis). Thus Comolli and Narboni insist that their critical theory has implications for a potential aesthetic practice capable of producing a real as opposed to an imaginary form of knowledge. Functioning implicitly as an a priori condition of their argument, this idea underwrites Comolli and Narboni's description of seven critical categories that define a crestline differentiating films dominated by an ideological function from films that stage a reflexive critique of that function. It is important to recognize that for Comolli and Narboni no film can entirely escape an ideological function. However, certain texts can produce knowledge of their formal relation to ideological representation. In "Cinema/Ideology/Criticism," the ability to either facilitate or contravene the dominant ideology is understood as a product of individual textual systems and of certain formal devices (e.g., continuity editing, diegetic verisimilitude, subservience of sound to image) that films can either adopt or reject. Moreover, by dividing considerations of representational form between a "politics of the signifier" and a "politics of the signified," Comolli and Narboni stage their argument in a manner that quickly became familiar to Anglo-American criticism. Therefore, their seven categories are defined according to the degree that a film can distance itself from both ideological form and subject matter. The first and largest category contains those films "which are imbued through and through with the dominant ideology in pure and unadulterated form, and give no indication that their makers were even aware of the fact" (CIC 5). Highly conventional, these are films characterized not only by a lack of political subject matter, but also by a complete acceptance of an ideology of realism at the level of their form. These films are opposed, first of all, by a category of filmmaking where formal experimentation is a dominant characteristic. Although not engaged in political argumentation, these films are political to the extent that they take as their object the formal means of ideological representation ("the traditional way of depicting reality"). Paradoxically, this category includes not only avowedly avant-garde films like Jean-Daniel Pollet and Philippe Sollers's *Méditerranée* (1963), but also commercial films like Jerry Lewis's *The Bellboy* (1960) that reflexively address the question of their own fictiveness as a condition of their narrative. However, the most important films for Comolli and Narboni are those

> which attack their ideological assimilation on two fronts. Firstly, by direct political action, on the level of the "signified," ie they deal with a directly political subject. 'Deal with' is here intended in an active sense: they do not just discuss an issue, reiterate it, paraphrase it, but use it to attack the ideology (this presupposes a theoretical activity which is the direct opposite of the ideological one). This act only becomes politically effective if it is linked with a breaking down of the traditional way of depicting reality. . . . We would stress that only action on both fronts, "signified" and "signifiers" has any hope of operating against the prevailing ideology. . . . (CIC 6)[11]

These are the films that Wollen characterizes as counter-cinema and that Mulvey describes as engaging in a theoretical level of film practice.

This category can be clarified by noting *Cahiers du cinéma*'s objections to that genre of filmmaking usually thought of as political. Comolli and Narboni define this genre as a category of films "which have an explicitly political content . . . but which do not effectively criticise the ideological system in which they are embedded because they unquestioningly adopt its language and its imagery" (CIC 6).[12] Comolli further developes this argument in a critique of Constantin Costa-Gavras' *L'Aveu* (1969), a popular commercial film critical of Stalinism similar to his *Z* (1969).[13] Comolli proposes that in every film there is a "double articulation" with respect to the production of dominant ideology. There is a primary articulation that reproduces the conditions of the ideological domination of the signifier (that is, a given economy of normative aesthetic and cultural codes), and a secondary articulation that transmits (either complicitly or critically) a given number of ideological "themes" or signifieds. According to Comolli, *L'Aveu* is problematic on both levels of articulation despite its political message. By utilizing normative representational codes, *L'Aveu* perpetuates and reproduces what Comolli terms (with implicit reference to Althusser's critique of empiricism) "an ideology of the visible": the aesthetic and technical means by which the cinema seems to give the world as seen, apparently without the agency of the signifier. Second, because it uses its means of representation instrumentally, it offers no resistance to norms of interpretation and criticism that could potentially assign it a meaning opposite to its political intent. Having thus allied itself to bourgeois cinema at the level of its economy and its form, *L'Aveu* offers no barriers to those who would, for example, equate its criticism of Stalinism with a critique of communism or socialism in general.

Clearly, what Comolli and Narboni draw most forcefully from Althusser is the concept of ideology as a form or a system of representation. In order to analyze what characterizes cinema's function in the "general ideological discourse," they posit the operation of an aesthetic effect or impression of reality as a code organizing ideological relations in the film text. According to this code, films will produce an imaginary form of knowing as opposed to a potentially real one. However, given that *Cahiers du cinéma* situates itself explicitly in an Althusserian framework, it is interesting to note the degree to which their position was not completely consonant with the Althusserian work on aesthetics extant at that time.[14]

In order to clarify the problems posed by *Cahiers du cinéma*'s assimilation of Althusser, the rhetoric of the break staged in Comolli and Narboni's essay must be reconsidered. Their desire to establish a scientific critical theory accounting for the possible relationships between art and knowledge is clearly consonant with Althusser's notions of what a Marxist aesthetics should provide. In "A Letter on Art in Reply to André Daspre," Althusser writes the following: "As you see, in order to answer most of the questions posed for us by the existence and specific nature of art, we are forced to produce an adequate (scientific) *knowledge* of the processes which produce the 'aesthetic effect' of a work of art. In other words, in order to answer the question of the relationship between art and knowledge, we must produce a *knowledge of art*. . . . Like all knowledge, the knowledge of art presupposes a preliminary *rupture* with the language of *ideological spontaneity* and the constitution of a body of scientific concepts to replace it."[15]

Clearly, Althusser's definition of the specific difference of art as the manner in which art allows us to *perceive* ideology responds to the objectives of an epistemological modernism. What must be emphasized, however, is that in questioning the relationship between art and knowledge, Althusser is interested in establishing art as a mode of cognition distinguishable from that of science, on the one hand, and ideology on the other. The specific difference between art and science is the different form in which they give us the same object—that is, science in the form of strict knowledge and art in the form of "seeing," "perceiving," or "feeling." According to Althusser art is a form of experience that although close to ideology is not identical to it. For art, in order to be defined as a practice in the Althusserian sense, must transform a given raw material in the production of a given product. Art's specific relationship with ideology is that it works on the materials of representation offered by ideology in order to produce them in another form, what Althusser and Macherey call that of "internal distantiation": "What art makes us *see* . . . is the *ideology* from which it is born, in which it bathes, from which it detaches itself as art, and to which it *alludes*. . . . Balzac and Solzhenitsyn give us a 'view' of the ideology to which their work alludes and with which it is constantly fed, a view which supposes a *retreat*, an *internal distantiation* from the very ideology from which their novels emerged. They make us 'perceive' (but not know) in some sense *from the inside*, by an *internal distance*, the very ideology in which they are held" ("A Letter on Art," 222-23).

Art is, then, a definite practice, and what it produces in the transformation of its raw material is given in the form of an "aesthetic effect." Even if art does not give us knowledge of ideology (in the form of the "knowledge effect" specific to scientific or theoretical practice), it nonetheless renders ideology perceptible, cognizable, and thus accessible to the knowledge of a scientific criticism in the form of symptomatic readings.

These propositions are clearly evident in "Cinema/Ideology/ Criticism," especially as they come to bear on Comolli and Narboni's most influential critical category, the "progressive text." This category includes those commercial, narrative films that seem to have an ambiguous relationship to ideology.

> Looking at the framework one can see two moments in it: one holding it back within certain limits, one transgressing them. An internal criticism is taking place which cracks the films apart at the seams. If one reads the film obliquely, looking for symptoms; if one looks beyond its apparent formal coherence, one can see that it is riddled with cracks: it is splitting under an internal tension which is simply not there in an ideologically innocuous film. The ideology thus becomes subordinate to the text. It no longer has an independent existence: it is *presented* by the film. (CIC 7)[16]

Although these statements seem to correspond with the general project of an Althusserian criticism, they are contradictory for the following reasons. First, for Althusser and the literary critics associated with him, art was a general, formal structure independent of specific texts. Second, even though this conception was evaluative in certain respects (Althusser speaks of "authentic art"), Althusserian criticism had to this point never exhibited the desire to establish a formal typology adjudicating the degree of ideological implication of various kinds of texts or formal strategies. Primarily a theory of critical reading, it had little to say about the development of a potential revolutionary artistic practice, nor did it wish to differentiate between reactionary and progressive texts. In this sense, all aesthetic practice was considered to be ideological. The task of criticism was to define the specific difference of art in its special relationship to ideology.[17]

It is important to remember that this last category of films is for Comolli and Narboni only the center of a sliding scale halfway between those texts that are entirely complicit with the dominant ideology and those that are beginning to break with it. There is little doubt that Althusser's writings on ideology, and his specific reconciliation of Marxist and psychoanalytic terminologies, were extremely influential and adopted wholesale into the emerging field of post-'68 film theory. Moreover, Althusser's reflection on the specific difference of art as a form of cognition was also attractive. For example, there is an understood, even unthought, relation between aesthetic form and perception in Althusser's writings on art, where an implicit relation of identity is construed between spectator and text in the form of "seeing," "perceiving," "feeling," and so on. This notion was consonant in many respects with ideas on textual production and analysis operational in *Tel Quel*. There was an insistence in *Tel Quel* that the ideological positioning of the subject was intrinsically bound to given textual economies. Conversely, the modernist text disrupted those positions by disturbing the formal economies supporting them. However, in Althusser's thoughts on aesthetics there is neither the question nor the desire of dividing the avant-garde text from the normative text, or the work of modernism from the work of realism. And this, it must be recalled, was an absolutely determinate proposition in the post-'68 period, especially since it maintained an association between aesthetic activity and political activity. In this respect, *Cahiers du cinéma* implicitly accepted that whatever knowledges might be produced by aesthetic texts would be either scientific or ideological. By developing a typology of texts in this manner, they conceded (consciously or not) to the demands of an epistemological modernism that films could produce or occlude knowledge of their relation to ideology by means of their intrinsic, formal organization. Rather than differentiating between ideology, science, and art as specific forms of cognition, differences between aesthetic forms were posed through a critical theory that privileged Althusser's work on epistemology and ideology at the expense of his and Pierre Macherey's writings on art. In this manner, Comolli and Narboni's critical theory was founded on the opposition between ideology and science in order to preserve the radical possibility of defining a cinema of "theoretical practice."

This particular and selective reading of Althusser through the grid of epistemological modernism is even more forceful in the early editorial position of *Cinéthique*. The most thorough statement of *Cinéthique*'s position is Jean-Paul Fargier's "Parenthesis or Indirect Route: an Attempt at Theoretical Definition of the Relationship between Cinema and Politics." This essay outlines the main points of *Cinéthique*'s theory of textual production, drawing most of its philosophical arguments from Althusser with references to Jacques Derrida and Philippe Sollers. Significant terms used with caution by Comolli and Narboni come forcefully into play here, including the metaphor of the break, the impression of reality, the opposition between science and ideology, the concept of theoretical practice, and so on. The inaugural questions of Fargier's essay are also similar to those posed by Comolli and Narboni: What constitutes the differential specificity of cinema in its currently received forms and how may films be differentiated according to the political knowledges they produce? However, as opposed to *Cahiers du cinéma*'s interest in critical reading and evaluation, *Cinéthique* presents a different emphasis: How can cinematic practice develop in the direction of what Althusser calls theoretical practice? Or if the so-called dominant cinema is implicated within an idealist philosophy of representation, how can it be opposed by a "dialectical materialist" cinema?

Fargier's argument develops obliquely through two metaphors—the "parenthesis" and the "indirect route." For Fargier, the structure of "parenthesis" perfectly describes idealist philosophies of representation because language is rendered as a hierarchical system of signs where the signifier is subordinated to the signified. Meaning is understood here to have an a priori relation with a language that only renders or expresses it more or less exactly. In this manner, Fargier claims that society has placed the cinema in parentheses in two ways:

first, by marginalizing cinema as a leisure activity, society defines cinema going as superfluous with no direct relation to
social or political life; and second by negating cinema's material nature as a discourse by supposing that it merely and
instrumentally communicates the "world as it is."

However, the metaphor of the indirect route has greater
bearing on *Cinéthique*'s theory since it articulates cinema's potential for staging a critique of its ideological function. In order
to institute a truly materialist understanding of the cinema,
Fargier argues that we must comprehend not only the physical
materiality of films—how they produce images and sounds—
but also the material relations constituting cinema as a social
practice. Like Comolli later on, Fargier insists on the power
of the impression of a reality as a normative "aesthetic effect"
underpinning cinema's ideological function in the capitalist
economic system. A film that does not question its style, he
argues, at the same time as its dissemination and reception, or
a film that compromises itself aesthetically in order to reach
a wider audience by conforming to the expectations of those
who control the marketplace, can never achieve a rupture with
ideology. Of necessity, these films serve in the reproduction
of the economic system through which capital enforces it
power, regardless of their political message. As an ideological
and cultural norm, the impression of reality is inextricably
linked to the capitalist system of production; to reproduce one
is to reproduce the other.

Referring explicitly to Althusser, Fargier argues that the intelligibility of "cinema" is governed by its specific relation to
the various practices (economic, political, ideological) that
constitute the totality of a given society.[18] Fargier claims that
cinema can have neither a direct nor specific relation to political struggle because, according to Althusser, "*politics* is a
practice which transforms its raw material (given social relations) into a given product (new social relations) by the systematic use of given means of production (the *class* struggle)"
(PIR 26). To imagine a cinema that inspires a revolutionary
transformation of the relations that organize men and women
into social groups would be the worst form of utopianism.

Therefore, work in the areas of film theory and practice is most productively defined in relation to ideological practice.

Cinéthique, like *Cahiers du cinéma*, reproduces a definition of ideology directly from Althusser: " 'An ideology is a system (possessing its own logic and rigour) of representation (images, myths, ideas or concepts as the case may be) existing and having a historical role within a given society.' (Louis Althusser: 'Marxism and Humanism' in *For Marx*)" (PIR 28). Fargier claims that the cinema's specific ideological function coincides with this general definition, and in order to explain, offers a two-tiered model not unlike Comolli's in the later essay on *L'Aveu*.

(a) It REPRODUCES, it reflects existing ideologies. It is therefore used (consciously or unconsciously, it makes little difference) as a vector in the process of circulating ideologies. (b) It PRODUCES its own ideology: THE IMPRESSION OF REALITY. . . . The first thing people do is deny the existence of the screen: it opens like a *window*, it "is" *transparent*. This illusion is the very substance of the specific ideology secreted by the cinema.

If one understands that ideology always presents itself in the form of a body of ideas and pictures of reality which people spontaneously accept as true, as *realistic*, it is easy to see why the cinema, by its specific nature, plays such a privileged role in the general ideological process. It REINFORCES the impression that what looks realistic must be real, and thus reinforces the ideology it reflects. It presents it as true, by virtue of its self-evident existence on the screen. (PIR 28)

Like Comolli, Fargier supposes that the cinema both reproduces ideologies as a content and produces an ideology (the impression of reality) as a form determining particular relations of knowing. Moreover, as an ideological structure of representation, the impression of reality exerts an overdetermining force. Encoding a realist vocation in cinema's technology and forms, these structures must be transformed before film practice can be developed for any other use.

Therefore, unlike *Cahiers du cinéma*, who differentiate seven categories of films according to their internal and formal displacement of ideology, Fargier insists that there are only ideological and nonideological (that is, "scientific") texts. And he attempts to differentiate the cognitive status of these texts, at least initially, not only on the basis of their formal negotiation of ideology, but also on that of the class position of the audience. In this respect, Fargier could be criticized for promoting an idealized and homogenous view of proletarian class consciousness, as well as lapsing into the kind of unthought reflectionism that Althusser was fond of criticizing. This position leads Fargier to divide the ideological effects produced by the impression of reality into two types, what he calls "recognition" and "mystification." According to Fargier, the economically dominant classes identify with and recognize themselves on the screen because its ideology is coextensive with their worldview, or the ideological position that empowers them. However, this cannot be the case for the disenfranchised classes—"They identify with what happens on the screen (mechanically) but they *cannot*, or ought not to be able to recognise themselves in it"—and if they indeed submit to the "impression of reality," it must be in the form of a "mystification" (PIR 29).[19] In other words, Fargier shifts the grounds for theorizing the subject positions offered by cinema onto a problem of *illusionism.* What is a social reality for the empowered classes—because it perpetuates an ideology in which their class position coheres in its domination of the economically disenfranchised classes—is simply a bribe of identity or a fiction pacifying the proletariat. Thus, in Gerard Leblanc's companion essay, "Direction," he states that

> The true interest of the bourgeoisie is that the cinema should make up for what people do not have in life. The pseudo-satisfaction they find there may be sexual, political, emotional or metaphysical, there is something for all the different kinds of alienation engendered by capitalism. The audience tacitly delegate their power to change the world to the characters on the screen. The famous 'window' that the bourgeois cinema is supposed to open on the world is never anything other than a method of permitting the audience to live an imaginary life within a non-existent reality. ("Direction," 15)

Therefore, the principal task of an oppositional cinema is to interrupt this process where the audience is asked to passively identify with the class that exploits them and that substitutes an imaginary pleasure for the material satisfaction denied them in real life.

However, even if the cinema cannot be directly allied to political practice, Fargier suggests that it may have an indirect relationship if one understands how it has been placed with respect to economic practice, on the one hand, and ideological practice on the other. In his example, the cinema of the present day may be understood as having a special relationship with economic practice, since capitalist society assigns its value in the form of a commodity and its function as entertainment or the consumption of leisure time. Moreover, by reconsidering the idea of the parenthesis, it is possible to understand that this economic definition of aesthetic practice has ideological implications for three reasons. First, capitalism's economic definition of cinema as a nonproductive or leisure activity elides the potential uses of film in relation to other practices such as the political or theoretical. Second, this bracketing of aesthetic practice demonstrates how capitalist society determines what constitutes the field of political life by legitimizing certain kinds of political action and censoring others. And third, remembering that this bracketing is itself a decisive form of cultural representation, it suppresses the problem of aesthetic representation, and work on representation, within the field of the political. This economic censorship situates the problem of representation in general, and cinema in particular, specifically within the field of ideology. Unlike political practice, a film cannot contribute to the process that revolutionizes social relations; however, it can, "at a given historical moment, hold back, mask, or reactivate the class struggle, *by modifying the subjective factor in the struggle*, ie the class consciousness of the proletariat . . ." (PIR 27; emphasis mine). In other words, the political effectivity of film can be judged only on the basis of a specific transformation of subjectivity as the inculcation of a relation between ideology and knowledge on the part of aesthetic practice.

Whereas *Cahiers du cinéma* asks which texts communicate the dominant ideology and which make it visible by revealing its mechanisms, *Cinéthique* asks: "[Can] the film transmit a proletarian ideology? And can the cinema have any other than an ideological function: a *theoretical* one for example?" (PIR 29; emphasis mine). The rhetoric of the break in Comolli and Narboni, which progressively drives a wedge between form and ideology, is radicalized here and forged in a binary logic. According to Fargier, the subjective transformation that is the object of oppositional aesthetic practice is accomplished by a passage from illusion to knowledge in relation to ideology. And to the extent that the problem of illusionism is solely identified with an idealist conception of cinematic forms, then a critique of cinema's ideological function can only occur as a materialist deconstruction of those forms.

In sum, Fargier stresses that work in the cinema can never influence the balance of forces in political struggle, but it can and must intervene indirectly through the field of ideology in the conflict between idealism and materialism. Given his insistence that the cinema cannot serve the proletarian cause since the history of its forms has been massively determined by an idealist ideology (the impression of reality), what, then, does his argument specify for aesthetic practice? Fargier's solution is that of an "impossible reversal" which, opposing a materialist aesthetic to an idealist one, dislodges the cinema from the juncture of economic and ideological practice and replaces it on the terrain of theoretical practice. In this manner, the cognitive relations specified as recognition and mystification would be dispelled by a "knowledge effect." By forcing an "epistemological break" with its ideological predecessor, Fargier proposes that a cinema of theoretical practice can be constituted.

This insistence on the overdetermination of the impression of reality in cinematic representation is equally forceful in *Cahiers du cinéma* and *Cinéthique.* On this basis the discourse of political modernism emerges in French film theory as a series of binary oppositions leading from ideology/theory, through idealism/materialism, to what might be called code/deconstruction. In attempting to describe the conceptual system of the discourse of political modernism, the idea of "code" refers to the confluence of aesthetic means that yield the impression of reality as an ideology-in-general produced by the cinematic apparatus. But it is the reciprocal linking of the concept of code to that of "deconstruction," as the possible foundation of a materialist and theoretical film practice, that must now be specified.

The opposition of code to deconstruction in the discourse of political modernism suggests that the formal system supporting the impression of reality in the cinema contains within itself the potentiality for its own negation or critique—in short, its reversal will found a possible epistemological modernism. Although the theoretical agenda for this project was clearly set by the fall of 1969, neither *Cahiers du cinéma* nor *Cinéthique* had yet been able to clearly specify the elements for a theory of epistemological modernism. Several problems had to be resolved before this theory could be adequately formulated. Having established a link between the problem of cinematic form and the transmission of an ideology of realism, and having targeted that link as the means for achieving a break with cinema's ideological function, how could one specify the properties of cinematic representation that sustain it as an ideological apparatus? In what ways could these properties be understood as producing subjective relations in the cinema? And what precisely would it mean to release the cinema from its marginalization as mass entertainment, considering it instead as a philosophical instrument capable of producing "theoretical" knowledge in the conflict between idealism and materialism?

These questions were largely unanswered until Jean-Louis Baudry published his influential, "Cinéma: effets idéologiques produit par l'appareil de base" in *Cinéthique* 7/8 (1970).[20] One cannot overestimate the impact of Baudry's work in this period. He was subsequently credited for being among the first to introduce Lacan to contemporary film theory and for asserting the importance of psychoanalytic theory in comprehending cinema's relation to ideology in the production of subjectivity. In retrospect, Baudry's reductive reading of Lacan is open to criticism and in many respects the psychoanalytic dimensions of his essay have been overstressed.[21] Of greater importance is his response to Pleynet's call for a full philosophical understanding of the epistemological foundations of the cinema as a representational apparatus, and of this apparatus' correspondance to the conceptual system of empirical knowing criticized by Althusser as ideological.

In this respect, Baudry's essay is better understood by referring to the influence of Althusser rather than to that of Lacan. Baudry's argument can be characterized as trying to accomplish two principal tasks. The first task is to define cinema's differential specificity with philosophical precision by comparing the camera's mental appropriation of reality with the process of knowledge constituted by empirical science. Here Baudry plays continually on the dual sense of "apparatus" [*appareil*], considering the cinema both as a technological machine and a conceptual system. Second, by thoroughly defining the system of interaction between metaphysics and representation, Baudry desires to uncover the possibility of a radical, modernist cinematographic practice. According to Baudry, what unites these two "systems" is a particular ideology of vision. If both empiricist epistemology and the process of photographic inscription represent themselves as the condition of an optics—the construction, attenuation, and management of a gaze—then Baudry asks: "Does the technical nature of optical instruments, directly attached to scientific practice, serve to conceal not only their use in ideological products but also the ideological effects which they may provoke themselves?" (IEA 25).

To answer this question, Baudry describes the specificity of cinematic inscription as the "specularization" of the subject in three moments: the delimitation of the frame, the negation of difference between the series of frames in projection (which provides the illusion and continuity of movement), and the phenomenon of double identification (with characters in the film and the camera's own "visioning" of the world) in which the specularization of the subject-spectator is assured.

In perfect accordance with Pleynet's views but extending them, Baudry asserts that the delimitation of film space by the camera lens is organized according to the conventions of *perspectiva artificialis* developed in Quattrocento painting.

> Contrary to Chinese and Japanese painting, Western easel painting, presenting as it does a motionless and continuous whole, elaborates a total vision which corresponds to the idealist con-

ception of the fullness and homogeneity of "being," and is, so to speak, representative of this conception. In this sense it contributes in a singularly emphatic way to the ideological function of art, which is to provide the tangible representation of metaphysics. The principle of transcendence which conditions and is conditioned by the perspective construction represented in painting and in the photographic image which copies from it seems to inspire all the idealist paeans to which the cinema has given rise. . . . (IEA 28)

However, given that the cinema takes up the code of scientific perspective from optics, its specificity relies more on its temporal aspects—its particular registration of images through the mechanical instrumentation and regulation of the series of individual frames. Paradoxically, this signifies that meaning is only constituted in the cinema according to the suppression of a radical discontinuity, the relationship of difference and multiplication of points of view offered by a serialized photographic space.

The projection operation (projector and screen) restore [sic] continuity of movement and the temporal dimension to the sequence of static images. . . . The meaning effect produced does not depend only on the content of the images but also on the material procedures by which an illusion of continuity, dependent on the persistence of vision, is restored from discontinuous elements. These separate frames have between them differences that are indispensible [sic] for the creation of an illusion of continuity, of a continuous passage (movement, time). But only on one condition can these differences create this illusion: they must be effaced as differences. (IEA 29)

Baudry describes the constitution of meaning in cinematographic "writing" on the model of Freud's notion of the "dream-work," the serialized passage of individual frames standing in for the moment of primary elaboration in the dream. But this analogy holds true only with the understanding that the cinematographic apparatus is a more perfect form of "consciousness." The apparatus not only selects the minimal units of difference, it represses them in projection so that meaning is constituted only in one direction: linearity, continuity, movement. Unlike language per se where subjectivity is split—

the conscious mind or thetic subject being disordered by the
irruption of the unconscious in the form of parapraxes or hysterical symptoms—the mutually reinforcing operations of the
perspectival organization of the frame and the negation of difference in projection work together to enforce the positioning
of the spectator as what Baudry calls "the transcendental subject."

The ideological effect of the apparatus thus resides in the
form of a substitution that mimics the psychical constitution
of the subject while remodeling it more perfectly. Comparing
this process to the institution of subjectivity described by Lacan's concept of the mirror stage, Baudry then characterizes
it in the form of a double identification. Unlike the mirror
stage, what is reflected on the screen is not the spectator's
body, but the world already given as a meaning or as an idealized look. Even though the spectator unquestionably identifies
with the fictional characters and their point of view, this secondary identification is subtended by a primary one.

> . . .this is the transcendental subject whose place is taken by
> the camera which constitutes and rules the objects in this
> "world." Thus the spectator identifies less with what is repre-
> sented, the spectacle itself, than with what stages the specta-
> cle. . . ; this is exactly the function taken over by the camera as
> a sort of relay. . . . It constitutes the "subject" by the illusory
> delimitation of a central location—whether this be that of a god
> or of any other substitute. It is an apparatus destined to obtain
> a precise ideological effect, necessary to the dominant ideology:
> creating a fantasmatization of the subject, it collaborates with
> a marked efficacity in the maintenance of idealism. . . . Every-
> thing happens as if, the subject himself being unable—and for
> a reason—to account for his own situation, it was necessary to
> substitute secondary organs, grafted on to replace his own de-
> fective ones, instruments or ideological formations capable of
> filling his function as subject. In fact, this substitution is only
> possible *on the condition that the instrumentation itself be hidden
> or repressed.* (IEA 34; emphasis mine)

For Baudry, the cinematic apparatus summons its subject
with a bribe of identity, or the promise of an imaginary completion of the subject's own lack-in-being. Through the ac-

complishment of a phenomenological experience where all contradictions are overcome and all conflicts resolved, the apparatus promises the fulfillment of a desire for self-identical being and the completion of meaning. At the most specific, material levels of signification, the organization of space within the frame and the imposition of continuity and fixed temporality in projection together accomplish a phenomenological reduction: "the world offers up an object endowed with meaning, an intentional object, implied by and implying the action of a "subject" which sights it" (IEA 31). The institution of a "look" at the level of the apparatus, as a structure that manifests the visible, establishes both a position of continuity necessary for the constitution of meaning and a subject to occupy that position as an attribute of meaning, effectively reversing Godard's famous *cogito*: "The cinema exists, therefore I think." Moreover, without placing his argument exactly within Pleynet's definition of the problem, Baudry theorizes the differential specificity of cinematic inscription, recalling precisely Althusser's description of the three constitutive errors of empiricist thought: (1) cognition is reduced to the form of an optics since all knowledge resides in the domain of the visible world; (2) knowledge about the world is confused with the world itself; and (3) the instrumentality (theoretical and/or technical) conditioning and formulating that knowledge is suppressed.[22]

However, the continuity imposed by the apparatus at its primary levels of articulation, which is reproduced at the level of conventional spatial continuity in the form of narrative codes, can only take place at a risk. Between the ontological centering of the camera's reproduction of monocular perspective, and the linear organization of space according to the continuity system of editing, the material discontinuity on which the cinema relies for the illusion of movement also exists as a potentiality for rupture and for disturbing the placement of the spectator. Retrospectively, each stage of Baudry's argument can be read as building a series of binary oppositions where an element of realist code contains within itself the cell of its own deconstruction—for example, the elaboration of a motionless and continuous whole produced by Western perspective is countered by the example of a decentering Oriental perspective, and the illusion of spatially continuous movement is understood as possible only at the price of reducing the difference between the individual frames serialized contiguously on the filmstrip. The cinematic *appareil* is therefore conceived as a system of interlocking parts that—organized hierarchically from a technological base to a set of narrative conventions for the presentation of spatio-temporal continuity—are aimed at a precise effect. The search for narrative continuity, which seems to overdetermine the history of cinematic forms, may only be accounted for by elucidating the ideological stakes involved: "it is a question of preserving at any cost the synthetic unity of the locus where meaning originates—the constituting transcendental function to which narrative continuity points back as its natural secretion" (IEA 32).

This question of risk recalls the point of origin of Baudry's essay: what forms of cognition are instituted by the technological base of cinematic inscription, what ideological stakes are reproduced there, and where may one discover the potentiality that recovers cinema for the purposes of its own deconstruction? To comprehend adequately the position enabling Baudry to ask these questions and stage their answers, it is necessary to understand that it is not precisely the mechanics of cinematic recording nor the economics of film production that are at issue. Rather, it is an understanding of the constitution of the cinematic signifier as a given *work,* where the cinematographic apparatus intervenes between a determinate raw material in the form of "objective reality" and a determinate product in the form of an ideological subject-positioning. In this respect, Baudry places the cinematic apparatus at the center of a process of transformation.

> Between "objective reality" and the camera, site of the inscription, and between the inscription and projection are situated certain operations, a *work* which has as its result a finished product. To the extent that it is cut off from the raw material ("objective reality") this product does not allow us to see the transformation which has taken place. Equally distant from "objective reality" and the finished product, the camera occupies an in-

termediate position in the work process which leads from raw material to finished product. (IEA 26)

It is necessary to comprehend fully how Baudry exploits the multiple senses of the French term *appareil* to bring together lines of thought drawn from Marxism and semiology and to direct them toward a theory of epistemological modernism. The *Petit Robert* furnishes two interesting definitions where *appareil* signifies both a "scientific" recording technology (e.g., the camera) and the unfolding of a public spectacle before the eyes of its audience. Clearly, the polarity described by these two senses of the term responds to Baudry's desire to "question the privileged position which optical instruments seem to occupy on the line of intersection of science and ideological products" (IEA 25). However, Baudry continues shaping this term to achieve deeper philosophical ends. By stressing the sense of *appareil* as a given system of concepts, Baudry attempts to bring Marxism and deconstruction onto common ground. By emphasizing cinematic specificity as a particular, technologically founded *conceptual* apparatus—a determinate mental appropriation of reality—Baudry attempts to define cinematic representation within the frame of Althusser's critique of empiricist epistemologies.

Baudry is undoubtedly sensitive to Althusser's outline for analyzing how various ideological apparatuses (*appareils idéologiques*) such as the educational system, the church, or public communication, serve to determine and constrain categories of subjectivity.[23] But this equation of aesthetic and epistemological concerns is motivated by a more compelling desire on Baudry's part: to preserve within his account of cinema as an ideological apparatus, the possibility of defining a "deconstructive" theoretical practice; that is, the possibility of transforming aesthetic practice from an affirmative ideological function into a critical or theoretical one. This is accomplished only in part by staging his argument according to the theory of knowledge outlined in "On the Materialist Dialectic" in *For Marx*.[24] Theoretical practice is defined by Althusser here as one step of a three-stage process describing the generation of scientific knowledge. More precisely, it is the intermediate transformational step (defined by a historically variable corpus of concepts) between the raw material that theory works on (in the form of the questions or problems it is able to designate) and the system of knowledge that theory is finally able to produce. Brutely characterized, the function of the ideological structure of empiricist thought is the forceful suppression of this intermediate step. Empiricism simply designates an existing reality as immutable by construing an identity between the first and last stages of knowledge, rather than reflecting dialectically on the theory that has selected, filtered, and worked over the elements of potential knowledge.

The proposition that the cinematic apparatus preserves a representational bias within its claim to offer the spectator an omniscient specularity is fundamental. But Baudry pushes the sense of *appareil* as a system of optical/conceptual reproduction yet further. As a metaphor powerfully mobilized by Freud, Marx, and others, Baudry asserts from the first lines of his essay the importance of the identification of optical models with the psychical constitution of subjectivity in the history of philosophy. More importantly, it is Derrida's reading of Freud that is manifested in a rhetorically significant way.[25] The optical metaphor—in its association with light, perception, clarity, focus, and mirroring—has all the characteristics for asserting the neutrality of a system whose function is the precise rendering of a mimetic reciprocity between mind and nature. Here optics becomes the tangible representative of a metaphysical conception of Being whose identity can only be maintained by the exorcism of that difference that Derrida argues through a metaphorics of "writing." Baudry's argument begins and ends on the following points. The ideological function of the cinematic apparatus resides in its disingenuously simple "designation" of a preexisting reality that it in fact manufactures. It produces and preserves the illusory self-identity of a transcendental subject by suppressing any awareness of the technological and semiotic machinery that intervenes between the object and subject of the gaze in the form of a "writing." Baudry's description of the filmstrip as a field for the regulated inscription of difference is a constant reference to this idea.[26]

Despite Baudry's appeals to Derrida, his description of cinematic writing as a semiotic materiality suppressed by an ide-

alist and illusionist system of representation could not correspond less to Derrida's meaning. Rather than questioning the
self-evidence of the visible or the perceptible, Baudry simply
substitutes one criterion of visibility for another by inscribing
"writing" within a logic of binary reversibility. The illusionist,
ideological apparatus thus preserves the terms of its own materialist and scientific "deconstruction." According to Baudry,
in order to accomplish a "deconstruction of the ideology produced by the camera," the question then becomes "is the work
made evident [Il s'agira de savoir si le travail est montré], does
consumption of the product bring about a 'knowledge effect,'
or is the work concealed?" (IEA 26). Unequivocally, Baudry
specifies that cinema's potential for achieving a break with its
ideological function corresponds to the degree in which the
work of its instrumental base—photographic inscription, serial
regulation of movement, the process of identification in projection—can in fact be made legible [lisible] within the text:
". . .concealment of the technical base will also bring about a
specific ideological effect. Its inscription, its manifestation as
such, on the other hand, would produce a knowledge effect,
as actualization of the work process, as denunciation of ideology, and as critique of idealism" (IEA 27).

These remarks, which conclude the opening section of Baudry's essay, clearly demonstrate how his argument is ordered
by a dialectic of visibility and suppression aligned with an opposition of illusion to knowledge, idealism to materialism, and
ideological to theoretical practice. Further, this logic reprises
exactly that of Fargier's editorial whose position, one imagines,
was supposed to be deepened and corrected through the publication of Baudry's work. However, both arguments are structured by a common desire where the possibility of integrating
aesthetic and theoretical practice is contingent upon the following rule: "IN THE CINEMA THE COMMUNICATION OF KNOWLEDGE
IS ATTENDANT UPON THE PRODUCTION OF KNOWLEDGE ABOUT THE
CINEMA" (PIR 32). According to Fargier, the cinema can and
must participate in the communication of genuine, scientific
knowledges, but its ability to do so is contingent upon the
production or autodesignation of the material and social facts
of its existence. As opposed to the idealist cinema, which ef-

faces the marks of its textual production, *Cinéthique* proposes
a materialist cinema structured by the reflexive designation of
its material processes of signification: "In these films, images
and sounds at last no longer deny the process by which they
came to be imprinted on the film stock. The work embodied
in the film becomes scientific in the measure to which it puts
on view the ideologies struggling to penetrate the signs (bodies, faces) and abstract them from the body of the film. This
break is materialism. One of its effects is to permit a new critical understanding of idealist films" ("Direction," 16).

This quote recalls Wollen's notion of the modernist text as
being defined by the autodesignation of code, for the two conceptions of an epistemological modernism are readily compatible. However, the editors of *Cinéthique* are more specific
in their insistence that a materialist cinema take as its object
not only the autodesignation of code, but also film's physical
substance of expression. In Fargier's formula:

> A Materialist Film is one which does not give illusory reflec-
> tions of reality. In fact it 'reflects' nothing. It starts from its own
> material nature (flat screen, natural ideological bias, audience)
> and that of the world, and shows them both, all in one move-
> ment. This movement is the theoretical one. . . .
> A Dialectical Film is one made in the consciousness, which it
> is able to transmit to the audience, of the exact process whereby
> an item of knowledge or a depiction of reality is transformed
> by degrees into *screen material* to be then re-converted into
> knowledge and a view of reality in the audience's mind. (PIR
> 35)

Here, despite the criticisms that Comolli and Narboni would
subsequently express, *Cinéthique* does not quite lapse into the
mechanical materialism that this position suggests. By placing
their aesthetic theory within the Althusserian concept of practice, two defenses of *Cinéthique* present themselves. First,
"theoretical" cinema understands its materiality as a *process*
where the camera, refusing the ideality of communication
without a channel for which it was designed, takes account of
its transformation of its object. Second, it is not the "world"
given as some idealized referent that this cinema acknowledges
as its object or takes as its raw material, but rather, ideologies,

already systems of representation in and of themselves, that have to be worked upon and transformed.

However, there is little doubt that *Cinéthique*'s proposed integration of cinema and theoretical practice is a utopian move, something that Comolli and Narboni were quick to note. In a thorough critique of *Cinéthique* 5, with special reference to their adoption of an Althusserian philosophical vocabulary, Comolli and Narboni justly pose this utopianism as a confusion between the concepts "theory" and "theoretical practice."

> It is clear that *Cinéthique* are seriously confused about the concept of *theoretical practice* (the mode of production of scientific knowledge), confounding it totally with the simple "theory" of a practice (technical, empirical or ideological). "Theory" in this application simply means the special set of concepts needed by these practices in order to accomplish the tasks assigned to them. These sets of concepts are never more than a reflection of what is to be accomplished in the means used to attain it, and has nothing to do with theoretical practice. . . . On the other hand it is extremely possible to apply a theoretical practice to films which have none. This is the essential role of criticism.[27]

Comolli and Narboni thus clarify their notion of what critical theory brings to aesthetic practice. Although they are ready to concede the possibility of a cinema in which a theoretical reflection could be joined to aesthetic practice (Eisenstein, for example), Comolli and Narboni nonetheless insist on Althusser's thesis that ideology is a necessary component of society, capitalist or socialist. They emphasize that the cinema is overdetermined as a product of ideology—it must of necessity work within and against the terrain of ideology, distancing itself by degrees. Therefore, according to Comolli and Narboni, aesthetic practice can never become an instrument of science for three reasons: "(1) because a film 'works on the theoretical level' it does not necessarily mean it retains any explicit traces of the theoretical process; (2) to accumulate 'knowledge' does not inevitably imply leaving the ideology, for the process of accumulation takes place *within* the ideology as well; (3) 'truths' never came to be 'known theoretically' through a film: known, yes; theoretically, no" ("Cinema/Ideology/Criticism (2)," 41).

In the degree to which Baudry's critique of cinema as an ideological apparatus is meant to recover its potential for a formal deconstruction through an aesthetic of reflexivity and antiillusionism, his argument is similarly flawed. Although his solution regarding a possible theoretical level of film practice is ultimately both imaginative and compelling, he slips into a fundamental error that Althusser in his own writings is careful to elucidate—that of the difference between "theoretical" and "technical" practices. Despite Baudry's attempt to equate the technical process of cinematic inscription with the project of metaphysics, and despite the number of analyses that have now informed our knowledge of how subjective relations may be inscribed in both technological and textual codes, Baudry mistakenly assumes that although theoretical practice may act as the support of a technical practice, a technical practice can never in and of itself serve in the production of knowledge. In this manner, Althusser writes:

> Theoretical practice produces knowledges which can then figure as *means* that will serve the ends of a technical practice. Any technical practice is defined by its ends: such and such effects to be produced in such and such an object in such and such a situation. . . . Any theoretical practice uses among other means knowledges which intervene as procedures: either knowledges borrowed from outside, from existing sciences, or "knowledges" produced by the technical practice itself in pursuance of its ends. In every case, the relation between technique and knowledge is an *external*, unreflected relation, radically different from the internal, reflected relation between a science and its knowledges. (*For Marx*, 171)

For Althusser, theoretical practice can only be given in the form of a conceptual apparatus or what he calls a *problematic*: a set of knowledges, and a series of procedures or relations among knowledges, that achieve the status of disciplines. To define a given aesthetic practice (cinematic or otherwise) as a theoretical one is to ascribe to it a level of generality and a degree of autonomy with respect to which it must always fall short. However, in the various relations that might exist between a theoretical practice and an aesthetic/technological practice, one cannot discount the possibility of importing a theoretical practice to serve in the production of aesthetic work. Far from being a process of internalization where the aesthetic message takes "theory" as its object of representation, this implies instead a dialectical relation where aesthetic practices are transformed and renewed by the systems of intelligibility that determine their potential meanings—the kinds of knowledge that can accrue to, or be produced in an external relation with respect to them. In fact, this is the principal intent of *Cahiers du cinéma*'s editorial policy of the period. And to the extent that their ideas were meant to establish a theory of critical reading as a "scientific" practice, their particular assimilation of Althusser can be understood as exact and consistent.

Despite *Cahiers du cinéma*'s qualifications, however, the specific difference between the two journals was one of degree, not kind, for both positions are subtended by a common rhetorical structure. Comolli and Narboni, for example, legitimately insist that if aesthetic practice cannot itself become an instrument of theoretical practice, a critical theory of the cinema can and must achieve a break with *its* ideological predecessors. Moreover, to assert that the cinema cannot produce *scientific* knowledge about itself or the world is not to suggest that it does not produce knowledge of any kind. At this point, however, neither journal can be said to have given proper thought to the nature of aesthetic practice as a *practice* defined according to Althusserian theory, which is the explicit task that Baudry's essay sets for itself. Committed to the idea of the revolutionary potential of film, both journals argued, over and against the existing work of Althusser on the differential specificity of the "aesthetic effect" as opposed to a "knowledge effect," that the cognitive status of the work of art was a matter of degree, negotiated by the formal structure of the aesthetic message, not an a priori category as Althusser argued. In this respect, both *Cahiers du cinéma* and *Cinéthique* retained, implicitly or explicitly, the opposition of ideology versus science, especially in its correspondence with the opposition of realism versus modernism, as set into place by *Tel Quel* through its work on textual semiotics and modernist literature.

Economic, ideological, formal: it is now possible to account for the transposition of terms which, in the assimilation of Althusser to the discourse of political modernism, substitutes the category of the "formal" for that of the "aesthetic." This assertion in no way implies a defence of Althusser's description of the aesthetic as an a priori "epistemic" category that mediates ideological and scientific knowing. Rather, it is the logic that determines this substitution as a struggle between ideology and theory *within* the structure of aesthetic form, and as a property of the generic distinction between aesthetic forms, that must now be clarified.

Here the rhetoric of the epistemological break must work hardest to sustain an opposition between code and deconstruction as the crest line dividing the forms of realism, idealism, and illusionism from those of modernism, materialism, and theoretical knowing as intrinsic properties of the film-text. In this manner, the "deconstructive" text was conceived as "theoretical practice" and as a critique of illusionism and ideology. But to the extent that this critique of illusionism and the strategies of reflexivity it prescribed persisted in identifying the possibility of knowledge with the criterion of the visible, it is necessary to ask whether the emerging discourse of political modernism was ultimately able to break with an empirical conception of the text and its presumed subjective effects, or whether it unconsciously reproduced this conception as the result of a simple dialectic between code and deconstruction.

In this respect, several ideas concerning a "politics of the sign" held in common by *Cahiers du cinéma* and *Cinéthique* are now clear. First, for these two journals the possibility of a politics of the sign relied on the definition and differentiation of formal properties *intrinsic* to the aesthetic text and the apparatus that sustains it. It is especially clear in *Cahiers du cinéma*'s definition of the "progressive text" that the possibility of an "internal critique" is a property of the textual object that only waits for recognition on the part of an informed gaze.[28] Second, the criterion of a reflexive criticism is based on a division within the text itself between a politics of the signifier and a politics of the signified. Despite the influence of Derrida on *Tel Quel*, a Saussurean definition of the sign persists here as a criterion of the formal self-identity of the aesthetic text. In *Cahiers du cinéma*'s critical categories, for example, the possibility of a critique of ideology is the property of a dialectical ratio between the two parts of the sign. Without digressing too far into Derrida's critique of Saussure, it should be stressed how this binary conceptualization of the sign preserves in the "signified" the guarantee of a transcendental truth to which the signifier must refer regardless of the vicissitudes of its forms.[29]

Similarly, these critical theories reproduce a contradiction that Paul Hirst criticizes extensively in Althusser's own opposition of ideology to science by requiring the effects of falsity or illusion in order to specify the condition of a repressed but nonetheless "real" knowledge.[30] Finally, and paradoxically, what the reading of Althusser through the discourse of political modernism reveals is the reproduction, within the "deconstructive" critique of a Hegelian epistemology, of a theory of knowledge that also requires the unity of the subject and object of thought.

What Baudry's critique of the ideological effects of the cinematic apparatus evidences is ultimately and ironically an ontology of the text as the final yield of the opposition between code and deconstruction governing his argument. The "impossible reversal" submitted by Fargier as the criterion for the text of theoretical practice similarly relies on a binary structure that identifies knowledge with the evidence of a suppressed but ultimately renderable visibility. It is in fact the optical metaphor criticized by Baudry that finally turns Oriental perspective against a Western optical centering, difference against continuity, and a knowledge-effect against the illusory fantasy of an omniscient, transcendental subject. Even in the discourse of political modernism, the metaphor of visibility retains its power as the measure of the unity of subject and object in the field of perception, posing self-identical being as the locus of knowledge and the mastery of the world that is its object of thought. Although in his reading of Althusser and Derrida, Baudry begins by proposing a critical analysis of the ideology of representation informing the development of cinema as a technology of illusionism, the actual aim of this essay is to locate an autodeconstructive force within the body of the apparatus itself. Moreover, this insistence on reflexivity as the measure of a cinematic materialism and an epistemological modernism resembles more and more what Derrida criticizes as the discourse of autoaffection characteristic of logocentrism; or more simply, as an ontology defined by a self-authenticating meaning. There is no break with Hegel here, where vision is the most theoretical of the senses and the eye is the site of truth. Rather, in Baudry's argument the subject-spectator is displaced as origin of the gaze, becoming instead the product of a logic of perception determined by and identical to the structure of the apparatus itself, which may be turned either to the ends of illusion or to those of knowledge.

Finally, it is to Pleynet's credit that he did not simply equate the problem of empiricism with that of realism or illusionism. In fact, Pleynet warns against an "avant-garde empiricism" that takes formal deconstruction as an end in itself. On this basis, Baudry's argument, and in fact most arguments reducing the problem of ideology to a politics of textual form, paradoxically reveal their complicity with the aesthetic philosophies they set out to criticize. Considered as a clarification of how Althusser's critique of Hegel could illuminate an understanding of cinema's technological foundations as a vehicle for ideological representation, Baudry's argument is original and convincing. However, the extension of these insights, here and elsewhere, as a justification for a cinema of theoretical practice, and as the effort to preserve within the self-identity of aesthetic forms the potential for a deconstructive critique of illusionism and ideology, must now be understood as problematic. What remains to be resolved is how these theories in the discourse of political modernism addressed concretely the differential relation between "deconstructive" aesthetic practices and their potential spectators. We will turn to this problem in the next five chapters.

NOTES

1. Trans. Elias Noujaim in Sylvia Harvey's *May '68 and Film Culture* (London: British Film Institute, 1978): 159-60; cited hereafter

as EIF. This interview with *Tel Quel* editors Marcelin Pleynet and Jean Thibaudeau originally appeared in *Cinéthique* 3 (1969): 7-14.

2. For an interesting history of this attitude, see Wollen's "Semiotic Counter-Strategies: Retrospect 1982" in *Readings and Writings* (London: Verso, 1982): 208-15.

3. An in-depth survey of French film culture in this period is provided in Sylvia Harvey's *May '68 and Film Culture*. Of additional interest is Colin MacCabe's "Class of '68: Elements of an Intellectual Autobiography 1967-1981" in his *Tracking the Signifier* (Minneapolis: University of Minnesota Press, 1985): 1-32. The arguments that follow are fundamentally indebted to these accounts.

4. *Cahiers du cinéma* 216 (octobre 1969): 24-39.

5. Laura Mulvey and Peter Wollen, "Written Discussion," *Afterimage* 6 (Summer 1976): 36-37.

6. "The Politics of the Sign and Film Theory," *October* 17 (Summer 1981): 5-22.

7. Throughout the fifties and sixties, the editorial policy of *Cahiers du cinéma* was marked by a commitment to *auteur* criticism and its celebrated association with the French New Wave. *Cahiers du cinéma*'s immediate response to the political events of May and June 1968 was inconsistent at best, although several points deserve comment. Issues appearing in the spring of 1968 (Nos. 200/201 in particular) included extensive reportage of the "Langlois affair," which precipitated the May events by rapidly politicizing the film community and preparing them ideologically for the revolt. However, the French political upheaval did not affect editorial policy directly until the August 1968 issue where a shift in critical priorities was announced: the focus of the magazine's attention was to be displaced from the Hollywood cinema of the present day to either those films shown at the Cinémathèque and cine clubs or at the receiving end of political and economic censorship. With respect to theory development, *Cahiers du cinéma* began a project of Eisenstein translations (prefiguring a commitment to Russian Formalism and the Soviet avant-garde of the 1920s), as well as developing an interest in psychoanalytic criticism (cf. Oudart's work on "the suture" beginning in No. 211 [April 1969].) However, it was not until the publication of the editorial entitled "Cinema/Ideology/Criticism," drafted by Jean Narboni and Jean-Louis Comolli for the Oct./Nov. 1969 issue, that *Cahiers du cinéma* proposed a critical theory of the cinema to be carried out within a Marxist (explicitly Althusserian) framework, an act that sealed their commitment to political criticism and initiated a crisis of ownership in the magazine.

Cinéthique began publication in January 1969 and more or less
quickly organized itself in an adversarial position toward *Cahiers du
cinéma* by announcing a complete renunciation of Hollywood cinema. Alternatively, *Cinéthique* wished to contribute to building a
"parallel cinema" by revolutionizing the existing means of production, distribution, and exhibition. In other words, as opposed to *Cahiers du cinéma*, *Cinéthique* wished to build a theory of aesthetic as
well as critical practice whose object would be "materialist film," a
concept strongly influenced by *Tel Quel*'s championing of the revolutionary potential of modernism. The first nine issues of *Cinéthique*
witnessed the publication of interviews with Marcelin Pleynet, Christian Metz, and Julia Kristeva, as well as articles by Pleynet, Philippe
Sollers, and Jean-Louis Baudry. Just a month before *Cahiers du cinéma* published "Cinema/Ideology/Criticism," *Cinéthique* published
their two most cogent articles theorizing the proposed "materialist
film practice": Jean-Paul Fargier's "Parenthesis or Indirect Route:
an Attempt at Theoretical Definition of the Relationship between
Cinema and Politics" and Gerard Leblanc's "Direction." Both essays
originally appeared in *Cinéthique* 5 (septembre/octobre 1969).

All three of these essays appeared fairly quickly in English and
had a strong impact on Anglo-American film theory. "Cinema/Ide-
ology/Criticism" [hereafter cited as CIC] was translated in *Screen*
12.1 (Spring 1971), followed by "Direction" and "Parenthesis or
Indirect Route" [hereafter cited as PIR] in *Screen* 12.2 (Summer
1971). All three were subsequently anthologized in *Screen Reader*
1 (London: SEFT, 1977) and all citations refer to that edition.

It should also be noted that *Screen* continued to translate essays
from both *Cahiers du cinéma* and *Cinéthique*, developing their rep-
utation as the most influential journal of Anglo-American film theory
through a continued commitment to Parisian thought. For an in-
depth analysis of *Screen*'s relationship both to Althusser and Parisian
theory in general, see Philip Rosen's *The Concept of Ideology and
Contemporary Film Criticism: A Study of the Position of the Journal
Screen in the Context of the Marxist Theoretical Tradition*, dissertation, University of Iowa, 1978. For a more complete historical account of the situation in France, see Sylvia Harvey's excellent *May
'68 and Film Culture*, especially 33-41, and "Les Cahiers du cinéma,
1968-1977: Interview with Serge Daney," *The Thousand Eyes* 2
(1977): 18-31.

8. Althusser used the concept of the break specifically to describe
Marx's separation from Hegelian thought, which thereby constituted
the "science" of dialectical materialism in the *1857 Introduction* and

Capital. For a deeper discussion of this concept, see his essays "On the Materialist Dialectic" and "Marxism and Humanism" in *For Marx* (London: Verso Editions, 1977) and *Reading Capital* (London: Verso Editions, 1979), both trans. Ben Brewster. For Althusser's autocritique of this position, see his *Essays in Self-Criticism,* trans. Grahame Locke (Thetford: New Left, 1976): 112-13, 147-48, and 189-90.

9. This proposition caused a number of interesting debates, typified by the response of Jean-Patrick Lebel in the pages of *La Nouvelle Critique.* Lebel's essays were collected into a book entitled *Cinéma et idéologie* (Paris: Editions Sociales, 1971). For a summary of these debates, see James Spellerberg's "Technology and Ideology in the Cinema," *Quarterly Review of Film Studies* 2.3 (August 1977): 288-301.

10. For additional useful commentaries, see Alex Callinicos's *Althusser's Marxism* (London: Pluto Press, 1976) and Norman Geras' "Althusser's Marxism: An Account and Assessment," *New Left Review* 71 (Jan.-Feb. 1972): 58-87.

11. This category has a parallel documentary category that not only takes as its object political events, but also organizes its material so as to problematize traditional documentary codes of realism.

12. This group of films also has a corresponding documentary category.

13. "Film/politique (2), *L'Aveu:* 15 propositions," *Cahiers du cinéma* 224 (octobre 1970): 48-51.

14. An Althusserian position on aesthetics was already developed by 1966. Of Althusser's three essays on aesthetics, "Le 'Piccolo' Bertolazzi et Brecht (Notes sur un théâtre matérialiste)," appeared in *Esprit* in December 1962, "Une lettre sur l'art en reponse d'André Daspre" appeared in *La Nouvelle Critique* in 1966, and "Cremonini, peintre d'abstrait" was published in *Democratie Nouvelle,* also in 1966. Moreover, Pierre Macherey's *Pour une théorie de la production littéraire* (Paris: Librarie François Maspero) also appeared in 1966, reprinting his important essays on Jules Verne and Vladimir Lenin and Count Lev Nickolayevich Tolstoy.

15. In *Lenin and Philosophy,* trans. Ben Brewster (New York and London: Monthly Review Press, 1971): 225-26.

16. Not only did this critical category have the greatest influence on Anglo-American criticism, in the long run it was also the category from which *Cahiers du cinéma* produced their strongest efforts in textual analysis. Among these were analyses of John Ford's *Young Mr. Lincoln* in No. 223, Joseph von Sternberg's *Morocco* in No. 225, and Fritz Lang's *Hangmen Also Die* in Nos. 286, 288, and 290/291.

17. Thus Althusser writes: ". . . as the specific function of the work of art is to make *visible*. . . , by establishing a distance from it, the reality of the existing ideology (of any one of its forms), the work of art *can not fail to exercise* a directly ideological effect . . . and . . . it is impossible to think the work of art, in its specifically aesthetic existence, without taking into account the privileged relation between it and ideology, i.e. *its direct and inevitable ideological effect.*" "Cremonini, Painter of the Abstract," in *Lenin and Philosophy*, 241-42. Also see Tony Bennett's *Formalism and Marxism* (London: Methuen, 1979), especially 111-26.

18. Here Fargier cites Althusser directly: " 'By *practice* we mean, in general, any process *transforming* a given raw material into a given *product*, the transformation being effected by a given expenditure of labour using given means (of production).'

"This general definition of practice includes within itself the possibility of particularity. There are different practices which are really distinct from each other, although belonging organically to the same complex whole." (Louis Althusser: "On Dialectical Materialism" in *For Marx*.)

"This complex whole is social practice. It implies a structured totality comprising all the practices of a given society" (PIR 26).

Considering the influence of Maoist theory on Althusser and other French intellectuals in the late sixties, we might also note Mao's dictum concerning the three types of struggle (economic, political, scientific) that intervene in the various practices comprising the social whole, as well as Godard's insistence that aesthetic work be considered under the rubric of "scientific struggle." For more discussion of these issues, see Colin MacCabe's *Godard: Images, Sounds, Politics* (Bloomington: Indiana University Press, 1980), especially Chapter Three, and Mao's essay "On Practice," in *Selected Works* (New York: International Publishers, 1954), II: 282-97.

19. To resolve these problems, Fargier suggests that three types of cinema exist that attempt to serve the proletarian cause: socialist films of the people's democracies, "social" films in bourgeois democracies, and militant films that appear in both. When laying out his typology of texts, a curious displacement occurs across the ideology/science opposition with respect to the kinds of films attacked or defended. Each of these types of films is differentiated only on the basis of the ideologies they reproduce and thus each is deemed complicit with a cinematic idealism due to the lack of reflection on the "ideology-in-general" produced by their form. In socialist films, produced in countries where the proletariat is supposedly in pos-

session of the means of production, both economic and political, this problem is judged to be negligible since the ideological effect (the impression of reality) serves the humanist element of socialist realism by reinforcing the credibility of proletarian representation of itself to itself in the consolidation of its victory. However, with social films, produced in a conjuncture where capital reigns, this cannot be the case. Arguing once again in a manner close to Comolli, Fargier explains that despite the best intentions of the filmmaker, these films can only enhance the ideological effect produced by their form because "in a capitalist society, where the cinema is automatically aimed at the entire public, without distinction of class, these films can only reproduce (and so are produced by) the image of 'real life' acceptable to that section of bourgeois ideology known as 'the guilty conscience' " (PIR 31). Militant filmmakers are judged to be in a somewhat better position since they attempt to alter film's relation to economic practice by developing oppositional modes of production, distribution, and exhibition, but in the last instance, they too are judged complicit with idealism to the extent that they may have ignored the ideology-in-general produced by cinema at the level of its form.

20. Trans. Alan Williams as "Ideological Effects of the Basic Cinematographic Apparatus" in *Cinematographic Apparatus: Selected Writings* (New York: Tanam Press, 1980), ed. Theresa Hak Kyung Cha: 25-37; hereafter cited as IEA. I will cite the original text in brackets when necessary. A better edited version of this essay has recently appeared in Philip Rosen, ed., *Narrative, Apparatus, Ideology* (New York: Columbia University Press, 1986): 286-98.

21. The most interesting critiques of Baudry specifically, and arguments concerning the cinematic apparatus in general, have come from feminist film theory. See especially Jacqueline Rose's "The Cinematic Apparatus: Problems in Current Theory" in *The Cinematic Apparatus*, eds. Teresa de Lauretis and Stephen Heath (New York: St. Martin's Press, 1980): 172-86; Joan Copjec's "The Anxiety of the Influencing Machine," *October* 23 (Winter 1982): 43-59; and Constance Penley's "Feminism, Film Theory and the Bachelor Machines," *m/f* 10 (1985): 39-59.

22. See Geras, especially 63-66, and Althusser's critique of Hegel in "On the Materialist Dialectic" in *For Marx*, 161-218.

23. Althusser's influential essay, "Idéologie et appareils idéologiques d'état," *La pensée* 151 (juin 1970), was published in the same year as Baudry's article.

24. See for example the section entitled "The Process of Theoretical Practice," 182-93.

25. See his "Freud and the Scene of Writing" in *Writing and Difference*, trans. Alan Bass (Chicago: University of Chicago Press, 1978): 196-231.

26. For example, Derrida writes that "We have already defined elsewhere the fundamental property of writing, in a difficult sense of the word, as *spacing*: diastem and time becoming space; an unfolding as well, on an original site, of meanings which irreversible, linear consecution, moving from present point to present point, could only tend to repress, and (to a certain extent) could only fail to repress. In particular in so-called phonetic writing. The latter's complicity with logos (or the time of logic), which is dominated by the principle of noncontradiction, the cornerstone of all metaphysics or presence, is profound" ("Freud and the Scene of Writing," 217).

The opening move of Derrida's essay, of course, is to examine Freud's rejection of the optical metaphor in favor of describing the psychical apparatus in the form of a "writing machine," the popular toy called "The Mystic Writing Pad." Thierry Kuntzel and others have noticed the startling analogies between cinema and "writing" in both Freud's and Derrida's essays. See Kuntzel's "A Note Upon the Filmic Apparatus," *Quarterly Review of Film Studies* 1.3 (August 1976): 266-71.

27. "Cinema/Ideology/Criticism (2): Examining a critique at its critical point," in Susan Bennett's trans., *Screen Reader 1*: 45-46. Originally published in *Cahiers du Cinéma* 217 (November 1969); trans. originally published in *Screen* 12.2 (Summer 1971). For more discussion of the Althusserian terminology in question, see Ben Brewster's glossary in *For Marx*, especially the entry entitled "theory, 'theory,' Theory": 256.

28. Barbara Klinger has dealt with this problem at length in her essay "Cinema/Ideology/Criticism Revisited: The Progressive Text" *Screen* 25.1 (January/February 1984): 30-44.

29. Derrida's extensive critique of Saussure is found most prominently in *Of Grammatology*, trans. Gayatri Chakravorty Spivak (Baltimore: The Johns Hopkins University Press, 1976), especially pages 27-73. I will address these problems in relation to film theory and the discourse of political modernism in much greater depth in Chapters Six and Seven.

30. See Hirst's *On Law and Ideology* (London: The MacMillan Press, 1979), especially Chapter 3, p. 63.

FOUR

Formalism and "Deconstruction"

Unquestionably, an implicit theory of history informs the notions of theoretical practice in film confronted so far. Noel Burch's discussions of modernism and history in film perfectly exemplify this aspect of the discourse of political modernism. Whereas Peter Wollen's objective in the argument of the two avant-gardes is to realign the history of modernism in film with the history of semiology, Noel Burch's view of film history describes a Manichean struggle between a materialist or antiillusionist potential intrinsic to film form and its suppression by an ideology of realism imposed from the "outside."

The most concise statement of Noel Burch's views on cinematic modernism is "Propositions," an essay coauthored with Jorge Dana and published with Jean-Louis Baudry's "Writing/Fiction/Ideology" in *Afterimage* 5.[1] Burch and Dana begin their essay, not unlike Baudry, by asserting that the modernist text is the subject of a doubly repressed history—of the cinema's specific potential as an aesthetic form, and of the systems of intelligibility, theoretical and critical thought, that could articulate the possibility of this potential. Since their essay is offered as an intervention in the field of criticism and theory, they expressly define their project as taxonomic; that is, to define an aesthetically decisive discontinuity between various film practices according to their particular negotiation of problems of ideology and form. Burch and Dana's theoretical project can therefore be understood as reconsidering problems discussed in Chapter Two (the negotiation of points of contact between the history of modernism and that of semiology), as well as Chapter Three (the definition of a political modernism according to formal criteria able to distinguish the degrees of ideological implication of various kinds of texts). Having noted the elaboration of a retrospective crest line of exemplary modernist practices in the other arts—for example, by Pierre Boulez in music (Machault-Gesualdo-Bach-Beethoven-Wagner-Debussy-Schoenberg-Webern-Varèse-Cage) and by the *Tel Quel* group in literature (Dante-Sade-Lautréamont-Mallarmé-Roussel-Artaud-Bataille)—Burch and Dana set out to devise a similar "paternity based on modernity" for the cinema. In this manner, they hope to divide the films of a Dziga Vertov, Carl Dreyer, or Kenji Mizoguchi from those films that constitute the "anonymous machinery of ordinary cinema." Moreover, they suggest that such a taxonomy is only possible through the assimilation of a theoretical practice so far (at that time) excluded from the history of cinema criticism. Implicitly defined as Formalism, its own crest line is described by Burch and Dana as descending from Victor Shklovsky and Roman Jakobson to Umberto Eco, Julia Kristeva, and Jacques Derrida.

The importance of Formalism for Burch is that it enables him to define film history as the history of a critical modernism. For example, in Burch's study of the Japanese film *To the Distant Observer*, "deconstruction" in film is defined as "the inscription of its [the Western or Institutional Mode of Representation] basic mechanisms within the film, so that one could read the filmic text *relative to the mode as such, considered in its historical dimension*, and not merely *through* it, as if it were a 'natural language.' "[2] This proposition can be clarified by examining Burch's definition of what he calls the Institutional Mode of Representation (IMR. Although he offers a more complete account in a later essay, a more economic and prototypical definition is offered in "Propositions" itself.[3] What Burch calls the IMR (as he abbreviates it), resembles what is more typically known as the "classic realist text." In "Propositions," Burch refers to the IMR as a narrative discourse based on a linear form of exposition. "Linear discourse" is used throughout the essay to define an ideological determination of codes that ensures the suppression of paradigmatic forms of textual organization in favor of those syntagmatic articulations that guarantee the transparent expression of the diegesis (denoted elements of story) through a mechanistic relation of cause and effect and the subordination of signifier to signified. In the cinema, the domination of linear discourse overdetermines the organization of codes to maintain the univocality of spatial and temporal articulations: ". . . in other words, all those codes contributing to the reproduction, within the cinema, of the spectator/stage relationship in proscenium theatre, the representation of deep space as evolved by the Quattrocento and the ideally transparent narrative time associated with the 'bourgeois' novel of the nineteenth century, and whose function may be summed up as the camouflaging of the material discontinuities attendant upon the filmic process" (PPS 49).

Fundamental affinities with the work of Baudry are apparent here. First there is the notion of an ideological determination of representation as the repression of a material system of differences as the base of cinematic presentation. A second affinity is the equation of narrative or the "novelistic" with this ideological determination as the operation of an extrinsic, nonspecific cinematic code. However, where Baudry specifies a politics of *écriture* to reverse this situation, Burch and Dana propose what might be called a dialectics of form. In this manner, they oppose their notion of linear discourse to that of the aesthetic message, defined by Roman Jakobson and Jan Mukařovský as the transmission of an "internal system through which a work contests the validity of the system of codes in force within the artistic practices of the ideology dominant in a given time and place" (PPS 41). In an interview published in *Women and Film*, Burch links this concept directly to one of deconstruction.[4] On this basis, Burch and Dana construct a taxonomy that may be considered a more formal elaboration of Comolli and Narboni's. This taxonomy designates a range of films bounded on one end by "films totally accounted for and informed at all levels by the dominant codes," and on the other by those

films which are informed by a constant designation/deconstruction of the codes which, however ideologically determined at the strictly diegetic level, implicitly question this determination by the way they situate the codes and play upon them. . . . (PPS 48)

[It] is precisely through the work of "deconstruction" and "subversion" of the dominant codes of representation and narrativity that these films distinguish themselves so strikingly; and that this implicit critique is consubstantial with a redistribution of signifiers *according to the parti pris peculiar to that particular film*, choices which in fact generate what we call its *form*. (PPS 41-42)

Burch and Dana argue that any genuine theory of the film-text has to be founded on a formalist definition of the aesthetic message. What Burch means by *form* here is not specifically reducible either to material or technological codes of representation. Instead, following Umberto Eco's argument in *La Structure absente* (Paris: Mercure de France, 1972), Burch and Dana consider the problem of film form as the "dialectisation" of two kinds of structure, the *structural* and the *serial* or structured. Structural relations are conventional, involving, according to Burch and Dana, the production of socialized meaning through the operation of code. Following Pierre Francastel, Burch and Dana submit that films dominated by structural relations have ceased to be combinatory or paradigmatically organized in order to become institutional or normative. This in fact is the source of Burch's characterization of the Hollywood cinema as the "Institutional Mode of Representation." Opposed to structural relations are serial or structured relations that involve "the negation of socialised meaning above and beyond the simple ambiguity of the aesthetic message" (PPS 42). Examples of aesthetic practices dominated by structured relations include serial music, nonfigurative painting, nonnarrative dance, or any other art form that organizes and distributes its signifiers according to para-mathematical models. Citing Umberto Eco, Burch and Dana suggest that the serial method induces a crisis of code in the formulation of the aesthetic message. It could be thus considered "like the other dialectical face of the structural method. The pole of becoming as opposed to the pole of permanence. The contribution that the semiotics of the message can bring to the semiotics of the code. The attempt to insert diachronic development into a synchronic view of communicative conventions. The series would then no longer be the negation of structure, but structure questioning itself and recognising itself as part of history" (PPS 42).[5]

Devolving from a code/deconstruction opposition, this theory of the aesthetic message establishes as the precondition for a history of modernism the full elaboration of a system of normative and institutionalized codes. In fact, this is the source of Burch's interest in "primitive" cinema and the premise has been rehearsed time and again in his essays on that subject.[6] In "Propositions," for example, Burch designates 1895-1919 as marking out the period where specific codes of representation and narrativity in the cinema were institutionalized. According to Burch, this process is motivated by a specific ideological and economic necessity. In order to ensure its economic and cultural survival, the cinema had to attract and maintain a middle-class audience by adopting codes of narrativity and spatial representation from the bourgeois novel and theater. The date of 1919 is not arbitrary. The closure of the first period of institutionalization of film form is marked by the appearance of *The Cabinet of Dr. Caligari*, which inaugurates the modernist project as "the first film to devolve fully and deliberately upon a deconstruction of the then barely instituted codes of transparence and the illusion of continuity" (PPS 43). According to this logic, which defines the aesthetic message in the structure of a dialectic, it seems that, paradoxically, the history of the IMR could not really become intelligible until its principal devices and conventions were formulated through their reversal or negation in the modernist text. Similarly, the cinema could not be defined in its aesthetic function until the operation of a dialectic between structural and serial forms could be identified. The outline of *Caligari*'s aesthetic strategies offered by Burch and Dana may thus be read both as a lexicography of dominant, "ideological" codes and as a prospectus for a "deconstructive" cinema. For Burch, *Caligari* inaugurates the aesthetic function in film through its use of four basic procedures:

1. The elimination of linear causality so as to stress the autonomy and spatial integrity of individual shots: "The expulsion and/or radical contestation of the codes of orientation (contiguous/ continuous links) by a strategic return to 'frontality,' and 'archaic' tableau shots. . ." (PPS 43).

2. The elimination of depth and concomitant emphasis on the dimensionality of the picture plane: "The dialectical negation of the illusion of spatial depth by explicitly opposing it to the material flatness of the screen. . . . This is achieved by exaggerating the perspective by means of artifices related to two-dimensional design. . ." (PPS 44).

3. The rejection of guarantees of continuity in the articulation of diegetic space including the historical and stylistic homogeneity of costuming, decor, props, and verisimilitude in acting, all of which usually function as additional supports for the illusionist effect.

4. The subversion of the linear exposition of the narrative through a strategic foregrounding of repetition, redundancy, and ellipsis.

In fact, Burch and Dana's understanding of how the modernist text can escape the ideological attitudes inherent in illusionist forms may be summarized as follows: the aesthetic message emphasizes the paradigmatic level of textual production through the operation of anaphora or the systematic repetition of morphological units of code. In Burch's description the modernist text becomes a dictionary of devices that are designated or "defamiliarized" (Burch's use of this Formalist term is omnipresent) through their formal distribution across the syntagmatic plane according to a system of structured or serial repetition. Following Annette Michelson, Burch and Dana characterize Vertov's *Man With A Movie Camera* (1929) as inaugurating "an 'epistemological' approach within the filmic discourse itself, whereby the form of the film is no less than the inscription of its process of production into the 'text' " (PPS 45).[7] In a similar manner, Dreyer's *Vampyr* (1933) is characterized as one of the few films that on "the technical and physical level of the substance of which its signifiers are made, on the level of the differential nature of the signifiers, on the level of its connoted signifieds, the level of the system of psychological expectations to which the signs relate . . . it establishes a system of homologous structural relationships as if all the levels were definable, as indeed they are, on the basis of a single code which structures them all."[8]

This code, defined explicitly by Burch and Dana as "the actual Form of the film," determines the deconstructive capacity of the aesthetic message as a specific relation established between structural and serial forms of textual organization. Moreover, Burch and Dana subsequently refer to the generative Form of the deconstructive text as a "dialectic"; alternatively, "the dialectic that is established between the ideologically determined codes and their critique" or the "dialecticising" of ideological content.

Although somewhat obscure on these points, Burch's argument is much clearer when his implicit ties to Russian Formalism are understood. Burch's opposition of ideology to form, which centers his theory as the dialectic between structural and serial modes of textual generation, is founded on a notion of aesthetic perception as defamiliarization. Thus the systematic designation and cognition of ideological devices is the object of the deconstructive text. In Victor Shklovsky's original formulation, defamiliarization is a technique that unsettles habitual or conventional modes of perception and cognition. For Burch and Dana it functions as what Roman Jakobson calls "the dominant" of the aesthetic text: "The dominant may be defined as the focusing component of a work of art: it rules, determines, and transforms the remaining components. It is the dominant which guarantees the integrity of the structure."[9] In other words, defamiliarization, as the structured feature termed as *dominant* in Formalist parlance, is reconsidered by Burch and Dana in the concept of dialectic as Form. The problem of aesthetic perception is crucial for Burch. In his view, what the ideological and structural (as opposed to formal and serial) determination of codes suppresses is in fact "the central 'problematic' of picturo-filmic space, of the projection of the pertinent traits of depth onto a flat surface (the screen). And what is being refuted here is the very corner-stone of the illusionist edifice: the presentation of the pro-filmic space as 'present,' the camouflage of the representational character of filmic space, as well as that of the process by which the two communicate" (PPS 63).

This idea recalls Jakobson's definition of the aesthetic function as devolving from an emphasis on the nonidentity of sign and thing. Comparisons are also possible with the Althusserian distinction between the aesthetic and the ideological as structurally related though competing modes of cognition. However, whereas in the last chapter I suggested that the code/deconstruction opposition valorized the relative autonomy of the aesthetic as distinct from the ideological, Burch takes a radical step beyond the formulations of both Jakobson and Althusser by stressing the absolute autonomy of aesthetic form, opposing it to ideology as an obfuscating "content"—the structural expression of bourgeois spatial and narrative codes—that dissimulates aesthetic perception.

The ramifications of Burch's argument are clarified by elaborating the latent assumptions that govern his use of the term *dialectic*. For in its strategic expression of the relation of ideology to Form, it defines not only the history of cinema in its rapport with modernism, but also the history of class struggle in the cinema.

This idea is explained in Burch's interview with the editors of *Women and Film*, entitled "Beyond Theory of Film Practice." Early in this interview, and after introducing some problems in the history of primitive cinema, there is a passage where Burch criticizes the work of Christian Metz in a discussion of the dangers confronting a semiology of the cinema as opposed to the study of speech. The framework of this criticism concerns the applicability of diachronic analysis. Burch draws an analogy that depicts language change as an inherently dialectical process, the protean and mercuric quality of popular speech in the working classes opposing the conservative nature of writing whose codicity is preserved by the bourgeoisie. To those familiar with Derrida, such a proposition, advanced within the context of a theory of deconstruction, is immediately suspect. However, Burch continues by extending the analogy to the cinema: "By comparison, the reasons for the evolution of verbal language are complex, but they can be found in part within the framework of language itself. The diachronic study of language is something which is legitimate and admissible scientifically speaking. The examination of cinema that way is completely absurd because the reasons for these codes lie entirely outside of film—but 100% outside of film. They are ideological. And they are 100% ideological" (BTFP 21).

According to Burch, the history of cinema *qua* cinema cannot be understood in its temporal dimension because its stylistic evolution has been governed by a radical exteriority—a vocation for realism and linear narrative that has determined its ideological functioning in the service of a specific class-audience, the bourgeoisie. The history of cinema is portrayed as the continuing suppression of an aesthetic potential that should have evolved according to the materials of expression proper to it.

This representation of the historical dimension of aesthetic form resembles the Formalist distinction between practical and poetic language, but with a crucial difference. In Burch's analogy, language change is dialogical and "naturally" dialectical to the extent that it "mirrors the class struggle," the permeability of popular speech opposing itself to the petrification of bourgeois writing. History and diachrony are at the center of this process. In the cinema, however, codicity is monological and dominated by the expressive means of a single class. The cinema has explicitly rejected dialectics, which Burch all too readily confuses automatically with the problem of class struggle. In this view, the history of the cinema is nothing less than the history of its ideological contamination by noncinematic codes: in sum, bourgeois "writing" as related, on the one hand, to the incorporation of Quattrocento perspective and the illusion of depth achieved dramaturgically on the nineteenth-century stage, and on the other, to the adoption of novelistic conventions of linear causality, diegetic verisimilitude, psychological determination of events, and so on. Here Burch's arguments resemble, in an extreme form, Roland Barthes's opposition of myth and history in that bourgeois writing—in its determination as a hegemonic and monolithic code—attains a universality that sublimates the history that could reveal its limits, its transience, and its relativity.

Paradoxically, there was a moment when history, in the sense given above, was a possibility for Burch: "... we believe it can be shown that the pre-Griffith period of cinema contained a potential for non-linearity which is often perfectly manifest: 'uncentred' tableau-shots in Lumière, 'mobile' close-up in *The Great Train Robbery*, 'a-chronological' editing in *The Life of An American Fireman*—both by Porter—, acknowledgment of the depth-illusion as such in the films of Méliès" (PPS 65). For Burch, primitive cinema is a archive of "modernist" techniques. And combined with his continuing assertion that the preindustrial phase of cinema history was mandated by a proletarian public, whose relationship to film as a popular art was only later supplanted by the middle classes, the primitive cinema is a utopian moment for Burch. In this period, the cinema "spontaneously" produced those antiillusionist strategies whose systematic deployment could only later restore a dialectic to film, defining its aesthetic function as a "structure questioning itself and recognising itself as part of history" (PPS 42).

In their recent critique of Burch, Kristin Thompson and David Bordwell have demonstrated convincingly that, both empirically and theoretically, Burch's assumptions with respect to the history of primitive film—its style, audiences, and technology—are highly debatable. Considering Burch's avowed materialism, it is interesting to note how Bordwell and Thompson easily demonstrate that his historical account of the constitution of the IMR is purely formal and teleological: "When Burch discusses historical changes after the constitution of the Codes [the IMR], he falls into a static expressive causality: the eternal struggle between ideologically complicit films and deconstructive films" (LMC 12). With these comments, Bordwell and Thompson touch upon the central contradiction of both Burch's theory of history and aesthetic practice. This theory is founded not on a dialectic but a simple binary logic—code versus deconstruction. Burch's arguments are therefore not historical in a Marxist, materialist sense; instead they present little more than an autonomous theory of devices: "Deconstruction is deconstruction, no matter when it happens. . . . Techniques are considered outside of any context in the films' formal systems and are never related to conditions of production or reception or to other spheres (other arts, social and economic history, etc.)" (LMC 12). In sum, the code/deconstruction opposition is radically ahistorical. And in this respect, Burch's account of the aesthetic function can hardly be differentiated from Clement Greenberg's conservative definition of modernism as preserving, in the autonomy of Form, the values of "culture" in an ideologically troubled world. It is therefore a pristine example of a traditional art historical argument that pits Ideology against Form, such that the political function of art is thought to be proportional to the degree in which perception of its intrinsic materials of expression can be restored.

But it is more important to understand how this binary logic sustains the formal system of the text (as devolving from its aesthetic function) as well as the subjective relations that are ineluctably identified with that system. I suggested earlier that Burch's notion of deconstruction relies fundamentally on a theory of aesthetic perception as defamiliarization. However, the degree in which this concept—so central to his theory—is consistent with Formalist and Prague School writings must now be questioned. Burch's specific use of this term is actually more closely allied to that of the Russian Futurists who argued that avant-garde techniques wrested artistic reality away from its deformation in older forms to reveal it in its purity. As Tony Bennett points out, in "On Realism in Art," Roman Jakobson demonstrated that all aesthetic forms were equally conventional, that is, bound by definable codes in their means of expression.[10] Defamiliarization constitutes only one possible mode of aesthetic cognition and it is tied to the historical situation or reception of given texts. Devices that served to defamiliarize codes or conventions canonized in earlier historical periods can themselves become conventional and perceptually neutral. Burch's notions of defamiliarization and of the aesthetic function therefore lacks the historical dimension given explicitly by Formalist theory.

Even in its contradictions Burch's theory observes a resolute and systematic logic, especially where the problem of the spectator is concerned. In the series of binary terms that runs from code/deconstruction through structural/serial forms to (bour-

geois) writing/(proletarian) speech, Burch's version of defamiliarization governs the truth or knowledge proper to the modernist text according to the "dialectical" rule of speech. There
is little doubt that the outline history of cinema that Burch
proposes—where cinema is recuperated from the class to which
it was "naturally" allied in its beginnings, co-opted by the
bourgeoisie, and developed industrially according to a style
that contravened its "proper" forms—is forged decisively in a
rhetoric of illusionism and its critique so characteristic of the
theory of epistemological modernism.

But it is the other side of this equation, so closely tied to
the problem of "speech," that is of special interest here. For
according to the binary structure of this rhetoric, in order to
posit the function of ideology as the willful suppression of
cinematic materiality, and as the elision of any perception of
cinema's intrinsic forms, Burch implicitly offers an ontological
theory of aesthetic value. Moreover, this is an ontology both
of the text (as an essential and self-identical form, subject to
degrading and falsifying uses) and of the subject. The proletariat, for example, is characterized as a fully self-identical
class-subject that is intrinsically capable of nonideological
knowing. Without the aid of any theory, proletarian subjectivity is understood as able to recognize the truth in itself and
in the (cinematic) forms where truth presents itself. Curiously,
Burch's history of film as the history of modernism is founded
as a kind of origin myth. At the beginnings of cinema, he imagines the existence of a once integral unity of subject (a hypostasized class audience) and object ("primitive" cinema as
both the "speech" of the working classes and as identical to
the forms proper to cinematic expression), now divided but
potentially restorable once the cinema is stripped of its ideological function. The entire system of canonization proposed
by Burch and Dana requires the figure of Truth or "scientific"
perception as, on one hand, the integral property of the class-
subject to which cinema is naturally allied, and on the other,
as the property of textual systems produced by "artists"
(Dreyer, Mizoguchi, Vertov) capable of recognizing cinema's
inherently modernist vocation. This aspect of Burch's theory
is present even in the forms of his binary rhetoric; for example,

"structural" versus "structured" textual systems. Paradoxically, "structural" forms describe an "open" system—"open,"
that is, in the sense of vulnerable to ideological contamination
from an outside—where both texts and subject are passively
swept up in the force of mass identity. Conversely, "structured" forms indicate a sense of independence, completion,
or closure. They seem to be the result of an intentional, artistic
activity, as well as the restoration of an integral self-identity
(of the modernist text, the subject of truth, and of the perceptual relation sustained between them). (The irony, of course,
is that these terms are borrowed from Eco who, contrariwise,
theorizes the open text as the avant-garde form and the closed
text as the norm.)

The binary logic of Burch's version of political modernism
proposes the liberation of cinema's integral form as a truth
verified by its original class-subject, and as a self-conscious,
critical perception produced by and in the text as opposed to
the passive reproduction of an aesthetic status quo. But the
simplicity of this opposition is suspect. In its dedication to
modernism and Formalism, Burch's theory begins with the radically antirealist assumption of the *nonidentity* of sign and referent. But in order to accomplish its critique of ideology, this
theory must propose an equally powerful *identity* as the essential Forms of cinema and the perception they encourage in
the spectator. In this respect, any sense of history as the continual possibility of transformations in textual form, meaning,
and contexts of reception, is excluded from Burch's arguments.

In Burch's formulation, deconstruction as a critical practice
is reduced to a formal, aesthetic system intrinsic to the function
of modernist texts. Although Burch's arguments are provocative in their critical distinctions, and I do believe he has made
a genuine contribution to film semiotics, they are flawed as
the basis for a history of cinema or for a political criticism.
They do not acknowledge their own historical placement as
establishing a particular system of intelligibility—theoretically
informed, critical readings—of the texts Burch wishes to promote, and thus fall short of fulfilling the basic conditions of a
genuine theoretical practice. As Steve Crofts and Mark Nash
point out, Burch's understanding of the production of textual

meaning is restricted solely to an internal dynamics of form. In this he exemplifies a "formalist tendency to freeze this process of circulation of meanings between film and viewer/reader into formal effects at the filmic level and a view of the audience as irredeemably 'manipulated' by the media. . ."[11] Since Burch implicitly refuses to situate films in a complex network of political, economic, and ideological determinations, or to accept that their potential meanings and uses may be negotiated or renegotiated by differing theoretical and critical frames, his views are actually an ahistorical, essentialist, and intractable account of textual meaning.

NOTES

1. Noel Burch and Jorge Dana, "Propositions," *Afterimage* 5 (Summer 1974): 40-66, trans. Diana Matias and Christopher King; referred to in subsequent citations as PPS.

2. Noel Burch, *To the Distant Observer: Form and Meaning in the Japanese Cinema* (Berkeley: University of California Press, 1979): 123; hereafter cited as TDO.

3. See, for example, Burch's "Film's Institutional Mode of Representation and the Soviet Response," *October* 11 (Winter 1979): 77-96.

4. "Beyond Theory of Film Practice: An Interview with Noel Burch," *Women and Film* 5/6 (1974): 22; hereafter cited as BTFP.

Earlier, in *Theory of Film Practice* itself, Burch compares a similar notion of dialectic to Brecht's concept of distantiation. It is interesting to note that Burch was convinced of the importance of Brecht's ideas concerning a non-Aristotelian theater as the basis for a theory of deconstruction in cinema as long as one eliminated "Brecht's concern for content." I thank Dana Polan for this observation. Further discussion may be found in his essay "Brecht and the Politics of Self-Reflexive Cinema," *Jumpcut* 17 (April 1978): 29-32.

5. *La Structure absente*, cited in PPS 42. Similar arguments have been revised and updated by Eco in *A Theory of Semiotics* (Bloomington and London: Indiana University Press, 1976) and *The Role of the Reader* (Bloomington and London: Indiana University Press, 1979).

Burch's use of Eco to define an aesthetic function for film through the presence or absence of serial structures began as early as 1967 with the publication of a series of essays in *Cahiers du cinéma* that were later published as a book, *Praxis du cinéma* (Paris: Editions Gallimard, 1969). On the importance of serial composition for Burch's aesthetic, see Annette Michelson's "Introduction" to *Theory of Film Practice* (New York and Washington: Praeger Publisher's Inc., 1973): v-xv.

6. Primitive cinema has in fact become the focus of Burch's theoretical interests as evidenced in a series of recent essays including "Beyond Theory of Film Practice"; "Porter, or Ambivalence," *Screen* 19.4 (Winter 1978/79): 91-105; "Film's Institutional Mode of Representation and the Soviet Response," his program notes for *Correction Please, or How We Got Into Pictures* (London: Arts Council of Great Britain, n.d. [c. 1979]); and "Charles Baudelaire v. Dr. Frankenstein," *Afterimage* 8/9 (Winter 1980/81): 4-21. Moreover, the importance accorded to this thesis, linking primitive cinema historically to a certain conception of the modernist text, is demonstrated by Burch's prominence in *Afterimage* 8/9, a special issue dedicated to this proposition.

Here I will only be concerned with discussing Burch's arguments concerning the history of modernism in film. For a criticism of his assumptions concerning film history and historiography in general, see David Bordwell and Kristin Thompson's "Linearity, Materialism, and the Study of Early American Cinema," *Wide Angle* 5.3 (1983): 4-15; cited hereafter as LMC. The arguments that follow are deeply indebted to this essay.

7. Annette Michelson's influential discussion of Vertov is " 'The Man with the Movie Camera': From Magician to Epistemologist," *Artforum* (March 1972): 60-72.

8. *La Structure absente*: 127; cited in PPS 46.

9. Roman Jakobson, "The Dominant" in Ladislav Matejka and Krystyna Pomorska, eds. *Readings in Russian Poetics: Formalist and Structuralist Views* (Ann Arbor: Michigan Slavic Publications, 1978): 82.

10. *Formalism and Marxism* (London: Methuen, 1980): 50-56.

11. "Form and Politics: the Work of Noel Burch," BFI Summer School paper, n.d., 1. Crofts and Nash also extend their critique in a direction that ultimately undermines Burch's arguments for the applicability of his theories for a socialist politics as outlined in "Avant-Garde or Vanguard?," *Afterimage* 6 (Summer 1976): 52-63.

FIVE

Anti-Narrative,
or the Ascetic Ideal

In his "Afterword" to Peter Gidal's essay "The Anti-Narrative," Stephen Heath compares Gidal's film theory and practice to Walter Benjamin's apology for surrealism. As surprising as it is exact, this parallel is drawn in the following citation: "To organise pessimism means nothing other than to expel moral metaphor from politics and to discover in political action a sphere reserved one hundred per cent for images."[1]

Gidal is not being represented as a "Benjaminian filmmaker" here, much less a surrealist one. However, this passage holds the heuristic interest of illustrating the utopianism of Gidal's self-proclaimed "ultraleftism," both as an avant-garde artist and as the principal theoretician of structural/materialist film. My use of the word *utopia* here refers to T. W. Adorno's sense of the term. In the culture of late capitalism, dominated in its totality by the demands of ideology and affirmative culture, the best hope of political art is its commitment to a relentless negativity. To organize pessimism in aesthetic practice thus requires the formulation of a dialectic powerful and flexible enough to perform the seemingly impossible task of maintaining a space outside of an ideology whose power to recover countercultural forces for affirmative ends seems uncontested.

Heath continues his gloss by defining Gidal's negativity as rehearsing the end of cinema in films. Structural/materialist

film, the "truly materialist practice" which is the constant object of Gidal's theoretical and polemical writings,

> is then necessarily the fully reflexive knowledge of the history
> of cinema that at any moment a film—a materialist film—must
> hold and present, "a dialectically constituted 'presentation,' of
> film representation, film image, film moment, film meaning in
> temporalness, etcetera." The film must be the event of that
> material presentation ("the historical moment is the film mo-
> ment each moment"), the only way to end the implications of
> cinema, the place-image, identification, narrative-sign, illu-
> sion—of the spectator there. ("Afterword," 95)

More simply put, in Heath's reading of Gidal, the history of
cinema—its forms, meanings, and politics—are replayed, re-
circulated, and re-presented in every conventional, narrative
film. In Sartrian terms, the text of each narrative film "re-
totalizes" the history of cinema stylistics in its ideological function and subsequently produces a subject for ideology there.
Alternatively, the objective of antinarrative or the goal of a
structural/materialist film practice is to perform the seemingly
impossible task of defining, over and against the massive domination of film by narrative style and ideology, a series of negative strategies capable of derailing that history. In dividing
narrative from the intrinsic possibilities of cinematic representation, structural/materialist film desires "to expel moral
metaphor from politics and to discover in political action a
sphere reserved one hundred per cent for images."
    The particularly intricate relation between narrative and
ideology in Gidal's theory will be discussed in a moment. But
first another dimension of Gidal's rhetoric of antinarrative
should be introduced. The interest of Heath's reading of Gidal
is not only his deployment of the key concepts in Gidal's theoretical writing (for example, reflexivity, materialism, temporality, and dialectic, defined as the negating terms of illusionism, narrative, meaning, and subjectivity), but also in
Heath's reconsideration of the strategic opacity of Gidal's rhetoric. Deke Dusinberre, who along with Heath is one of Gidal's
more sympathetic apologists, has called this strategy "consistent oxymoron."[2] Dusinberre argues that the style of Gidal's
writing demonstrates the inextricable relatedness of his theory

and practice. The difficulty of Gidal's theoretical prose and the importation of theoretical concepts to his aesthetic practice is comparable in this respect to Adorno's justification of "dialectical sentences." By imposing difficulties in reading, the dialectical text engages its reader in the process of knowledge by resisting the utilitarian logic of most critical prose with its rationalist and empiricist connotations of completely comprehending its object. According to Dusinberre, Gidal adopts contradiction as his trope to emphasize the materiality of discourse and to problematize the activity of reading. Gidal's negativity—his contradictions and restatements of former positions; his avoidance of any linear form of exposition; his fragmentation of discourse; and the collage effect of his citations—resembles not only the aesthetic strategies of his films, it also globally defines his project as the disintegration of any unified subject of representation by ceaselessly deferring the temptation of final closure or meaning.

To clarify Gidal's positions, his relation to the Co-op movement in England must be explored. For structural/materialist film by no means exhausts the history of British experimental cinema, and the theoretical problems that Gidal addresses, although crucially determined in this context, should also be understood as diverging from it. In an essay entitled "Technology and Ideology in/through/and Avant-Garde Film: An Instance," Gidal discusses the influence of the London Filmmakers' Co-op as the attempt to define an alternative social space of production.[3] This included not only the development of an alternative economic practice (e.g., cooperative ownership of the full means of production and distribution), but also a theoretical one. In Gidal's essay, ownership of the full apparatus of production (especially printing technology) is understood as enabling concrete theoretical and practical work on the kinds of ideological determinations acting at the level of film technology in image production. The Co-op is also credited with linking economic and ideological practice to define a context where different social relations of production surrounding aesthetic work and its reception could be developed. In this manner, the work of the Co-op has also included the publication of catalogs, program notes, and a journal—originally *Cinim* and now *Undercut*—the organization of screenings, conferences, the building of a film library, and so on. In sum, the Co-op was an acknowledged pioneer of what is called "integrated practice," or the recognition that the construction of meaning in film is determined by a network of different material practices including those of production, exhibition, and the theoretical or critical practices that subtend or augment them.[4]

According to Dusinberre, this situation fostered three basic aesthetic issues in the history of the English avant-garde: a decisive rejection of narrative and narrativity, the subordination of image-content to image-production, and an emphasis on the temporal dimension of the film process as the basic structure of cinematic articulation.[5] All of these concerns target narrative as the object of a "deconstructive" critique of illusionism and all are central to Gidal's theoretical and aesthetic work. However, as opposed to a theorist like Burch who understands deconstruction as a dialectical process where the aesthetic message foregrounds or defamiliarizes codes of narrative representation, Dusinberre considers that the decisive element in the history of the British avant-garde has been the complete rejection of narrative either as structure or metaphor for structure. Dusinberre is especially sensitive here to the implications of readings such as P. Adams Sitney's definition of structural film as a teleological or goal-directed elaboration of structure, or Annette Michelson's characterization of Michael Snow's *Wavelength* (1966–67) as "a grand metaphor for narrative form."[6] In fact, in its more radical formulations the antiillusionist current in the British avant-garde is resolutely opposed to any hermeneutic element. Dusinberre notes that the emphasis on specifically cinematic devices (e.g., flicker effect, time lapse, rephotography, loop printing, strategic alterations of focus, focal length, and exposure) in these films is equivalent to an assertion of the primacy of cognition over meaningfulness, especially at the level of perception or what Freud called the perception/consciousness system: "English avant-garde cinema asserts the firstness of apprehension, setting as a condition for comprehension. This places the spectator in a continual moment of reflection, demanding an awareness of the act of apprehension tantamount to constant reflexiveness" ("St. George in the Forest," 14).

Gidal is easily situated in this context; it is more difficult to reduce him to it. Despite his antagonistic attitude to mainstream British film theory (above all *Screen* and its "unrepentant Parisianism"), and Gidal's own frequent citations from Louis Althusser, Jacques Derrida, and Michel Foucault, there has so far been little serious examination of Gidal's relationship to the most radical elements of French theory, including the theories of political modernism presented by the *Tel Quel* group. Gidal's precise interest here is that he does not fit, either into the problematic where the English avant-garde has attempted to write its history or that of British film theory in its conceptualization of problems of film form and ideology. Serious consideration of Gidal, then, has the advantage of illuminating a whole other system of reference with respect to the discourse of political modernism in contemporary film theory.

Paradoxically, Gidal is best understood when separated from his historical context. The situation of Gidal in the well-worn modernist arguments of the "pure film" or "film as film" genre (as, for example, in Malcolm LeGrice's otherwise useful *Abstract Film and Beyond*) have done more to obfuscate his work than to clarify it. Therefore, it is necessary to unravel a series of otherwise familiar concepts that take on unfamiliar meanings in the context of Gidal's theory. Foremost among these are: the relation between material and structure; dialectic, as a form organizing the film-text and its spectatorial relations, defined in relation to narrative; and finally, reflexivity as a form of mental activity presupposed by the avant-garde text. Each of these terms is present in the rhetorical strategies of political modernism. However, it is important to recognize at the outset that Gidal refashions them in ways unique to his theory of structural/materialist film.

Justifiable criticisms have been brought against the modernist current in the avant-garde film for its ontological impulse—the definition of its history as the systematic eradication of noncinematic elements in order to achieve a perception divorced from signification and therefore, it is implied, ideology. In Gidal's writings, however, both "material" and "structure" are resolutely antiontological concepts. For Gidal material refers not to a purely physical, mechanical, or substantive concept, but rather to an effect of spatial and temporal ordering. Of course, this does not divorce the problem of the substance of expression from that of signification any more than Derrida's concept of the trace renders unnecessary any consideration of the phonic or graphic material of language. The point is that one is simply not reducible to the other. Gidal is better understood as part of an aesthetic tradition of materialist theories of representation that begin with the problem of codical material—in the example of cinema, codes of perspective, framing, exposure, focus, movement, and so forth—in order to emphasize the productive transformation of the referent (here the profilmic object) by the technique or the technology of the artistic process. In his essay on structural/materialist film, Stephen Heath stresses the irreducibility of the term *materialist* in the following manner: " 'Materialist' stresses process, a film in its process of production of images, sounds, times, meanings, *the transformations effected on the basis of the specific properties of film in the relation of a viewing and listening situation.* It is that situation which is, finally, the point of 'structural/materialist film'. . . ."[7]

In Gidal's "Definition and theory of the current avant-garde: materialist/structural film," the concept of structure receives similar emphasis as the "art of relations, of structuring, in which the shape of the material is primary to any internal content. . . ."[8] Michael Snow's *Wavelength* perfectly illustrates this idea with its resolute and deliberate zoom absorbing not only the diegetic space of the loft, but also the film's multiple temporal ellipses, changes of shot, and optical manipulations of the image in an overdetermined figure of duration and process. Similarly, in tracing his relationship to past art movements such as Abstract Expressionism and Minimalism, Gidal takes care to define structure as a process irreducible to material. For Gidal, the influence of action painting resides in the problem of the "trace" in that the activity of inscription remains visible in the aesthetic product as the mark of its construction and constructedness. Here process achieves an ethical dimension in that the artist sublimates choice for procedure. In order to circumvent the existential dimension that this position might suggest, Gidal balances it with the analytical impulse of Minimalism with its emphasis on semiotic reduction through serial or repetitive structures. The tension between Abstract Expressionist and Minimalist impulses in Gidal's work is exemplified in his 1978 film *Silent Partner*. This film resembles Gidal's *Room Film* (1973) and *Conditions of Illusion* (1975) in its exploration of the limits of image legibility through shifts of focus, exposure, and random framing, that is, strategies that foreground the materiality of cinematic signification through the use of the handheld and hand-manipulated camera. But what radically divides Gidal from a similar emphasis in Stan Brakhage's work, for example, is a process of semiotic reduction aimed not at maximizing the expressivity of the image (especially as the product of the subjective manipulation of the artist), but rather at undermining it. In *Silent Partner*, this is achieved by the repetition of units of duration—shots of relatively equal length separated by black leader cut to relatively equal lengths—that in their predictability and their nonteleological orientation empty the image of any hermeneutic interest.

This last point is the key to Gidal's antiillusionism. His emphasis is in no way ontological. Gidal has no interest in recovering the purity of cinematic expression from narrative, or in rendering the film-text a purely autonomous or autoreferential object. In fact, by constantly introducing the *question* of referentiality, the concept of structure in Gidal's films yields a strategic tension in the desire to read the image—as the equation of iconic semblance with the identity of the photographed object—*through* the material opaqueness of cinematic materials of expression: grain, emulsion density relative to exposure, instability of framing and focus, and so on. In this manner, Gidal defines the objective of structural/materialist film as an "attempted demystification of the film process. . . . An avant-garde film defined by its development towards increased materialism and materialist function does not *represent*, or *document*, anything. The film produces certain relations between *segments*, between what the camera is aimed at and the way that 'image' is presented. The dialectic of the film is established in that space of tension between materialist flatness, grain, light, movement and the supposed real reality that is represented. Thus a consequent attempted destruction of the illusion is a constant necessity."[9] Gidal requires the question of referentiality and at least a liminal legibility of the image in order to frustrate strategically the spectator's desire to ascribe meaning to an image. Or more precisely, Gidal films attempt to undercut the drive to identify an image according to the criterion of iconic semblance and to force the spectator to recognize the material conditions producing that semblance.

In his efforts to constrain rigorously the spectator's relation to the image, Gidal's theory is predicated on the desire to produce an account of the organization of structure in film, and in the perception of the viewer as mutually determining instances. Gidal's materialism does not refer to the physical substance of cinematic materials of expression, but to the *material effects* devolving from the organization of filmic structure as, specifically, relations of subjectivity. In Gidal's theory, the critical term is *dialectic*, a concept that refers both to the differential ordering of elements within the film and to the perception of difference between film and viewer that this ordering is supposed to inculcate. On this basis, structural/materialist film is designed to contravene the formal and ideological effects of narrative film. In Gidal's view, as in Baudry's, narrative codes function for the systematic repression of difference in film. They also serve to cancel the distance in space where the viewing subject is led to believe in an identity between sign and thing: "Narrative is an illusionistic procedure, manipulatory, mystificatory, repressive. The repression is that of space, the distance between the viewer and the object, a repression of real space in favour of illusionist space" ("Theory and definition," 190). This repression is equally that of the space between signifier and signified in the designation of given meaning. In the continuity system of editing, this entails the suppression of material heterogeneity and discontinuity both at the level of units of code (e.g., shot-to-shot relations) as well as that of the serial regimentation of frames. Finally, according to Gidal this repression is also temporal. The viewer's perception of cinematic "real time" relative to its material organization in the form of shot duration is displaced by the illusionist "story time" determined by the strictures of narrative.

Gidal's use of the term *dialectic* is ultimately an attempt to redefine fundamentally the spectatorial relations implied by the concept of structure in film that Gidal resolutely opposes to the idea of film narrative. A useful means of exploring Gidal's hostility to narrative is provided by Emile Benveniste's differentiation between *histoire* and *discours* as distinctive forms of linguistic activity, the latter being defined by a situation where the subjective markers of enunciation are in evidence whereas in the former they are suppressed. In "History/Discourse: Notes on Two Voyeurisms," Christian Metz applies this distinction to a discussion of subjective relations in film.[10] Playing upon the ambiguity in French where *histoire* may indicate either "history" or "story," Metz suggests that the aim of narrative in film is to efface film's material conditions as a discourse in order to better present itself as story; in sum, the diegesis or fictional world is given as the expression of a signified without a signifier. In Metz there is no doubt that this situation is ideological, but for Gidal it is radically so. Taking a position similar to that of Baudry and Burch, Gidal argues that conventional narrative form, or indeed narrative in any form, is resolutely ideological and extrinsic to the potentialities of film. However, when Gidal characterizes his own project as "anti-narrative," this does not necessarily mean that he is posing "pure film" as escaping ideological determination, nor is he promoting a strategy of deconstruction where avant-garde film enters into a "dialectical" relation with narrative codes in order to defamiliarize them. Instead, in Gidal's view the precise danger of narrative is its reproductive ubiquity. For Gidal, narrative is first of all the cultural agent that best serves ideology as the carrier of those pregiven meanings where capitalist society ceaselessly recirculates the representational structures (familial, political, sexual, economic) necessary for the reproduction of its social relations of production. Second, narrative dominates every aesthetic medium and reduces the material differences between genres and media to the singularity of its forms—the authority of signified over signifier, "history" over "discourse," closure over difference, transparency over materiality, and so on. Similarly, when stating the project of the antinarrative, Gidal's constant emphasis is the opposition of production to re-production and presentation to re-presentation. Here the suspicion of deconstruction, as manifested in Burch for example, is that negation simply means reproduction in a new form.

Gidal is also critical of narrative theories that reduce the concept of diegesis, as the level of cinematic denotation, to narrative as the signified or content for which film form is the signifier. When Metz speaks of diegesis in *Film Language,* for example, he obviously understands it as the signified produced by the signifiers of spatial and temporal articulations in film. The relation between the two, and the specific economy that binds them, defines the possibility of cinematic language for Metz and that language derives from narrative. Gidal strategically rereads this proposition by emphasizing Metz's commentary on the derivation of *diegesis* as the Greek for narration in the sense of the judiciary recital of facts.[11] In this rereading, narrative becomes a structure that denies the facticity of discourse. As such, narrative restrains cinematic spatial and temporal articulations by assuring the dominance of the signified as the expression of (ideological) meaning. Therefore, if narrative is eliminated, diegesis remains as the prosaic expression of denotation—not self-reference, but the simple designation or presentation of specifically cinematic spatial and temporal codes. Moreover, with the elimination of narrative goes connotation and any meaning or signified extrinsic to the sum of all possible cinematic denotation.

In this manner, Gidal's emphasis is on principles of semiotic reduction, refusal, or resistance to any potential meaning beyond that generated by the internal dynamics of cinematic signification. Like Sollers, Gidal is characterized best by his commitment to a "non-representational dynamics of the signifier," or what he prefers to call "a theory of non-interpretive or non-expressive art." For Gidal, the work of Samuel Beckett exemplifies this kind of aesthetic practice by postponing or deferring the signified through a processual ordering and intensification of the signifier. In an essay entitled "Beckett &

Others & Art: A System," Gidal writes: "To begin with, radical
art, an art of radical form, deals with the manipulation of materials made conscious . . . *with the inexpressible, the unsayable,*
i.e. not with content [the signified], as it is understood as distinguishable and primary, positing a transparent technique."[12]
For Gidal, the principal issue is not the separation of ideology
from form or material, but rather the division of signification
from meaning. Derailing the force of narrative readings, the
goal of structural/materialist film is to interrupt the spectator's
passage from signifier to signified, from filmic denotation,
strictly defined, to a connotative field whose boundaries are
determined by narrative conventions in a unilateral and irreversible movement. In his "Theory and Definition of Struc-
tural/Materialist Film," Gidal writes that

> Signifiers approaching emptiness means merely . . . that the im-
> age taken does not have a ready associative analogue, it is not
> a given symbol, metaphor or allegory; that which is signified by
> the signifier, that which is conjured up by the image given, is
> something formed by past connections but at a very low key,
> not a determining or overdetermining presence. . . . And that
> low level signifier in momentary interplay with other low level
> signifiers, foregrounds, brings forth a materialist (possibly) play
> of differences which don't have an overriding hierarchy of
> meaning, which don't determine the ideological reading, which
> don't direct into heavy associative symbolic realms. . . . Thus is
> presented the *arbitrariness* of meaning. . . . The unnaturalness,
> ungivenness, of any possible meaning is posited. Such practice
> thereby counters precisely the ideological usages which are
> dominant; the usages which *give meaning* to images, things, signs,
> etc, meanings which are then posited as natural, as residing
> within. The whole idealist system is opposed by a materialist
> practice of the production of meaning, of the arbitrariness of
> the signifier. (Meaning is *made*). ("Theory and Definition," 191)

What Gidal argues here is that meaning is produced ideologically, that it is not innate, natural, or given, and that the
function of ideology may be understood as suppressing the
production of meaning as a relational, open-ended, and conditional process. The strategy of semiotic reduction—dedicated to the elimination of narrative, symbol, allegory, or met-

aphor—is based on the argument that any level of connotation overdetermines an image, tipping the balance against perception of its conditions of representability in favor of a natural or transparent representation that seems to exist without the agency of a material support or the work of perception. If Althusser defines the work of ideology as the elision of perception, Gidal believes that it is possible to produce an alternative aesthetic situation where the operations of ideology are recognizable in the specific processes and procedures that materially produce cinematic images.

But this emphasis on semiotic reduction reveals a second, more utopian objective in Gidal's work. If cinematic processes of signification can be dismantled or deconstructed by these aesthetic strategies, then perhaps meaning can be reconstituted differently. In this respect, Gidal draws a specific relation between duration and perception as the keystone of his theory. For Gidal, duration is the basic unit of structure in film, defined by the material segmentations both at the level of the shot and of the filmstrip. As the limit of semiotic reduction, duration defines the specificity of cinematic denotation as the point where spatial and temporal articulations converge in the material instance of the filmstrip. Thus the valorization of real time in Gidal's writings is understood as a relative rather than an absolute value—temporality is materially structured and regulated by the aesthetic organization of film segments. Grounded in the problem of duration, film is a particularly apposite medium for materially establishing a relation of correspondence between aesthetic presentation and perception. In Gidal's definition, "real time" or "actual duration" consists in structuring a proximate 1:1 relationship between the work and its viewer, or between "production-time" and "viewing-time." In his examples, this situation is pioneered in Bach's preludes and fugues, the experimental music of Terry Riley and Steve Reich, and the paintings of Frank Stella.

Therefore, semiotic reduction is geared toward delimiting and regulating the spatial and temporal relations incumbent upon the spectator. Following Klee, Gidal calls this a problem of "reading duration"; or alternatively, the establishment of a "dialectic" as a mutually determining relation between structure in film and perception in the viewer. Gidal calls this potential perception—which is meant to inculcate a nonidentificatory, active relation with the image—the "reflexive attitude":

> . . . the reflexive attitude of the viewer is inculcated by filmic manipulations, and one is made conscious of the manipulation through various technical means; also the form of the manipulation is different, it is not towards a specific or even ambiguous interpretation of the work. Rather, it is utilized toward noninterpretive perceptual investigation, analyses of the full material. . . .
> The procedural interaction between viewer and "viewed" is primary, within a non-associative structure. . . .
> The mental dialectical activation of the viewer is necessary for the procedure of the film's existence. Each film is not only structural, but structuring. . . . The viewer is either forming an equal and more or less opposite film in his or her head or else constantly anticipating, correcting, recorrecting, . . . constantly re-determining the confrontation with the given reality, i.e. the isolated chosen area of each film. ("Definition and theory," 54)[13]

In Gidal's view, the reflexive attitude establishes a conscious relation in the spectator that develops step by step with the material shape of the film as "a non-hierarchical, cool, separate unfolding of a perceptual activity. That perceptual activity is *not* to be understood as relegating the primary function to the individual perceiver, who of course is embedded in ideological structures/strictures" ("Theory and Definition," 192). Here the relation of ideology to perception is understood as a structure of meaning that is unconscious, unthought, and unreflected. Therefore, the problem of reading duration is conceived by Gidal as the intensification of the viewer's perception/consciousness system through the assertion of a meaninglessness that drives a wedge between signifier and signified, perception and knowledge: "A film can inculcate positionings which force attempts—moment to moment attempts—at knowledge, attempts at delineating precisely the perception of distance between perception and (absent) knowledge. The apprehension of the functioning of that distance is a position in knowledge" (AN 78). This is why "self-reflexivity" in film is anathema for Gidal. It falsely signifies or represents "consciousness"—whether in the forms of self-reference characteristic of the Hollywood film, the personal or gestural codes of Abstract Expressionism, or as the autodesignation of code characteristic of epistemological modernism—as a more perfect substitute for the viewer's own consciousness. For Gidal, these forms of representation are illusory by virtue of a simple, literal fact: consciousness cannot be materially attributed to film or any of its devices; it can only arise in the activity of perception between viewer and viewed.

Because of this emphasis on perception and consciousness, Gidal's writings have been criticized for being too phenomenological. Although Gidal would not deny certain affinities with phenomenology, especially in his earlier essays, his version is not an orthodox or transcendental one. In the first place, Gidal's theory is certainly not ontic. Any notions of self-presence, both with respect to a possible theory of the subject of the avant-garde text or the autonomy of the aesthetic dimension, are vociferously denied in his writings.[14] Instead, the function of *difference* is emphasized in Gidal's formulation of dialectic as a "system or process of consciousness." If narrative imposes a passive identification and an (illusory) completion of consciousness in the (false) identity constructed between image and spectator, Gidal alternatively attempts in his films something closer to Lacan's "fading" as a constant slippage between the signifier and the subject it determines.[15] The utopian moment of Gidal's theory resides in his definition of the special reflexivity of structural art. Here duration and process support an autoreflective consciousness against the potentiality of its loss, even if this "presence" must be defined as an unrelenting negation. Thus Gidal's adoption of Derridean concepts such as *"différance"* and "presence" must be understood as an attempt to reinvigorate the concept of consciousness through process-oriented art, even if the dialectical relation enabling this concept implies a negativity that disables it and causes the autoreflective consciousness to fail. By a curious turn of dialectical thinking, the radical relativity that for Derrida undercuts any attempt to assert a fixed basis for ultimate truth or rational thought, becomes for Gidal, in its very negativity, the only possible basis for imagining history in the form of a rational consciousness opposed to the reification of ideological thought.

In this manner, the most radical aspiration of political modernism in film can be characterized as the attmept to offer an articulation of the subject different from that of ideology where, according to Gidal, "The individual . . . becomes posited as static, as essence, as ideal (or referring to the possibility of such) . . . as unitary, 'free' view, centered in deep perspective space away from the screen, and invisibly solidified, ever present" ("Theory and Definition," 190). However, it is also necessary to point out that this aspiration requires, as the condition for a future break, the present exclusion of contemporary history. Because history is given in the form of social meanings or representations of the social, Gidal views it as always already contaminated with traces of the ideological:

> Contemporary social formations cannot be adequately given *through* cinema . . . and the present assumption that the ideological nature of social constructions (of "society") can be the problematic around and through which a film operates, is incorrect. That any problematic *external* to cinema's *representations* of the social, economic, sexual, political can be somehow portrayed, dialectically or otherwise, or even operated upon and through in cinema, in relation (somehow) to social practice of the extra-cinematic (ie all the rest of life including non-cinematic codes) is useful for academic(s') hope(s) but nothing else. (AN 77)

Here the "impossibility of history" becomes the impossibility of the political in film, if one means by that the positive transformation of the social practices through which capitalist society maintains its hegemony. In this respect, Gidal's pessimism in relation to film, which is much deeper than the utopian pessimism that Benjamin describes for surrealism, is similar to Samuel Beckett's, whose strategic negativity claims that "there is nothing to express, nothing with which to express, nothing from which to express, no power to express, no desire to express, together with the obligation to 'express.' "[16] The concept of the sign can only be used "under erasure." Even when the necessity of a politics of representation is accepted,

the presence of any meaning or signified—"political" or otherwise— always presents for Gidal a definite risk in the form of
the reproduction of the ideological. Gidal's radical asceticism
thus poses itself between the impossibility of escaping the ideological in aesthetic signification, and the obligation to "express the political in art." In this manner, structural/materialist
film can at best only offer resistances to the reproduction of
ideology by diminishing any traces of the signified in aesthetic
work. Thus there is one overdetermining opposition (in a theory that attempts to resist the bind of oppositions) that colors
and organizes Gidal's writings—that of the external versus the
internal, or alternately, exteriority versus interiority. The
"phenomenological reduction" that Gidal performs is not between the camera and its objects, as Dusinberre argues in an
admittedly mistaken early assessment of Gidal, but rather in
the relation between history and aesthetic structure/percep-
tion/cognition.[17]

Heath ultimately takes issue with Gidal's practice on this
point, self-defined in "The Anti-Narrative" as "the undermining of determinate meaning, the latter being as always and
necessarily ideologically produced and arbitrary" ("Afterword," 97). Although he misunderstands several of Gidal's
points, to Heath's credit, he concludes with a fundamental
criticism of the "materialist" emphasis in Gidal's theory:

> (In what sense, moreover, *is* a determinate and ideologically
> produced meaning arbitrary? In one crucial sense at least, it is
> quite the reverse that has to be stressed; historical materialism
> indeed is the science of the non-arbitrariness of the given, in-
> cluding meaning(s)). . . . [And] that, precisely, Gidal's films are
> in meaning, crossed by meanings—those of the history of cinema
> they inevitably and critically engage included—and productive
> of meanings, not least the complex meaning of their, of that
> engagement. ("Afterword," 97)

In this context, Gidal's opposition of the interiority of the
viewer-text relation to the exteriority of history reveals a strategic weakness in his theory. What Gidal's aesthetic commitment excludes—in the effort to rigorously direct perception
through procedures of duration, repetition, reduction, and the
elimination of narrative and meaning—is precisely the material

and social existence of film. Gidal's refusal or denial of any element external to the specifically cinematic omits consideration of those cultural institutions (critical, technological, theoretical) where the conditions of meaning are socially and historically determined and determining. Every film encounters meaning in these contexts where the possible relations between viewer and text are constantly and inevitably produced and constrained by a heterogeneous network of cultural discourses.

To suggest that an avant-garde aesthetic signifying practice could disable, circumvent, or deconstruct this institutional network is utopian at best. But, as formulated by Adorno, the undecidability of this proposition is also utopian in the best sense of the term: "No general judgment can be made whether someone who does away with all expression is the mouthpiece of reified consciousness or the speechless, expressionless expression that denounces that consciousness."[18] However, to criticize Gidal for his disinterest and even antagonism to such an account—which undercuts his attempts not to objectify but to disambiguate the spectator's relationship with film—does not discount the real achievements of his work, even if they have not been theorized as such by Gidal himself. For his polemical and theoretical writings continue to articulate crucial problems in the theorization of film as a technical practice and as a medium of ideological representation. Moreover, Gidal's efforts to pose in a new way the determination of subjective relations in film must also be understood as forceful and influential rhetorical interventions in the problem of the production and direction of meaning through aesthetic and critical practices.

NOTES

1. Stephen Heath, "Afterword" to Peter Gidal, "The Anti-Narrative," *Screen* 20.2 (Summer 1979): 95. The citation is from Benjamin's essay, "Surrealism—the Last Snapshot of the European Intelligentsia," anthologized in *One-Way Street and Other Writings*, Edmund Jephcott and Kingsley Shorter, trans. (London: New Left

Books, 1979): 238. Heath's parallel is entirely out of the context of Benjamin's argument, but it does have the heuristic interest of illustrating Gidal's theory.

2. Deke Dusinberre, "Consistent Oxymoron—Peter Gidal's Rhetorical Strategy," *Screen* 18.2 (Summer 1977): 79-88.

3. In *The Cinematic Apparatus*, eds. Teresa de Lauretis and Stephen Heath (New York: St. Martin's Press, 1980): 151-71. A similar context for aesthetic production in Britain is examined in Rod Stoneman's "Film-Related Practice and the Avant-Garde," *Screen* 20.3/4 (Winter 1979/80): 40-57 and Malcolm LeGrice's "Towards Temporal Economy," *Screen* 20.3/4: 58-79.

I will not go into the history of the Co-op movement in greater depth. However, an excellent account is offered in Dusinberre's *English Avant-Garde Cinema, 1966-1974*, M.Phil thesis, University College, University of London, 1977. Other important sources include special issues of the following journals, dedicated to the contemporary European avant-gardes: *Art and Artists* 7:8.81 (December 1972), *Studio International* 190.978 (November/December 1975), and *Afterimage* 6 (1976). General contexts are provided by David Curtis's *Experimental Cinema* (New York: Universe Books, 1971) and Malcolm LeGrice's *Abstract Film and Beyond* (Cambridge: MIT Press, 1977).

4. See, for example, "Independent Filmmaking in the 70s," the influential position paper drafted by the Organising Committee for the Independent Filmmakers' Association Conference (May 1976), n.p.

5. Deke Dusinberre, "St. George in the Forest: The English Avant-Garde," *Afterimage* 6 (Summer 1976): 5. Dusinberre's comments on a possible stylistic history of the English avant-garde are supported not only by references in the previous two footnotes, but also by three important catalogues: *Perspectives on British Avant-Garde Film* (London: Arts Council of Great Britain and the Hayward Gallery, 1978); *A Perspective on English Avant-Garde Film*, eds. David Curtis and Deke Dusinberre (London: Arts Council of Great Britain, 1978); and *Film as Film* (London: Arts Council of Great Britain, 1979). More importantly, these references themselves demonstrate a desire to construct the historical intelligibility of the English avant-garde as "deconstructive" or as engaged with problems of cinematic illusionism, materiality, and the social and political implications of image production.

6. Annette Michelson, "Film and the Radical Aspiration" in *New Forms in Film*, ed. Annette Michelson (Montreux, 1974): 16.

7. Stephen Heath, "Repetition Time: Notes around "Structural/ Materialist Films", *Wide Angle* 2.3 (1978): 4; emphasis mine.

8. Peter Gidal, "Definition and Theory of the Current Avant-Garde," *Studio International* 187.963 (February 1974): 56.

9. Peter Gidal, "Theory and Definition of Structural/Materialist Film," *Studio International* 190.978 (November/December 1975): 189.

10. Trans. Susan Bennett in *Edinburgh Magazine* 1 (1976): 21-25. I feel strongly that the application of Benveniste to studies of subjectivity in film serves a mostly heuristic interest. In my own view, while Metz's brief homage to Benveniste is interesting, subsequent attempts to define a cinematic theory of enunciation have undoubtedly reached an impasse because of their equation of subjectivity with the structure of speech and the reduction of all discursive phenomena to the model of speech acts. I discuss this problem in greater detail in my "The Figure and the Text," *Diacritics* 15.1 (1985): 34-50.

11. For example, Gidal footnotes the following passage from Metz: " 'For also, and even first of all, through its procedures of denotation, the cinema is a specific language. The concept of diegesis is as important for the film semiologist as the idea of art. The word is derived from the Greek "narration," and was used particularly to designate one of the obligatory parts of judiciary discourse, the recital of facts. The term was introduced into the framework of the Cinema by Etienne Souriau. It designates the film's represented instance . . . that is to say, the sum of the film's denotation: the narration itself, but also the fictional space and time dimensions implied in and by the narrative, and consequently the characters, the landscapes, the events, and other narrative elements, in so far as they are considered in their denotated aspect.' Christian Metz, *Film Language*, pp. 97-98. Oxford University Press, London, 1974. Narrative in the end would have to be defined as story, inferrable or otherwise from (effect/affect of) the given, although the problem arises of the ideology of reading a text, in which viewers 'automatically' are placed in positions for themselves which do not necessarily have anything to do with the text/process/procedure/meanings in question." In "The Anti-Narrative (1978)," *Screen* 20.2 (Summer 1979): 76; cited hereafter as AN.

Oddly enough, in this essay Gidal paradoxically asserts that it is idealistic to oppose "non-narrative" film to "non-diegetic" film. In his commentary on Metz, Gidal argues that in its broadest determinations, diegesis resides in every film. In his example, to suppose that Peter Kubelka's *Arnulf Rainer* (1958/1960) (a film composed entirely of the serial alternation of black and white frames) is a non-diegetic film is "wishful 'thinking,' " and that, conversely, "the existence of diegesis in no way of necessity presupposes the existence of narrative."

12. *Studio International* 188.971 (November 1974): 183; my emphasis. Since the writing of this chapter, Gidal has published a major study of Beckett. Dusinberre's essay "Consistent Oxymoron" contains an excellent discussion of Gidal's relationship to Beckett's work.

13. "Definition and Theory of the Avant-Garde," 54. Also see the section entitled "The Viewer" in "Theory and Definition of Structural/Materialist Film," 189.

14. Compare, for example, these comments from "Theory and Definition of Structural/Materialist Film": "Self-consciousness, and consciousness *per se*, must in no way imply consciousness as deflecting onto a mythical subject; it must in no way imply transcendence or transcendent subjectivity; it does not set itself up in opposition to real relations, *ie* consciousness as knowledge in opposition to material relations as knowledge. . . ." ("Theory and Definition," 192). "The *self* posited here is situated in its self-alienation/distanciation, and this still refers to the concept, which must be fought, of self as centre (distanced though it be), self as unitary. This psychological centering of the self must be nullified in order to even begin to set up a concept of a dialectically posited, distanciated self. Merely to drop the usage of a word such as *self* does not fulfil the requirement of redefining the word. And the redefining must be done so that *self* is understood, not to be that unitary centre of knowledge, that 'I' through which the world is. For the 'I' does not form the world. Consciousness does not form the world. Material relations form the 'I.' The self is merely a clinical word for a cipher" ("Theory and Definition," 195-96).

15. A similar view is expressed by Stephen Heath in a taped discussion with Gidal: "In *Condition of Illusion* you are in a relation to the photographic image, but that relation is a constant slipping of the identifying relation which is the basis of classic film, which doesn't mean that there is no identification, it means that there is, like a constant slipping of identification, or a constant horizon of identifying. . . ." Cited from Heath/Gidal Cambridge Tapes (March 1976) in Gidal's response to Heath's essay "Repetition Time," published in *Wide Angle* 2.4 (1978): 86.

16. Cited in the frontispiece to Michael Robinson's *The Long So-*

nata of the Dead: A Study of Samuel Beckett (New York: Grove Press, Inc., 1969).

17. Cf. "The Ascetic Task" in Structural Film Anthology, ed. Peter Gidal (London: British Film Institute, 1976): 109-113.

18. Aesthetic Theory as cited in Peter Bürger's Theory of the Avant-Garde, trans. Michael Shaw (Minneapolis: University of Minnesota Press, 1984): 62.

SIX

Language, Narrative, Subject (1): The Critique of "Ontological" Modernism

The emergence of the discourse of political modernism in post-'68 film theory cannot be traced in a continuous or uniform fashion. Despite the overarching desire of its adherents to re-define modernist aesthetic practice along the lines of a se-miotically informed, Marxist critique of ideology, the idea of political modernism is best examined as an implied system of debates, discontinuities, divergences, and divisions, rather than as a tacit consensus of theoreticians and artists working toward a common objective: the definition and theory of a "materi-alist" film practice dedicated to a critique of ideology.

One of the most striking of these debates involved a critique of "ontological" concerns in the contemporary British and North American avant-garde cinemas as represented by two essays published in *Screen* in 1976: Peter Wollen's " 'Ontol-ogy' and 'Materialism' in Film" and Stephen Heath's "Nar-rative Space."[1] As I argued earlier, a fascination with the his-tory and practice of experimental cinemas was in part the result of a theoretical insistence that the problem of defining the relations between film and ideology necessarily involved ques-tions of aesthetic representation and form. Programs of ex-perimental cinema were organized regularly at the National Film Theatre in London from 1970, culminating in a retrospective of structural film in May 1976 organized by Peter Gidal. Gidal's *Structural Film Anthology*, which made available important theoretical writings on contemporary experimental cinema, was published by the British Film Institute in conjunction with this program.

Other noteworthy events, conferences, and workshops were programmed at the London Filmmakers' Co-op, the Institute for Contemporary Art, the Hayward Gallery, and the Edinburgh Film Festivals. That Wollen and Heath's essays both appeared in *Screen* in 1976, and were received as major theoretical statements concerning the relation of ideology to film form (or more precisely, film semiotics), is not coincidental. When read against the background of an abiding but contested interest in experimental film, and understood in the context of the presentations and publications associated with events such as the founding conference of the Independent Filmmakers' Association, the Edinburgh Festival events on psychoanalysis and avant-garde cinemas, and related day and weekend schools sponsored by the Society for Education in Film and Television, Wollen's and Heath's arguments, which are sympathetic to yet highly critical of this fascination, have a continuity that is not apparent at first glance. In this respect, they can be understood as representative of a genuine faultline in the discourse of political modernism that divides *Screen's* promotion of a "post-Brechtian aesthetic" in Jean Luc Godard, Jean-Marie Straub and Danielle Huillet, and Nagisa Oshima from the "ontological materialism" of Michael Snow, Paul Sharits, Malcolm LeGrice, and others.

The critique forwarded in these two essays is eccentric according to any philosophically accepted definition of ontological problems. Nevertheless, this critique reveals its own specific pattern of anxieties and concerns when placed in the context of the discourse of political modernism. In its alignment with the binary logic opposing realism to modernism and illusionism to materialism, the "ontological impulse" in the history and practice of avant-garde film is defined as the desire to exclude from the field of film practice any element that is not specific to cinema's intrinsic materials of expression. What is most worrisome to *Screen* is the antagonism toward narrative informing this position, most notably in the otherwise divergent theories of Noel Burch and Peter Gidal. In these theories, narrative is equated with the ideological and illusionist procedures of a realist style that has been imposed on film from the outside, obscuring film's intrinsic representational possibilities. Subsequently, narrative comes to represent a force that is antithetical to film's identity as such; it is only through the dialectical negation or radical eschewal of this force that the intrinsic identity of film form can be redeemed.

Malcolm LeGrice, an important experimental filmmaker and historian of the avant-garde, gives succinct expression to the position that Heath and Wollen find problematic. An authentic materialist attitude, argues LeGrice, is one that considers "film as film," in its reality as such: "Examination of the film's reality involves attention to its materiality/actuality as the essential basis of the film experience. . . . The only art which deserves the term 'realist' is that which stems from the confrontation of the audience with the material conditions of the work. Work which seeks to 'portray' a reality existing in another place at another time (and in another time) is illusionist."[2]

Like Peter Wollen, LeGrice is also interested in understanding the formal history of the avant-garde film as a political history. This is in fact part of the project of his *Abstract Film and Beyond.* Moreover, both understand this history as the development of an increased materialism in terms of "work on the signifier" and both abhor those lapses into idealist or mystical philosophies that often characterize past theories of abstract or nonobjective art. However, whereas Wollen wishes to protect the political impact of modernism by realigning its history with that of semiology, as Constance Penley points out, LeGrice is less concerned with the semiotic dimension of film than its relation to problems of perception and consciousness. For LeGrice, the political impact of an increased materialism is that it restructures or reorients perception: "In these films, which LeGrice refers to as 'perception training films,' the single sort of information is that which concerns filmic processes, but the concern is not with an *intellection* of these processes, a mental act involving a semantic dimension, but a direct apprehension: 'the primacy of current experience over the il-

lusory or retrospective.' ''[3] The strategies of semiotic reduction characteristic of this form of materialism are meant not
only to liberate film from a narrative and referential modality
in order to restore its proper identity, but also to delimit and
define the work of the aesthetic object as an "active, parti-
cipatory, structuring of the individual's direct experience"
(LeGrice, 3).

In his essay " 'Ontology' and 'Materialism' in Film," written
a year before LeGrice's book was published, Peter Wollen
fears that this particular version of the history of modernism
will produce "materialism" as the basis for a filmic ontology
indistinguishable from idealist theories of cinema such as André
Bazin's. According to Wollen, Bazin's idealist ontology promoted cinematic realism in virtue of the perception of the
world produced through the automatism of photographic registration. In Bazin's view, meaning is a property of the pro-
filmic event and the aesthetic function of film is to capture and
transmit meaning as the reproduction of a perception identical
to that of the event itself. Wollen implies that Bazin's views
are antithetical to a semiotic theory of cinema since Bazin's
ontology "transferred the burden of meaning outside the cinema. . . . The 'language' of film would virtually wither away
as cinema possessed itself of the integral reality which was its
mythic destiny" (OM 22). Alternatively, a "materialist" ontology defines realism as the perception of the particularity of
the filmic—grain, light, two-dimensional frame, splice marks,
and so on. In this view, argues Wollen, "light is no longer seen
as the means by which the pro-filmic event is registered on
film, but as the pro-filmic event itself, and at the same time
part of the material process of film . . ." (OM 14). The search
for the particularity of the filmic therefore excludes the reproduction of any signified, denotatum, or referent that is not
intrinsic to the physical materiality of film. In both situations
Wollen claims that "language wants to be overlooked," a position that is anathema because it displaces semiology from the
history and philosophy of modernism.

In his essay "Narrative Space," Stephen Heath voices similar
concerns in his assessment of contemporary experimental cinema. One striking feature of this celebrated essay is its distinct

rhetorical shift in the transition from the sections on the narrational economy of the classic, realist text—with its emphasis
on relations of perspective, point of view, and subjectivity—
to a nascent critique of theories of the avant-garde text culminating in a defense of Oshima's *Death By Hanging* (1968)
as a privileged model for a politically consequent modernism.
This essay, which otherwise seems fragmentary and digressive
in its organization, can be understood as a singularly directed
argument when read as an attempted theory of political modernism rather than as a theory of classical narration. In this
manner, "Narrative Space" delineates precisely the two main
theoretical interests of *Screen* in the middle seventies: to define
a materialist theory of cinema through a rapprochement between narrative semiotics and Lacanian psychoanalysis (best
represented by the work of Christian Metz in film theory and
Julia Kristeva in literary theory), and to define the possibility
of an alternative cinematic practice on the basis of a "narrative
representation of the political" aligned with what Dana Polan
has called the "formalizing interpretation of Brecht."[4] For example, Heath criticizes Snow's *Rameau's Nephew by Diderot
(thanx to Dennis Young) by Wilma Schoen* (1972-74) as

> something akin to an indefatigably prolonged version of Go-
> dard's *Le Gai Savoir*, but lacking the political insistence of any
> analysis as text; the film talks, jokes, accumulates, overlays, re-
> verses, confuses and tricks as though empty of any reflexive
> contradiction. Its work, as it were, fails to *carry*, in the sense
> in which the crucial filmic-narrative concerns of the previous
> films might have led one to expect, fails to transform—and to
> transform politically—the cinematic relations of form and con-
> tent, and the setting of narrative accordingly. (NS 103-04)

Heath's critique of Snow, Burch, and others reads as a menu
of potential, but ultimately failed attempts to theorize a trans-
gressive political cinema. Moreover, his arguments closely follow Wollen's account of "ontological modernism." Both understand this theory of film modernism as a desire for "re-
doing the history of cinema again from zero" in the search for
a "pure" cinema based on the "muting or exclusion of the
non-cinematic codes" (NS 102 and OM 14). Wollen notes that
specifically exiled codes include those of verbal language, nar-

rative, and iconic reference and Heath similarly describes this
tendency as a project of "destroying the narrative frame in
the interests of the action of the film as flow of images" (NS
102). Finally, both critique the ontological argument for its
reduction of cinematic codes "to their material—optical, photo-
chemical—substrate ('material support') to the exclusion of any
semantic dimension other than reference-back to the material
of the signifier itself, which thus becomes its own unique field
of signification" (OM 14).

There is no question here of deciding whether Heath is right
in his assessment of Snow's film or if Wollen is correct in his
implicit debate with LeGrice. Similarly, to read these debates
as an argument over how to refer theories of political modernism back to the example of Bertolt Brecht (as both paradigms often ask) simply obscures the theoretical issues at stake.
What is interesting is the encounter between these two positions within the discourse of political modernism. While sharing a similar context and set of theoretical assumptions with
the avatars of "ontological modernism," Wollen and Heath
nonetheless express concern over the lack of "the political
insistence of any analysis as text," or feel they must decide
the commensurability "of the relationship between an ontology of cinema—albeit perhaps a materialist ontology—and language or semiotic; the problem of illusion and anti-illusion; the
historic problem of the impact of sound" (OM 9-10). There is
no better way of exploring Screen's positions on political modernism than examining its fears concerning the elision of particular conceptions of language and narrative in the British and
North American avant-gardes of the seventies, or by establishing the criteria with which it was compelled to divide an
"ontological materialism" from a "post-Brechtian aesthetic."[5]

" 'Ontology' and 'Materialism' in Film" is a direct extension
of the pattern of concerns Wollen develops in "The Two Avant-
Gardes" and the 1972 "Conclusion" to Signs and Meaning in
the Cinema. Wollen begins his critique by tracing how in the
history of art criticism ontological arguments developed in the
definitions of modern art forwarded by Ortega y Gasset, Clement Greenberg, and others have become linked to "material-

ist" concerns in current avant-garde film. Wollen notes that Bazin, in order to assert what is specific to cinematic representation and meaning, accepted but downplayed arguments concerning cinematic language. Instead, he offered a teleological history where the technology of the image developes asymptotically with respect to reality itself. In Bazin's view, the photographic image is endowed with meaning only to the extent that it reproduces a perception identical to that offered by the represented object itself. However, as Wollen points out, the paradox of modernist criticism is that it left the ontological argument intact while turning it to different, though no less idealist, visions of reality as such. Michael Snow, for example, is shown to produce accounts of his films as representations of his interior, mental states: "a summary of my nervous system" or further as "attempts to suggest the mind in a certain state or certain states of consciousness. . . ."[6] Similarly, P. Adams Sitney argues that "Snow has intuitively discovered an image, in almost every one of his films, capable of evoking metaphysical notions of categories of being."[7] Unquestionably, ontological justifications of cinematic representation are displaced here from world to mind. And in this respect, Heath justly chastises Sitney for his "phenomenologico-romantic visionary" account of the avant-garde as the "cinematic reproduction of the human mind" (NS 102).

Clement Greenberg describes the identity of the modernist work of art in a related but different way and establishes the grounds for introducing "materialist" concerns to the ontological emphasis. In an imperfect and dehumanized society, he argues, the objective of the work of art is to express a state of integral object-hood or pure being by referring to nothing outside of itself. Greenberg conceives the history of art as a progressive autoreferentiality where each artistic medium searches out those forms coincident with the materials of expression unique and proper to it. Representation is not excluded here, it is reduced. What the modernist work is said to present is a reflexive consideration and explanation of its own formative principles and materials of expression. In contemporary theories of avant-garde film, this idea opens the way for what Annette Michelson calls a "critique of illusionism" consonant with the presumed epistemological project of modernist work.[8] The specificity of filmic expression is accounted for by the refusal to subordinate film space to the demands of narrative and by emphasizing the physicality of the filmstrip: its flatness, grain, the processing of light and color, and so forth. Here the demand for liberating film's *differentia specifica* clearly articulates a binary logic that opposes realist to modernist art, transparency to materiality, and illusion to knowledge, thereby conflating ontological and epistemological arguments.

Wollen is clearly sympathetic to the critique of illusionism as it appears in Michelson, Gidal, and elsewhere. However, whether or not this version of materialism could underwrite a theory of political modernism, dedicated to a critique of ideology and the establishment of an epistemological function for the work of art, is a question he finds more disturbing. His apprehension becomes explicit when he registers his concern for Michelson's extension of the critique of illusionism—as an explicit epistemological standard for political modernism—to an account of the "post-Brechtian aesthetic" of Godard and Straub/Huillet. A close reading of these passages in Wollen's essay reveals clearly the conflict between two competing versions of political modernism and the materialist theory of film, which are not necessarily aligned on the basis of acknowledged theoretical and aesthetic loyalties. The criticism of Michelson is joined by worries concerning Straub's account of his own work. And while Wollen credits Gidal as the most rigorously antiontological of these theorists, Gidal too comes up short in Wollen's desire to oppose the antiillusionist argument with his own vision of a film semiology and a "post-Brechtian sense of materialism, which must be concerned with the significance of what is represented, itself located in the material world and in history" (OM 13).

In Wollen's view, questions of referentiality and antiillusionism can and must be reconciled. And the best model for this reconciliation, he argues, is the "re-reading" of Brecht performed by the Dziga Vertov Group in the context of a now familiar triangulation of discourses:

Althusser's insistence on a materialist reading of Marx; Lacan's critique of neo-Freudianism and ego-psychology; the journal *Tel*

Quel and its development of a theory of the text, a semiotic based on the material character of the signifier and the practice of writing as a subversion of conventional codes, especially those of representation, and a "de-structuration" of the conscious (ie self-conscious) subject in favour of a subject fissured and split by articulation with the order of the unconscious and his or her own body. Thus the somewhat simple Brechtian concept of materialism in the theatre was translated to the cinema in terms of a re-reading and re-formulation (re-writing) which presumed a more sophisticated conceptual apparatus. . . . (OM 13)[9]

The historical argument concerning the two avant-gardes is unquestionably present here with Brecht as a specific touchstone. For Wollen, Godard has already demonstrated in practice that the emphasis on social referentiality in Brecht can be reconciled both with a "semiotic based on the material character of the signifier" and a theory of the subject as offered by Louis Althusser, Jacques Lacan, and Julia Kristeva. The critique of illusionism, however, with its emphasis on an ideal autoreferentiality, fails this objective in its insistence on the exclusion of "codes of verbal language, narrative, and iconic reference." With the exclusion of reference goes representation (social or otherwise) and the possibility that Brecht understood for a political aesthetics; with the exclusion of language and meaning goes semiology, which for Wollen is the only theoretical means for comprehending the political intelligibility of the cinema through a theory of the subject.

Wollen is therefore curious to test his interest in structural film and the critique of illusionism by asking to what degree a materialist ontology is commensurable with his understanding of film semiotics. In other words, could a materialist ontology articulate the possibilities of cinema as a language?

Wollen considers Paul Sharits's efforts to theorize a "cinematics" to be exemplary in this respect. In an essay published in *Afterimage*, "Words per Page," Sharits voices his desire to displace Bazin with an ontology of purely filmic concerns.[10] Wollen notes the degree to which Sharits is in a direct line of descent from Greenbergian modernism. Devolving from a painterly aesthetic exemplified by Frank Stella, Sharits's filmic ontology calls for "the achievement of 'objecthood' in nonobjective art, primarily through 'intensification of materiality,' but through serial systems as well," and strategies of " 'self-reference' through formal tautology" (OM 15). Wollen also notes that Sharits does not totally exclude iconic reference since recording or registration is a "physical fact" intrinsic to film. For Sharits, it is the specific tension between film's intrinsic appeal to referentiality and its optical/material processes of registration that defines the "problematic equivocality of film's 'being' " or "cinema's most basic ontological issue" (Sharits, cited in OM 15).

Sharits introduces linguistics to these issues by establishing the field of "cinematics," one of whose tools is the production of films that inquire into the nature of cinematic articulation by isolating its minimal, distinctive units below the level of the shot, for example, frame to frame articulations. However, Wollen argues that Sharits's real interests are practical rather than theoretical. He characterizes Sharits as searching for a "way in which a protocol can be devised to structure this material substrate—a serial system or calculus, perhaps a random system—so that the structuring is no longer dependent on a higher [and less cinematically specific one might add] level of organisation" (OM 16). In Wollen's reading, Sharits argues that ontology and semiology can coincide in a particular epistemological and aesthetic project. Material, cinematic phenomena (such as frame to frame articulations, splice marks, emulsion alterations, etc.) that are normally overlooked, bracketed out as mistakes or noise, or else suppressed by second-order articulations, may be isolated and examined through self-referential aesthetic procedures.

Wollen is clearly disturbed by this collapsing of an ontological project onto a semiotic one. Earlier in his discussion, he points out that, in its search for meaningful differences "below" those that have a clear semantic dimension, Sharits's cinematics is better characterized as a phonematics than as a syntactics. The structure of self-referential film, Wollen argues, is based on the problem of double articulation in its systematic commutation of cinematic codes from "meaning downwards"—from significant units at the syntactic level to those at the level of the substance of expression. Wollen cautions that schools of linguistics are by no means in agreement on how to handle this problem theoretically. But more importantly, he argues that although language cannot exist without a channel (whether it be vocalic, graphic, or gestural), the field of semiology is not reducible to a materiality conceived as a physical substance of expression. Wollen follows the linguist Louis Hjelmslev in this respect. Hjelmslev terms *figurae* those elements comprising the physical substance of expression in language. These elements have a place in linguistics, he argues, but falling below the level of expression or meaning, they cannot be classified as signs and therefore cannot be considered a constitutive object of semiology.[11]

For Wollen, then, cinematics is not a linguistics but a stylistics, aimed at problems of aesthetic perception rather than social meaning. The self-referential aesthetic procedures Sharits promotes are nothing more nor less than an example of what Prague school linguistics called "foregrounding" and what the Russian Formalist Victor Shklovsky theorized as "defamiliarization." Wollen does not object to these procedures. Brecht theorized and used comparable devices in the form of the *Verfremdung-effekt* and Wollen feels that they are clearly important for a political aesthetics when situated in the proper context. But, as earlier in "The Two Avant-Gardes," the possibility of comparison is also his point of contention. In Wollen's view, the cinematic avant-garde—which Stan Brakhage inaugurates and of which Hollis Frampton, Paul Sharits, Malcolm LeGrice and others are the logical point of culmination—has lost the specific political impact of its discovery by using foregrounding to conflate ontological and epistemological claims in the idea of a critique of illusionism. Alternatively, a Brechtian materialism could only be opposed to an ontological materialism: "For Brecht, of course, the point of the *Verfremdung* [estrangement or alienation] -effect was not simply to break the spectator's involvement and empathy in order to draw attention to the artifice of art, ie, an art-centred model, but in order to demonstrate the workings of society, a reality obscured by habitual norms of perception, by habitual modes of identification with 'human problems' " (OM 17-18).

In a similar vein, Wollen contrasts Brechtian and ontological
materialism through the opposition of knowledge to experience. Although Wollen does not, one might establish a critical
hierarchy rating various forms of political aesthetics on the
basis of his distinctions. For example, in Wollen's essay the
most suspect of all representational forms is bourgeois or "Aristotelian" theater. Such a theater offers an "experience" as
opposed to "knowledge" of society in the form of an imaginary
simulation or substitution; in other words, pure idealism. Next
would be ontological materialism. Here the modernist emphasis on the material specificity or autonomy of given aesthetic media either collapses knowledge onto, or replaces it
with, an experience of form. This experience is reducible, *mu-
tatus mutandis*, to the Bazinian desire for producing a perception identical with the object itself. Whereas the latter appears
to communicate its referent without the material agency of a
channel, the former, in its very insistence on materiality, brackets out every system of reference except that contained within
itself. Neither can adequately justify epistemological claims in
the Brechtian sense which, as Wollen has already argued, "must
be concerned with the significance of what is represented,
itself located in the material world and in history" (OM 13).

In this respect, Wollen asserts that the lesson learned by
Godard and Straub is that for Brecht there is neither a question
of abandoning the realm of social reference outside of the play
(or film) nor of equating antiillusionism with the suppression
of any signified. In a gloss on Brecht's notes for *Mahagonny*
("The Modern Theatre is the Epic Theatre") and "A Short
Organum for the Theatre," Wollen claims that Brecht's materialism reconciles antiillusionism and referentiality in his theory of distantiation (the *Verfremdung-effekt*) as an activity that
encourages a fundamental dissymmetry in the film/viewer relation—the opening of a "gap in space" between referent, representation, and spectator.[12] In these essays Brecht referred
to his plays as representations, or alternately, models, diagrams, or demonstrations, "to which the spectator remained
external and through which he/she acquired knowledge about
(not gained experience of) the society in which he/she, himself/
herself lived (not the life of another/others). Brecht's anti-il-

lusionism then should be seen not as anti-representationalism (Brecht thought of himself as a 'realist') but, so to speak, as anti-substitutionism" (OM 18). Similarly, Wollen stresses that "Brecht wanted to find a concept of 'representation' which would account for a passage from perception/recognition to knowledge/understanding, from the imaginary to the symbolic: a theatre of representation, mimesis even, but also a theatre of ideas" (OM 18-19).

Clearly, Wollen's critique of ontological modernism is produced within its own strict system of binary logic. "Ontologies" of every color—idealist (Bazin), romantic (Sitney, Snow), or materialist (Greenberg, Sharits)—are opposed to a "semiotic" modernism as the only basis for conceiving a materialist text. "If there is something in common between 'structural' or 'modernist' film and the 'post-Brechtian aesthetic' of which Michelson writes," says Wollen, "it consists neither of the movement toward 'objecthood' and exclusive self-referentiality, nor in the simple act of foregrounding the material substrate. This 'post-Brechtian aesthetic' is not postulated on the search for an ontology, albeit a materialist ontology. *It has to be approached from the side of language, here dialectic* (OM 18; emphasis mine).

For Wollen, the opposition of a linguistic (for want of a better term) to an ontological modernism forges the theoretical consensus that makes a "post-Brechtian aesthetic" possible. However, the explicit meaning of the terms *language* and *dialectic* are unclear despite their centrality in his argument. How are these terms to be understood in Wollen's version of political modernism? What roles or functions are reserved for the notions of sign and subject that Wollen fears have been excluded from ontological modernism due to its rejection of or resistance to a linguistically founded semiology? How might these terms inaugurate the possibility of a "materialist" relation of knowledge between the "post-Brechtian aesthetic" Wollen favors and its potential subject-spectators?

In an earlier chapter, I criticized Wollen's devotion to Saussurean linguistics and his account of cinematic signification where speech was considered as an ideological corrective to the image, that is, political argumentation as so many signifieds

to supplement the lure and ambiguity of the cinematic signifier. In " 'Ontology' and 'Materialism'," Wollen seems anxious
to correct any such assumptions by organizing his argument
around the problem of the sign: "The decisive revolution of
twentieth-century art can be seen in the transformation of the
concept, and use, of the sign rather than in the rejection of
any signification except tautology, the closed circle of presence
and self-reference" (OM 21). Similarly, he presents a notion
of text that attempts to reconcile his interest in the aesthetic
theory and practice of Brecht, *Tel Quel*, and structural film.
Wollen first compares his version of the text of political modernism to the Russian Formalist distinction between poetic and
practical language, where rules governing the order of the
signifier—for example, meter, rhyme, and other forms of pro-
sody—are understood as operating independently of the signified. Wollen argues that Shklovsky and Jakobson understood
the potentiality of foregrounding as a deautomatization of language that gave new meaning to our perception of the world
through language. He also notes and discusses Jakobson's later
account of the poetic function as defined by the autodesignation of code—an "antiillusionist" procedure based on the
bipartite structure of the sign, rather than an intensification of
materiality of the signifier and rejection of the signified.[13]

Subsequently, Wollen differentiates (but does not disasso-
ciate) himself from this position. Accordingly, he presents a
theory of the cinematic text as *écriture* whose axiom is: "Style
is a producer of meaning" (OM 20). But style is not meant in
the sense of supplementarity, embellishment, or even poetic
foregrounding. Instead Wollen compares his idea of a materialist style to the politics of form and meaning designated by
Roland Barthes's conception of *écriture* in *Writing Degree Zero*.
Despite Wollen's references to Philippe Sollers, however, this
is in many respects a pre-Derridean notion of *écriture*. Moreover, like Metz, Wollen draws Hjelmslev into this discussion
by distinguishing material from form. Therefore, when speaking of an element of style—including meter and rhyme as well
as loop-printing, shot duration, or rephotography—a dual relation in the ordering of the signifier is presupposed: its sub-

stance (phonic, graphic, etc.) of expression as well as its form per se.

> A text is structured primarily at the level of the signifier. It is the ordering of the signifiers which determines the production of the signifieds. . . . [A] mistaken signifier—a metathesis, the displacement of a phoneme—changes meaning, alters or negates the flow of signifieds, diverts, subverts, converts. Whereas Sharits is interested in the re-structuration of noise to provide second-order self-referential information, we are here talking about the production of new—unintended, unanticipated, unconsciously derived—signification from operations carried out on the signifiers. First-order signifiers remain, but they are no longer the sovereign product of the intentional act of a subject, a transcendental ego, the generator of thought which finds embodiment in language as an instrumental necessity for the communication and exchange of ideas between equivalent subjects, alternating as source and receiver. (OM 19)

Wollen places himself squarely within the Formalist wing of the *Tel Quel* group (Kristeva, Todorov) and thus in a direct line of descent from Saussure-inflected theories of poetic language such as Roman Jakobson's. Thus, he justifies his version of the "text" of political modernism by asserting that strategies resulting in a transformation of the material ordering of signifiers necessarily yield not only a transformation in the destiny of meaning, but also a transformation of the subject's relation to meaning.

In Wollen's account a materialist style designates a specific set of relations between formal and material determinations in the production of meaning. In light of this explanation, he offers a second version of his concept of text:

> This concept of text does not exclude, indeed is constructed on, the need to produce beyond signifieds, meaning. It sees meaning, however, as a material and formal problem, the product of material and formal determinations rather than the intention of an *ego cogitans*, a thinking and conscious (ie self-conscious) subject. Indeed, the very concept of such a subject is dissolved by textual production in this sense, as Kristeva and others have repeatedly argued. This does not mean, of course, that the conscious subject of ideology is simply replaced by an automatism

or by a random process. Rather, it transforms the thinker, or imaginer, or seer, into an agent who is working with and within language in order to make something which cannot be precisely pre-conceived, which must remain problematical and in a sense unfinished, interminable. This manufacture must not suppress its material substrate, the sensuous activity which is its process of production, but nor is that sensuous activity its own horizon. (OM 20-21)

Thus Wollen criticizes Sharits and other proponents of ontological modernism for treating the aesthetic object as an instrument identical with the intentional act of a self-present, creative ego. To contravene this tendency, Wollen supplements his semiotic modernism with a psychoanalytic theory of the subject. By introducing the idea of the unconscious and of the divided subject, Wollen criticizes the tendency of ontological modernism to reduce the identity of the aesthetic object to that of its creator, even in the form of Sharits-like random protocols.

Alternatively, Wollen offers his conception of the "dialectic" operating in language or symbolic systems of communication. "Illusionism should not be confused with signification," writes Wollen, and similarly, "anti-illusionism does not . . . necessarily imply anti-representationalism" (OM 21). With respect to the first assertion, it is obvious to Wollen that one constantly signifies and creates meaning without the agency of mimetic or even analogical codes. For Saussure, the first principle of the structure of the sign is its arbitrariness; for C. S. Peirce, the symbol is marked by its fundamental difference from the object it represents. And indeed an initial understanding of what Wollen means by requiring a "gap in space" between referent, representamen, and spectator in the text of political modernism would have to refer to this difference. By the same token, stressing the relation of difference or nonidentity between an object and the form or substance of its expression need not imply the absence of representation. For the concept of representation can include systems of correspondence and homology as well as those of mimesis and analogy.

Therefore, what Wollen offers in his concept of dialectic is not a theory of communication, but rather a theory of the subject that reverses the emphasis of ontological modernism. It is no longer the artist or intentional ego that produces the text; it is the text that "produces" the subject. Wollen's efforts to theorize the modernist text through the form of the sign is based, quite specifically, on the possibility of a transformation of the subject in relation to the signifier as a transition from passivity (consumer of the artist's message) to activity. Described in psychoanalytic terms, this transition is understood by Wollen as a "passing" of the spectator from the imaginary to the symbolic in the form of a "productive deciphering." Strategies of self-reference and reflexivity characteristic of the modernist text are important not so much as strategies of antiillusionism, but rather as devices, based on the arbitrary character of the sign, for encouraging the activity and productive capacity of the spectator.

> In this respect, the "multiple mapping procedures" described by Sharits are, like Brecht's plagiarism or Kristeva's "intertextuality," important anti-illusionist procedures which can produce the transition from the imaginary to the symbolic in the spaces and overlaps of a palimpsest. In this way, the illusory immediacy of "reading" is destroyed and replaced by a productive deciphering, which must move from level to level, within a volume—rather than following a surface which presents itself as the alterity of a depth, a meaning which lies elsewhere, in the ideal transaction/exchange between consciousnesses, rather than the material text.
>
> To say, however, that the two anti-illusionist currents being discussed are in many respects separate, different from each other, does not mean that they may not be combined. (OM 21)

However, a fundamental undecidability informs Wollen's characterization of the subject of the text of semiotic modernism as well as his location of that subject in the compromise between "literary" and "painterly" strategies of antiillusionism. Specifically, it is necessary to understand, and to question in its self-evidence, Wollen's emphasis on the function of the signified in its relations with the signifier. In his implicit insistence on linguistics as the foundation of a semiotic modernism, Wollen holds to a fundamental Saussureanism in his operative definition of the sign. Like Saussure, Wollen understands the signifier and signified as being intrinsically and indestructibly linked: "A text is structured primarily at the level of the signifier. It is the ordering of the signifiers which *determines* the production of the signifieds" (OM 19; my emphasis).[14] But even if this relation is intrinsic, in Wollen's reading at least, it is not evenly determined—it proceeds unilaterally from the side of the signifier to that of the signified. A potential activity is reserved here for the space of the sign: a transformation in the ordering of signifiers—equivalent in Wollen to strategic work on the formal and material properties of text—will yield a transformation in the character of signification per se.

But on what basis is this defense of modernism's formal and material experimentation extendable to claims concerning the subject's relation to signification and to ideology? The key to this problem is Wollen's particular emphasis on notions of reference in his conception of the role of the signified. In fact it is the question of reference and not representation that is the target of Wollen's critique and defense of principles of antiillusionism and autoreferentiality. In idealist theories, the signified is identified with a "meaningful world," communicated transparently by a signifier that, by effacing itself before the signified, is not capable of transformation. Modernism discovers the materiality but not the primacy of the signifier in its formal relations with the signified. It therefore theorizes its signified as equivalent or reducible to an anterior relation: the will, spirit, or mind of the artist. In Wollen's view, if modernism is to be reconciled with semiology, if the theory of language is to be introduced to it, modernism must recognize not only the primacy of the signifier, but paradoxically, the *arbitrariness* of the link between the two sides of the sign: that there is no necessary relation between the sign and what it purports to represent, and that the signifier is capable of material transformations independent of its relation to the signified. But this arbitrariness is strictly circumscribed, directing the field of reference in a particular way. In Wollen's view, the signified must include reference not to the world or to the cogito of the artist, but to the production of meaning *in* and *for* the subject. Wollen's insistence on the problem of the signified, and his anxiety concerning its subtraction from the equation of political modernism, is multiply and contradictorily determined. On one hand, a specifically semiotic conception of modernism entails a priori the problem of meaning since the bipartite structure of the sign is indestructible. At the same time, because the relation between signifier and signified is arbitrary, material transformations in the process of signification are possible. On the other hand, the definition of cinema as a language will be decided by an interior determination: the possible forms of relations between signifier and signified as criteria of textual identity (e.g., idealist, "ontological" materialist, or "post-Brechtian" aesthetics). And at the same time the signified must account for an *exterior* relation that includes the forms of subjectivity it may determine.

A relation that is both determined and arbitrary, intrinsic and extrinsic: in a moment, the theoretical consequences of this situation will have to be accounted for where the forms proper to the text, as decided in the ratio of signifier to signified, are redoubled in the forms of relations possible between text and subject.

But first the following question must be resolved: What justifies Wollen's identification of cinematic language with a dialectic and the possibility of knowledge on the part of its subject? He has already explicitly formulated these ideas by arguing for "a concept of 'representation' which would account for a passage from perception/recognition to knowledge/understanding, from the imaginary to the symbolic . . ." (OM 18-19). But what sort of dialectic is described here? Defining an imperative for reading as "productive deciphering," this "transition" is decisive for Wollen's theory of aesthetic subjectivity. In Wollen's writings, it is clear that the painterly tradition of the avant-garde fails his definition of "text" or of an art form concerned with the "transformation, and use, of the sign . . ." By refusing to incorporate the problem of language, the films of the painterly avant-garde cannot effect a "transition from the imaginary to the symbolic" which, according to Wollen, is the dialectic that potentially encourages a transformation of subjective relations in film. But how is the precise use of these terms to be understood in the light of

Wollen's rewriting of the history of modernism? Using a Peircean terminology to draw an opposition between iconic and symbolic sign systems, Wollen has already defined codes of photographic reproduction as iconic. Now he forges an explicit relation between symbolic codes and language. (Of course, such an opposition is not absolutely faithful to Peirce's classification of signs, but we will let it stand for the moment.)[15] In a virtual paraphrase of "The Two Avant-Gardes," Wollen states that "it is only with a symbolic (rather than iconic) system that concepts can be developed, that there can be contradiction and hence argument" (OM 19). Throughout his essay Wollen consistently equates his version of symbolic codes with the presence of language in the form of concepts, ideas, or arguments." Moreover, with his emphasis on linking together language, reference, and social meaning, Wollen's Peircean inflection of the term *symbolic* coincides with a more psychoanalytically informed usage where the subject is considered as an effect of the signifier.

But what of the *imaginary*? Here Christian Metz's reading of Lacanian psychoanalytic theory is important for Wollen. According to Metz, the cinematic signifier is the imaginary signifier for two reasons. First, it is "imaginary" because cinema is by and large dominated by forms of fiction. But second, its conditions of specularity—the relations established by image and look—are understood as reprising the Lacanian Imaginary as the series of unconscious identifications subtending the formation of the "I" and precipitating the Oedipal crisis wherein the subject is constituted in the symbolic order, that of culture and language. Thus Metz, Baudry, and others have equated determinations on subjectivity in the cinema with the situation of specular identification described by Lacan in his seminal essay "The Mirror Phase as Formative of the Function of the 'I'." Similarly, Constance Penley has argued in relation to the cinema that the "imaginary is the order of perception, whereas the symbolic is the discursive order."[16] Wollen would undoubtedly concur and add that the imaginary describes the lure of iconicity, or more precisely, the lure of presence given as self-identical meaning. Therefore, for Wollen the imaginary can be inflated in two directions. First is that of illusionist narrative that attempts to efface its semiotic character in order to appear as a message without a code or a material support— the referent given as transcendental signified. Second is the imaginary relation that is, conversely, an overvaluation (Penley would say a "fetishization") of the material character of expression. A materialist ontology might overlook or "dematerialize" symbolic codes to the extent that cinematic reflexivity or self-investigation posits the material substrate as a transcendental signified.

In sum, the dialectical movement from the imaginary to the symbolic, which defines the post-Brechtian aesthetic to which Wollen aspires in his films with Laura Mulvey, is designed to achieve a consensus where iconic and symbolic codes "counterbalance" one another, but only to the extent that a certain hierarchy of terms is maintained. If this movement encompasses a theoretical dimension, it ultimately rests, as in "The Two Avant-Gardes," on an opposition that reproduces the binary organization of terms previously set into play; for example, the imaginary:the symbolic :: iconic codes:symbolic codes :: perception:knowledge. As defined by Wollen in his critique of materialist ontology, the problem of the imaginary is tantamount to a theoretical iconoclasm. In Wollen's writing and filmmaking, there is always a limit where language, as the object of semiology, must "speak" theory in relation to the image that otherwise resists discursive conceptualization. The dialectic, or rather confrontation, between the imaginary and the symbolic, iconic codes and codes of language, image and sound, thus constitute, in Wollen's view, the only possibility for the articulation of theory (i.e., concepts, ideas, or arguments) in films. This logic is superimposed on the speech/image relation in Wollen's essay "The Field of Language in Film":

> Verbal language is a crucial component of film, both as signifier and as signified, as crucial as the image. Each is deprived of a dimension of its sense in the absence of the other. . . . [It] is in the dialectic of fit and misfit that the value of working with both word and image lies, as well as in the heterogeneity of the registers of each. *Language is the component of film which both threatens to regulate the spectator, assigned a place in the symbolic order, and also offers the hope of liberation from the closed*

world of identification and the lure of the image. . . . Hence the
fractured and dislodged body of language in our films.[17]

In Chapter Two I demonstrated that for Wollen semiology
is the only possible theory with which to articulate a politics
of the sign. In his essays he often speaks of a semiotics of films,
of language, and of speech, but he rarely, if ever, speaks of a
semiotics of the image. In fact, throughout his writings Wollen
implies that the image presents a clear danger to semiology.
In the two tendencies of modernism in film, the first, pure
cinema, is criticized for excluding language and speech, hence
semiology. The second, in its extreme reflexivity, either refuses
signification or presents itself as fully self-interpreting through
the agency of perception. In its proximity to the imaginary and
to identification, this perception is thought to be "noncon-
ceptual," to exclude symbolic and thus semiotic intelligibility.

If previously in Wollen's work semiotic theory superceded
modernism, now psychoanalytic theory takes precedence over
semiology. Speech can no longer be considered as an ideological corrective to the lure of the image, for as the agency of
the symbolic order it also represents the articulation of patriarchal power. Language still receives priority in Wollen's
theories—without language there is no theory—but now it must
be a "fractured and dislodged" language whose relation to the
image is problematic. Hence the specific link between Brecht's
emphasis on contradiction and Saussure's on the arbitrariness
of the sign that inspires Wollen to conceive of dialectic as ruled
by a metaphor of distance and of the externality of the spectator in the form of a "gap in space" between signifier and
signified, word and image, code and channel, the imaginary
and the symbolic. Contradiction—but a directed, strategic, informed contradiction—is important for Wollen because, in his
view, it preserves meaning and thus theory in film; in other
words, it strains against the imaginary while interrupting the
transition to the symbolic, the guarantee of an identification
with patriarchal power.

There is no doubt that this literalization does little justice
to the subtleties and complexities of Lacanian psychoanalysis.
Nor does it entirely justify Wollen's argument for the necessity
of a semiotically informed avant-garde aesthetic practice. His

particular version of the subject, and of text/subject relations, must be explained in other terms. By a paradoxical turn, Wollen's definition of a cinematic *écriture* relies on the theoretical priority of *parole*, or speech, thus entertaining a contradiction that threatens his argument. For only by equating speech with the potential of knowledge, and the presence of the subject to thought in the form of ideas or concepts, can Wollen's claims for the epistemological privilege of a post-Brechtian aesthetic be justified. Similarly, we are brought full circle to one of the opening moves of Wollen's argument where the problematic relationships between language or semiotic and materialist ontologies, on the one hand, and antiillusionism and illusionism on the other, are linked to "the historic problem of the impact of sound" (OM 10).

In this respect, Wollen's adoption of poststructuralist notions of text and *écriture* remain paradoxically limited, even in their rearticulation through Lacan's psychoanalysis, by a profound Saussurean bias. That the model of speech serves as the near exclusive basis for film semiology is nowhere more clear than in Wollen's equation of images with iconic codes and their subsequent banishment from the field of symbolic or discursive activity.[18] For example, there is little or no textual justification in Lacan for an opposition distributing iconic signs on the side of the imaginary and codes of verbal language simply on the side of the symbolic. This hierarchical distinction is entirely refuted by Lacan's insistence on the mutual and differential articulation of the imaginary and the symbolic. Moreover, such a distinction effectively banishes the image—for example, photographic representation—from the field of signification where different types of represention (phonic, graphic, iconic, narrational) could be analyzed according to their different investments in the imaginary and their specific manner of giving form to unconscious desire. Similarly, Wollen's identification of photographic reproduction with iconic signs is explicitly contradicted by Peirce who, unlike Hjelmslev, does not distinguish signs according to their materials of expression, but rather, acc rding to a pragmatics defined by their cultural context and use. A "sign" is therefore not a preconstituted identity with a given empirical or ontological status, but rather a shifting configuration of relations among sign-functions. Unlike Saussure, where the hierarchical relation between speech and writing (interestingly described as the image or photograph of speech on page 45 of the *Cours*) reveals a specific metaphysical bias, there is little evidence that Peirce's semiotic would recognize the a priori purity of words and images as qualifiably different types of signs (symbolic and iconic). Nor could Peirce's terminology justify a binary logic that banishes "iconic" signs from the field of "symbolic" activity to preserve the identity of speech as that which is closest to thought. Once again, it is only through reference to the phonocentrism of Saussure that the epistemological priority of Wollen's post-Brechtian aesthetic can be explained.

The compromise Wollen seeks with the more radical strategies of antiillusionism, and the particular style or *"écriture"* he wishes to theorize would redeem meaning and the social construction of meaning for the text of political modernism. But in its specific orientation of terms—its opposition of symbolic to iconic signs, speech to image, indeed the sensible to the intelligible; its insistence on describing the process of knowledge as a passage from the imaginary to the symbolic; its stress on the primacy of linguistics and the importance of sound—Wollen's notion of *écriture* can only be comprehended as the phonocentric writing criticized by Derrida in the transcendental phenomenology of Husserl.[19] Wollen's use of a poststructuralist vocabulary contravenes his demand for a "post-Brechtian sense of materialism, which must be concerned with the significance of what is represented." The insistence on the presence of the signified, which must arise in the character of the signifier, is equated here with the presence of speech in the text, at least in the sense of a phonocentric theory of representation if not that of verbal language per se. And more importantly, since Wollen offers no specific reflection on the conditions of subjectivity, while nonetheless pointing out the importance of the category of the subject for any theory of semiotic modernism, the status of the subject in Wollen's essays can also only be construed in the context of Saussure who in the *Cours* is more or less silent on this area.

Nevertheless, several pertinent observations can be made. Derrida notes how Saussure's setting up of linguistics as a master pattern for semiology is linked to a phonocentrism where the presence of thought—of self-consciousness or the presence of the subject to meaning in the form of self-consciousness— is strictly identified with speech in the conceptualization of the sign.[20] Saussure is unambiguous on this account. In effect *phone* is equivalent to thought as signified "concept"; Saussure even speaks of "thought-sound" and asserts that there is a natural link between sound and meaning, voice and thought. Moreover, the immutability of the sign reveals a specifically interiorized relation (where the self-identity of the sign becomes coextensive with a psychologism as the articulation of thought by sound) that Saussure insists is a *formal* one. To the extent that Saussure addresses the question of subjectivity, it is entirely reduced to the formal character of the sign, its intrinsic relation to meaning, and the specific privilege of the phonic signifier's yielding "signified-thought" in the material of sound.

Derrida's critique of Saussure emphasizes how this phonologism reduces the exteriority of the signifier and excludes everything in semiotic practice that is not psychical. Curiously, in the discourse of materialism produced by post-'68 theories of political modernism in general, and Wollen in particular, the privileging of a link between language and thought has produced an opposite emphasis. It is the *exteriority* of the signifier that is insisted upon—that is, the materiality, self-identity, and formal autonomy the avant-garde text achieves through its devices of heterogeneity, defamiliarization, and autodesignation—to the following paradoxical effect. To the extent that the presence of the subject to thought is equated with the production of a signified, and to the degree in which Wollen and others theorize the forms of political modernism according to Saussure's account of the structure of the sign, all psychical relations are reduced through an implied interiorization: the "forms" of subjectivity can only be identified *in* the system of the text. The phonologism of political modernism, in other words, reduces the exteriority of the subject, as an "effect" of the signifier, to exclude everything in semiotic practice that

is not *formal*. In Wollen's semiotic modernism, the metaphysical implications of Saussure's phonocentric conception of the
relations between signifier and signified are sublated and reproduced at a higher level of articulation—that is, in the relations between text and subject. If the subject is to "take
place," as it were, or to have a place in relation to meaning,
it can only do so in the form of a reduction where the subject
is identified with the formal structure of the aesthetic text. The
subject is only manifest in relation to the text's operations of
signification, and can admit of no prior existence or exterior
relation. Here a certain priority of Saussure's logic has been
turned inside out without in the least disturbing his idealist
conception of the sign.

The difficulties of Wollen's implicit characterization of the
subject of a semiotic modernism are explained in part by Saussure's own lack of reflection on problems of subjectivity in the
Cours. In fact, one of the *Cours'* more radical aspects is that
it does not recognize the *necessity* of the category of the subject. In the *Cours*, the simultaneous mutability and immutability of the sign (so crucial to Wollen's version of political
modernism) best explains the absence of the subject, especially
in its Lacanian insistence. Saussure asserts that the sign is immutable because it is a property of the linguistic community
and not that of a speaking subject. Even reference to the concept of *parole* cannot restore the punctual simplicity of the
subject in relation to discourse, since a unique utterance is
only meaningful in its systemic aspect as the *langue* of a linguistic collectivity. Simultaneously, Saussure recognizes that
relations between signifier and signified do undergo diachronic
transformations. But again the historical mutability of the sign
posits the irrelevance of any singular identity—whether in the
form of a unique utterance or individual speaker—to the sociality of the system. The potential mutability of the sign cannot be attributed to the originary gesture of a singular discursive act or subject. Transformations in the field of
signification are resolutely the property of a linguistic community and the language system; otherwise, Saussure's proposition could only be read as bald self-contradiction.

Wollen's insistence on attributing a subject to Saussure's theory (where in fact no subject is required) reveals a paradoxical necessity in his equation of modernism and semiology: the creation of a *formal object* that locates the field of ideology, as well as the scale of its possible relations to knowledge, *within the province of the aesthetic text.* The specific attributes that Wollen redefines in his "post-Brechtian aesthetic"—including procedures of reflexivity and autodesignation—serve to locate, circumscribe, and reinforce the self-identity of the aesthetic object as a tangible field capable of material transformation, including the possibility of a transformation of the subject. But in its emphasis on the provocative singularity of aesthetic practice in relation to ideology, the idealism of this argument is now apparent. It defines the text-spectator relation as a space of pure autoaffection that actualizes its subject independent of any historical or discursive context of textual presentation. Similarly, it cannot conceive the subject-spectator as situated differentially and contradictorily in its relation to other discursive practices (e.g., theoretical or critical) that might, in given historical contexts, either reinforce or contravene potentialities for the consumption or reception of a given aesthetic practice.

In this context, Wollen's assumptions linking the subject of political modernism to the Saussurean definition of the sign begin to unravel. Similarly, the degree of "knowledge" possible within the post-Brechtian text relies on two fundamental principles that are not reconcilable in the conceptual space reserved for the subject. On one hand, Wollen insists that the possibility of knowledge relies on the externality of the subject with respect to the text. Taking up the Brechtian concept of distantiation, he states that the subject's relation to knowledge is predicated on the opening of a "gap in space" in the field of perception. On the other hand, "ideas cannot be divorced from their material substrate . . ." (OM 19). In Wollen's consideration of text, the immutability of the sign requires that the signified—in the form of "ideas," "concepts," "argument," indeed the presence of the subject to thought—be inseparable from the (phonological) materiality of language. Therefore, in the series of correlations drawn between the system of representation (signifier/signified), the process of knowledge (from the imaginary to the symbolic), and the desired transformation of text/spectator relations (dialectic), the category of the subject is caught up in a fundamental undecidability. Both a production *of* the text as a function of the immutability of the sign, *and* its specific field of address or the external point to which it is destined, the category of the subject refers simultaneously in Wollen's writings to relations of interiority and exteriority that his theory of text can neither master nor resolve. Wollen's notions concerning how his post-Brechtian aesthetic can produce a "gap in space opened in perception," or "gaps and fissures" in the spectator's consciousness, are best understood, then, not as metaphors of distance or distantiation, but as a specific form of identity between subject and object characterized by the integral body of the sign and the autoaffection of the modernist text. If the text of semiotic modernism requires the transformation of the subject as a relation of distance in the form of "productive deciphering," paradoxically, that transformation can only take place as an interiorization that renders the form(s) of the subject identical to those of the text.

In his critique of the formal autonomy and tautological construction of the aesthetic object posed by ontological modernism, Wollen does not take issue with the autoreferentiality of the text. Rather, it is the rejection of language or more precisely speech from the body of the text that worries him. But to what extent could any aesthetic object "reject" language? The proposition is untenable from the point of view of semiotic theory. But this is exactly what Wollen requires when, in his critique of ontological modernism, he reduces semiotics to linguistics and poses a (phonological) theory of *écriture* as text. Wollen's theory must suppose an outside to language in the form of a pure figuration that makes language anxious by threatening its self-identity as well as its claims for the communication of truth and rationality. Similarly, the anxiety of the subject's stand outside of the language/knowledge equation (and thus "within" perception, the image, or the imaginary) must be mastered by the return of the signified and the interiorization of the subject within the formal space of the

text. By forging a consensus between strategies of antiillusionism and an intensified materialism of the signifier on the
one hand, and by restoring the functionality of the signified
on the other, Wollen has not fundamentally stepped outside
of the terms of the ontological theories of representation he
criticizes. For what links Saussure to Bazin, or to a romantic
conception of the avant-garde text, is the inability to think the
category of the subject as other than identical in form to the
aesthetic object.

Yet Wollen's reading and critique of ontological concerns in
film theory remains a complex and productive polemic. And
it is worth noting the terms and consequences of this critique
for an understanding of the discourse of political modernism.
Wollen rejects all the ontologies he considers as either effacing
or overvaluing the signifier while forgetting the "completion
of language" in the signified. But another analysis is possible.
In each case the ontological gesture can be understood as a
bracketing of the signifier in relation to a transcendental signified; for example, world (Bazin), mind (Sitney, Snow), or
material (LeGrice, Sharits, Gidal). By the same token, does not
Wollen's post-Brechtian aesthetic also function in this manner
through its desired production of the (knowing) subject as a
transcendental signified formulated by a phonological consideration of cinematic language? Indeed, a thorough excavation
of the Sausurrean framework subtending Wollen's writings
supports this reading. But if the problem of the subject is located with difficulty in Wollen's essays (as it is in the *Cours*),
it must also be said that the goal of these essays is neither to
present a theory of the subject, nor precisely to discuss problems of subjectivity in aesthetic discourse. (And to criticize
Wollen on this account does not subtract from the relevance
and brilliance of his critique of the avant-gardes.) To further
illuminate these questions in the discourse of political modernism, we must turn to the work of Stephen Heath.

NOTES

1. Peter Wollen's " 'Ontology' and 'Materialism in Film' " was
published in *Screen* 17.1 (Spring 1976): 7-23; hereafter cited as OM.

Stephen Heath's "Narrative Space" first appeared in *Screen* 17.3 (Autumn 1976): 68-112; hereafter cited as NS.

2. Untitled presentation, London Filmmakers' Co-op, London, England, 10 February 1976: 3.

3. "The Avant-Garde and its Imaginary," *Camera Obscura* 2 (Fall 1977): 8. LeGrice has updated his views in light of these criticisms in two noteworthy essays: "Towards Temporal Economy," *Screen* 20.3/4 (Winter 1979/80): 58-79) and "Problematising the Spectator Placement in Film," *Undercut* 1 (March/April 1981): 13-18.

4. See, in particular, Polan's essay "Brecht and the Politics of Self-Reflexive Cinema," *Jumpcut* 17 (April 1978): 29-32; and his book *Image-Making and Image-Breaking: Studies in the Political Language of Film and the Avant-Garde* (Ann Arbor: UMI Research Press, 1985). I am also indebted to Sylvia Harvey's critique "Whose Brecht? Memories for the Eighties: A Critical Recovery," *Screen* 23.1 (May/June 1982): 45-59.

5. I do not assume that the pattern of correspondences and theoretical concerns in Wollen's and Heath's essays are the result of some unified editorial policy on the part of *Screen*, or even the result of some intellectual collaboration between them. If these essays are exemplary of the (contradictory) unity of a position, it is a consensus that must be understood as devolving from debate as well as dissenting and divergent viewpoints developing in SEFT and BFI Education throughout the seventies.

6. Respectively *Cinim* 3 (1969): 3, and *Film Culture* 46 (1967): 4-5. Both cited in OM 10.

7. In *Michael Snow/A Survey* (Ontario: Art Gallery of Ontario, 1970): 83; cited in OM 10. Ortega's views on modernism are preented in *The Dehumanization of Art*, trans. Helen Weyl (Princeton: Princeton University Press, 1968).

8. See Michelson's "Paul Sharits and the Critique of Illusionism: An Introduction" in *Projected Images* (Minneapolis: Walker Art Center, 1974): 20-25. Wollen also refers to the formalization of these arguments in Regina Cornwell's influential essay "Some Formalist Tendencies in the Current Avant-Garde Film," *Kansas Quarterly* 4.2 (1972): 60-73.

9. Wollen's readings of Godard's positions derives from interviews that appeared in *Kinopraxis*, a broadside published in Berkeley, California in 1970. Similar arguments with respect to the contemporary influence of Brecht may be found in the late Martin Walsh's *The Brechtian Aspect of Radical Cinema*, ed. Keith M. Griffiths (London: British Film Institute, 1981). Also see George Lellis's *Bertolt Brecht,*

Cahiers du cinéma and Contemporary Film Theory (Ann Arbor: Michigan Research Press, 1982). Alternatively, one could argue that it is not precisely a defense or interpretation of Brecht that is at issue here, as much as the theoretical paradigm being argued through and forwarded by *Screen*, above all in relation to its two special issues on Brecht (15.2 [Summer 1974] and 16.4 [Winter 1975/76] that documented the special Edinburgh event on Brecht and Cinema). This is in fact Harvey's argument in "Whose Brecht?" What is at stake is the theoretical context governing the reception of Brecht rather than a specific appeal to Brecht's theories themselves. For a detailed analysis of this problem, see my *The Political Avant-Garde: Modernism and Epistemology in Post-'68 Film Theory*, dissertation, The University of Iowa, 1983, especially pages 234-95.

10. Paul Sharits, "Words per Page," *Afterimage* 4 (Autumn 1972): 26-42. It is interesting to note that this essay appears in the same issue as Wollen's "Counter-Cinema" article.

11. See Louis Hjelmslev's *Prolegomena to a Theory of Language*, trans. Francis J. Whitfield (Madison: University of Wisconsin Press, 1969): 41-47.

12. In *Brecht on Theatre*, ed. and trans. John Willett (New York: Hill and Wang, 1964): 33-43 and 179-205, respectively.

13. See, for example, Victor Shklovsky's "Art as Technique" in *Russian Formalist Criticism*, eds. L. T. Lemon and M. J. Reis (Lincoln: University of Nebraska Press, 1965): 5-57, and Roman Jakobson's "Concluding Statement: Linguistics and Poetics" in Thomas A. Sebeok, ed., *Style in Language* (Cambridge: MIT Press, 1960): 350-77. The identification of a Formalist concept of "defamiliarization" with the Brechtian notion of "distantiation" was the subject of considerable debate in *Screen*. See, in particular, Stanley Mitchell's essay "From Shklovsky to Brecht," *Screen* 15.2 (Summer 1974): 74-81; and Ben Brewster's response in the same issue, 82-102. I have analyzed the consequences of this debate for a theory of political modernism in my *The Political Avant-Garde: Modernism and Epistemology in Post-'68 Film Theory*, especially pages 261-72. Also see Phil Rosen's excellent account in his *The Concept of Ideology and Contemporary Film Criticism*, dissertation, University of Iowa, 1978.

14. Cf. Saussure's *Cours de linguistique générale* (Paris: Payot, 1982): 104-13.

15. Wollen takes Peirce too literally. Iconic codes, based on the factor of resemblance to their "object," might indeed encompass photography, but one would have to accept a priori that photography

is a language. One could not use Peirce to define it as such as does Wollen. (I would like to thank Alan Trachtenberg for confirming this suspicion.) In this particular case, it is relatively certain that Peirce, who is unconcerned with pictorial codes per se, is speaking of pictographic or hieroglyphic scripts. Here in fact is Derrida's interest. Peirce is more concerned with a general grammatics, logics relating signs, things, and meaning through several sets of triadic relations, only one of which is that of icon, index, and symbol. The important thing to note is that in Peirce's system all language cannot be reduced to symbolic codes, nor can all codes of photographic reproduction be reduced to the iconic. Cf. Peirce's "Logic as Semiotic: The Theory of Signs" in Justus Buchler, ed., *Philosophical Writings of Peirce* (New York: Dover, 1955): 98-119 and James K. Feibleman's *An Introduction to the Philosophy of Charles S. Peirce* (Cambridge: The MIT Press, 1969), especially 89-97. Also see Jacques Derrida's *Of Grammatology*, trans. Gayatri Chakravorty Spivak (Baltimore: Johns Hopkins University Press, 1976): 48-49.

In my opinion, Wollen offers a similarly simplistic reduction when later on he equates photography solely with Lacan's register of the imaginary. More recent accounts of cinema semiotics, especially those informed by Eco's reading of Peirce, have placed in doubt both the self-identity of an iconic sign and its simple equation with the notion of an image. See, for example, Teresa de Lauretis's brilliant argument in *Alice Doesn't* (Bloomington: Indiana University Press, 1984), especially 37-69 passim.

16. Constance Penley, "The Avant-Garde and its Imaginary," 28. Penley has subsequently presented a thorough critique of the adoption of these terms into film theory. See her "Feminism, Film Theory and the Bachelor Machines," *m/f* 10 (1985): 39-59.

17. *October* 17 (Summer 1981): 54; my emphasis.

18. This logic is itself ripe for an ideological critique in its expression of an anxiety concerning imagery that has haunted Western philosophical discourse since at least the Enlightenment, and indeed much longer. See, for example, W. J. T. Mitchell's *Iconology* (Chicago: University of Chicago Press, 1986). One could go much further, however, by questioning philosophy's stake in producing the opposition between "word" and "image" as ontologically specific representational activities.

19. See, for example, the essays collected in *Speech and Phenomena, And Other Essays on Husserl's Theory of Signs*, trans. David B. Allison (Evanston: Northwestern University Press, 1973).

20. Cf. *Of Grammatology*, 27-74, and *Positions*, trans. Alan Bass (Chicago: University of Chicago Press, 1981): 18-33 passim. In the *Cours* these arguments are stated in their most direct form in the section entitled "La langue comme pensée organisée dans la matière phonique," 155-58.

SEVEN

Language, Narrative, Subject (2): Narration and Negativity

In all fairness to Peter Wollen, the arguments of " 'Ontology' and 'Materialism in Film' " were not meant to inaugurate a theory of political modernism. Nor does Wollen explicitly set out to produce a rigorous definition of cinema's relation to language or to ideology. Stephen Heath's work on narrative and narrative space, however, may be understood as complementing the issues raised by Wollen in a more direct and thorough way. Inspired by similar anxieties concerning the consequences for a political modernism dominated by the formalist and ontological concerns of the British and North American avant-gardes, the primary objective of Heath's work of the middle seventies was to define the specificity of cinematic *discourse* through an elaboration of its deictic properties, that is, its designations of subjectivity and point of view. Or, in the Kristevan terminology adopted by Heath, the intent of these essays was to define cinema's "specificity as a signifying practice."[1]

Heath's essay on "Narrative Space" is exemplary in this respect. Although respectful of a certain formalism in both experimental film and in film theory, from the beginning Heath displaces any question of distinguishing the problem of narrative from an understanding of spatial and temporal articulations in film. Nor is there any question of portraying narrative as a structure or system that is *a fortiori* a literary modality extrinsic to film. Rather, according to Heath, the specificity of cinematic discourse is defined by its forms of address to a subject. Heath insists on this point from the very first. To understand film's historic relation to an ideology of realism, the era of a descriptive semiology that simply catalogs varieties of spatial and temporal articulations in film must be surpassed in favor of an understanding of cinematic language from the side of its deictic properties.[2] "That reality," writes Heath, "the match of film and world, is a matter of representation, and *representation is in turn a matter of discourse, of the organisation of images, the definition of the 'views,' their construction.* It is the discursive operations that decide the work of a film and ultimately determine the scope of the analogical incidence of the images; in this sense at least, film is a series of languages, a history of codes . . ." (NS 73-74; emphasis mine). In other words, it is the spatial organization of a coherent and continuous vision and point of view, according to the demands of narrative meaning and pleasure, that define cinema's appeal to the spectator and its status as a discourse.

Therefore, Heath's emphasis throughout the first half of "Narrative Space" is the importance of point of view constructions in the organization of space. The control of point view in film is understood as motivating strategies of spatial fragmentation, mobility, reframing, and linkage according to ideals of perspectival centering inherited from Quattrocento optics, as well as the codes of composition, framing, and scene construction embodied in the continuity system of the classic, Hollywood cinema (e.g., 30 and 180 degree rules, matching eyelines, angles, and actions, etc.). Thus Heath describes the formation of narrative space as a deictic process where cinematic discourse is understood from the side of its strategic address to the spectator:

> Within this narrativisation of film, the role of the character-look has been fundamental for the welding of a spatial unity of narrative implication. In so many senses, every film is a veritable drama of vision and this drama has thematically and symptomatically "returned" in film since the very beginning. . . . How to make sense in film if not through vision, film with its founding ideology of vision as truth? . . . [On] the basis of a narrative

organisation of look and point of view that moves space into place through the image-flow; the character, figure of the look, is a kind of perspective within the perspective system, regulating the world, orientating space, providing directions—and for the spectator. (NS 90-91)

Crucial to this conception is the assumption that cinema *qua* cinema has no a priori existence or pure spatial form from which it has deviated historically according to the demands of ideology and its commercial exploitation. Rather a regulated binding of different representational systems—narrative, spatial, figural—has defined historically the realized and unrealized possibilities of cinematic discourse. Here Heath introduces a second point that has profound implications for his particular understanding of the stakes of political modernism. If the exploitation of film by capital has produced an ideology of realism in the cinema, this ideology devolves neither from the imposition of narrative on the purity of spatial representation, nor exactly from the principles of continuity and symmetry that are often claimed as the foundation of the classic, Hollywood cinema. In the analysis of a fragment from Alfred Hitchcock's *Suspicion* (1941) that opens Heath's essay, the classical, symmetrical construction of the scene is found to rely fundamentally on a dissymmetry, an excess, something left over and not accounted for by the system of the film. In this case, it is the formulation of a Hitchcockian gag in the disturbing view of a "post-cubist" painting at the structural center of the scene. This painting momentarily derails the linear progression of the narrative through the enchaining of points of view by distracting and fixing the gaze of one of the police inspectors who have come to inform the character Lina of the death of a friend, a death that reinforces suspicions of her husband's pathological nature. For Heath, it is all the more important that this little allegory—which introduces an authoritative, legalized, indeed policing vision in relation to Lina's "unbalanced" view of her husband—demonstrates within a scene of exemplary classical construction the importance of the "problem of point of view, different framing, disturbance of the law and its inspectoring eye, interruption of the homogeneity of the narrative economy . . ." (NS 71).

Heath's description of the specificity of cinematic discourse
is predicated on two major points, then, and both are crucial
to his version of political modernism. First, Heath insists on
the displacement of an object-oriented film theory (concentration on film form, style, structure) in favor of a theory
founded on the placement of the subject-spectator; or the inscription within cinematic discourse of processes that engage
and direct the sight of the spectator. Second, and perhaps more
importantly, is the concept of *negativity* introduced in the analysis of *Suspicion*. This concept is intricately and insistently tied
to the chain of terms that Heath uses to describe the positioning of the spectator in relation to the narrativization of
space, namely, suture, heterogeneity, and montage. Heath argues that the basis of cinematic pleasure—its fundamental
spectatorial appeal in the potential for movement, mobility,
and continually changing views—is predicated on the strategic
introduction of threats to the system and continuity of the film
text.

In their potential for dissymmetry—for disorienting and decentering the ideal of an all-embracing center through the
linking of continually mobile frames and of movement within
the frame—the narrativizing operations of film incessantly engage a fundamental negativity. For Heath, narrative introduces
the possibility of significance and meaning in cinematic discourse only by preserving the possibility of coherent subjective relations across the erosions of a continually deviating
space: "Narrative contains the mobility that could threaten the
clarity of vision in a constant renewal of perspective; space
becomes place [i.e., a place for the subject to occupy]—narrative as the taking place of film—in a movement which is no
more than the fulfilment of the Renaissance impetus . . ." (NS
83). Negativity is not to be understood, however, as the simple
antithesis of the system of narrative; it is the enabling condition
of that system, its foundation and motive force. In every example, Heath emphasizes that continuity and discontinuity,
symmetry and dissymmetry, and system and negation, are
linked in an ineluctable dialectical ratio. For example, Heath's
discussion of the development of central perspective is organized around the problem of anamorphosis, which simulta-

neously demonstrates that Quattrocento perspective is based on the potential for distortion while serving as the measure for accomplishing the ideal of a unique and embracing pictorial center. Similarly, the allegory of *Suspicion* is meant to demonstrate that classical construction—the continuity, symmetry and pleasure of the scene—is based on the acknowledgment of a figural anamorphosis at its very heart: the deviation of the gaze and the narrative through the presence of a "modernist" painting. Therefore, negativity figures an ever-renewable potential for discontinuity that narrative must recover. And in the allegory of *Suspicion*, the negating force of modernism resides in the marrow of classical construction and its ideological implications.

Heath's conception of negativity does not simply represent a potential for disturbing the system of cinematic discourse. Through the figure of "narrative space" it describes the conditions producing that system. The coding of relations of spatial mobility and continuity, which guarantee the clarity of vision offered by classical narrative, also involves "the negation of space for place" or the constant creation of deictic locales serving to thread the spectator's vision through the linking of shots. Negativity is at the heart of the logic of an ideal center. The appeal of central perspective, with its formulation of an all-embracing and totalizing spectatorial sight, relies on a potential for disruption and destabilization so as to reenact continually the drama of its own centrality and stability. By the same token, it is no coincidence that the trajectory of Heath's arguments describes an arc beginning with Alfred Hitchcock's *Suspicion* in its exemplarity of classical construction, and concluding with an account of Nagisa Oshima's *Death by Hanging* (1968) as a privileged example of what the text of political modernism should hope to accomplish. For the concepts of negativity and narrative space that Heath develops are primarily meant to enable an understanding of how subjective relations in cinematic discourse can be transformed.

To understand Heath's version of political modernism, it is necessary to emphasize how his concept of negativity opposes him to a resolute antiillusionism grounded in an exploration of film's intrinsic materials of expression. Indeed this concept breaks down any strict opposition between realist and modernist forms on the basis of a critique of illusionism or auto-designation of code, which is one of the central tenets of political modernism. For example, Heath clearly states that the appeal to continuity and central perspective, which produces the conditions for a transcendental subjectivity as theorized by Jean-Louis Baudry and Christian Metz, is little more than an *ideal*. A condition that is never finally achieved, it persists only in the forms of its possible displacements. Alternatively, Heath also insists that the ideological effect of classical cinema relies neither on its "invisible" style, nor its effacement of its signs of production, which in turn could be rendered perceptible and cognizable in a modernist gesture. The function of classical narrative style is not to efface the signs of textual production but to *contain* them, or to assure that they are mobilized on the side of continuity, affect, and intelligibility. Heath writes that "film is not a static and isolated object but a series of relations with the spectator it imagines, plays and sets as subject in its movement. The process of film is then perfectly available to certain terms of excess. . . . 'Style' is one such area of such controlled excess, as again, more powerfully, are genres in their specific versions of process (NS 97).

While narrative cannot simply be targeted as the origin of ideological relations in the cinema, neither can cinematic reflexivity be identified unproblematically as a progressive or critical form. For the work of negativity in the form of stylistic excess—so characteristic of genres like the Hollywood musical—is perfectly conducive to the work of the Hollywood cinema and does not in the least challenge its control, regulation, or containment of contradiction.[3] Similarly, where the text of political modernism is concerned, strategies of cinematic "deconstruction" predicated on the autonomization or defamiliarization of cinematic forms (the explicit program of Noel Burch and Jorge Dana for example) must be understood as insufficient. Rather, Heath says, the object of a politically consequent film is to work through the specific forms of spectatorial address, which are functions of the binding of narrative and space, in a manner that disturbs and ultimately cannot be contained.

Therefore, Heath's critique of the antiillusionist argument is based on his suspicion of a formalism that to various degrees eschews narrative. In Heath's view, this is equivalent to misconstruing cinema's deictic and discursive properties, which alone establish the grounds for ideological containment or critique. The "materialist" emphasis of ontological modernism is mistaken, Heath would argue, because it is predicated on the overcoming of contradiction and of establishing with the spectator a relation of identity to the artwork in her or his recognition of the actual or material conditions of cinematic presentation. Alternatively, for Heath the force of negativity or contradiction is never absent from cinematic discourse and can never be fully mastered or contained within it. In fact, it *defines* the possibility of cinematic discourse as such. Thus the problem of political modernism is to decide how and according to what spectatorial relations this force of negativity will be directed.

These arguments are clarified by tracing the influence of Julia Kristeva on Heath's work, specifically in her attempt to establish a "theory of the speaking subject" and to mark the importance of the study of poetic language for any theory of ideology.[4] In a short but provocative essay, "The System and the Speaking Subject," Kristeva summarizes the principal arguments and critiques presented in her work of the late sixties and early seventies.[5] Here she announces the end of a period of semiology (beginning with Saussure and Peirce and extending through Prague school linguistics and structuralism) and inaugurates a "semanalysis" dedicated to the study of "signifying practices." Former conceptions of language, Kristeva argues, were unable to free themselves from the phenomenological foundations of a linguistics that descends from Descartes to Husserl. In this philosophical context, language is considered only as an act carried out by a "thetic subject" or "transcendental ego." This subject verifies its ideality and its presence to thought through the field of speech, and its mastery of truth through the concept of the linguistic *system*, by abstracting the subject from history, society, and the body. In this manner, rational communication is guaranteed through the construction of a totally immanent relation—a strict system of identity and exchange between linguistic system and subject. More importantly, this system is judged as idealist in its bracketing out of external forces that could disturb or disrupt its self-identity.

Kristeva admires these views for their advancement of formal logic. Nevertheless, she insists that their centrality in the philosophy of language must now be challenged by the discoveries of psychoanalysis; specifically, Freud and Lacan's demonstration of the subject's division in language between the conscious and unconscious mind, and in the relation of the symbolic to the imaginary in the articulation of the drives.

> The theory of meaning now stands at a cross-road: either it will remain an attempt at formalizing meaning-systems by increasing sophistication of the logico-mathematical tools which enable it to formulate models on the basis of a conception (already rather dated) of meaning as the act of a *transcendental ego*, cut off from its body, its unconscious, and also its history; or else it will attune itself to the theory of the speaking subject as a divided subject (conscious/unconscious) and go on to attempt to specify the types of operation characteristic of the two sides of this split; thereby exposing them to those forces extraneous to the logic of the systematic; exposing them, that is to say, on the one hand, to bio-physiological processes (themselves already inescapably part of signifying processes; what Freud labelled "drives"), and, on the other hand, to social constraints (family structures, modes of production, etc.). (SSS 6)

These "forces extraneous to the logic of the systematic," above all the force of the drives as the investment and regulation of desire in representation, are associated throughout Kristeva's work with the concept of negativity whose privileged space of analysis is poetic language, especially the avant-gardes represented by Stéphane Mallarmé, Lautréamont, Antonin Artaud, and Georges Bataille.

Kristeva's semanalysis also privileges a discourse of political modernism. For it is through the study of avant-garde poetic language, in the light of a marriage between semiology and psychoanalysis, that she hopes to renovate linguistics and open it up to the demands of a critique of ideology. Kristeva argues that the first semiology protracted its notion of system and the subject by barricading itself within a strictly utilitarian view of language. This conception of language—defined as an instrumental exchange between fully reciprocal parties through the agency of a common code—ignored the no less powerful social functions of language including transgression, pleasure, and the articulation of desire in art, ritual, and poetic language. Therefore, Kristeva founds semanalysis on a critique of linguistic science by uncovering "what is in the poetical process which falls outside the realm of the signified and the transcendental ego and makes of that which we call 'literature' something other than knowledge: the very place where the social code is destroyed and renewed."[6]

This notion of a force of exclusion or repression that both founds and exceeds the identity of the linguistic system is characteristic of Kristeva's definition of the work of negativity. Drawn explicitly from Hegel, this term situates semanalysis as a dialectical method that studies the process of meaning through the contradictions suppressed by the linguistic system, and that always return to confound the system's exclusivity, homogeneity, and continuity.

> We can now grasp all the ambiguities of *semanalysis*: on the one hand it demystifies the logic at work in the elaboration of every transcendental reduction and, for this purpose, requires the study of each signifying system as a practice. Thus intent on revealing the negativity which Hegel had seen at work beneath all rationality but which, by a masterly stroke, he subordinated to absolute knowledge, *semanalysis* can be thought of as the direct successor of the dialectical method; but the dialectic it continues will be one which will at last be genuinely materialist since it recognizes the *materiality*—the *heterogeneity*—of that negativity whose concrete base Hegel was unable to see and which mechanistic Marxists have reduced to a merely economic externality. (SSS 9)

By "materiality" Kristeva undoubtedly refers to the presence of the body to sense, that is, the grounding of signification in the biophysiological origination of the drives. The concept of "heterogeneity," which is ineluctably tied to her sense of materiality, thus introduces an idea already familiar from Heath's comments. Kristeva wishes to replace the study of the

language system with that of the "semiotic disposition" of signifying practices by "specifying just what, within the practice,
falls outside the system and characterizes the specificity of the
practice as such" (SSS 4-5). Heath's account of *Suspicion* is
exemplary of this logic. For what characterizes his view of the
classical conception of the scene, and what permits him to
specify this classicism in its continuity, symmetry, and systematic development, is the recognition that only by transgressing
its own rules can the Hollywood cinema celebrate the triumph
of its narrative and spatial system as the perpetual recontain-
ment of those elements threatening to disrupt or destabilize
it.

Similarly, Kristeva writes that "The moment of transgression
is the key moment in practice:

> we can speak of practice wherever there is a transgression of
> systematicity, i.e., a transgression of the unity proper to the
> *transcendental ego.* The subject of the practice cannot be the
> transcendental subject, who lacks the shift, the split in logical
> unity brought about by language which separates out, within
> the signifying body, the symbolic order from the workings of
> the libido (this last revealing itself by the *semiotic disposition*).
> Identifying the semiotic disposition means in fact identifying
> the shift in the speaking subject, his capacity for renewing the
> order in which he is inescapably caught up; and that capacity
> is, for the *subject,* the capacity for enjoyment. (SSS 7)

According to Kristeva, the forms of pleasure produced by a
signifying practice are measured by the relations of negativity
that inhabit it, transgress its borders, and open it up to ever-
renewable signifying chains. Similar to the way in which Freud
identified the work of the unconscious in jokes, parapraxes,
and slips of the tongue, the work of negativity is marked by
identifiable structural features of poetic language; for example,
deviations of syntax, disturbances of grammaticality, and the
play of metaphor and metonymy, as well as nonlinguistic features such as rhythm and intonation. But more importantly, a
necessary condition for comprehending the semiotic disposition of a given practice is understanding how these structural
features—which are part of its phenomemal form and its consciously derived symbolic system—are in fact generated by the

primary processes. The specificity of any practice is thus paradoxically described by locating *within* it a force that can only
be *external* to it; that is, the unconscious, the imaginary, and
the work of the drives.[7]

Heath's critique of a "phenomenological formalism" in the
discourse of the contemporary, cinematic avant-gardes, is clarified in light of Kristeva's shift to a poststructural semiotic.
Similarly, in Wollen's account strategies of semiotic reduction
in ontological modernism can be understood as equivalent to
the demand of a phenomenological linguistics to bracket out
all externalities, thereby producing the artwork as a totally
immanent object serving to predicate the subject of a pure
perception. Where Wollen's worry is a forgetting of "language," through Kristeva Heath targets another fundamental
problem. By concentrating on the production of a totally immanent object, which stands outside of society, history, and
ideology, ontological and phenomenological modernisms in a
sense forget the subject. They assume that spectatorial relations are solely determined by the formal procedures structuring the avant-garde text.

Therefore, the concept of negativity serves multiple functions in Kristeva's theory as well as in Heath's. Whereas Kristeva specifies poetic language as an example of one type of
signifying practice, in point of fact, the poetic avant-gardes are
the privileged origin of her theory. In other words, they do
not derive from the theory as a type; they are its originary
object. Similarly, I have argued that the questions of ideology
and of the ideological analysis of the classic, realist text in
contemporary film theory have in fact been superintended by
the discourse of political modernism and the attempt to define
a politically consequent avant-garde aesthetic practice. This is
nowhere more clear than in Heath's arguments concerning
narrative space. The centrality of the problem of pleasure and
the implication of the desire of the subject is also emphasized
in Kristeva's concept of negativity. Here the possibility of pleasure resides in the potentiality of transgression: that which is
heterogeneous to the system as the ordering of the drives. To
release pleasure, and to renovate and perpetuate its cultural
function, the aesthetic code must endanger itself. It must open

itself up to the articulation of the drives and to the production of new signifying chains and relations of desire that it might not be able to contain. This is a point that Heath finds provocative and appealing. The moment of transgression or negativity is proper to all aesthetic discourse. It defines precisely, for both Kristeva and Heath, the aesthetic function. And especially for Heath, the question of political modernism is whether transgression is mobilized toward containment—reaffirming the illusory unity of the transcendental ego—or whether it opens itself to the possibilities of contradiction that found the idea of a textual system.

Implicit in Heath, however, is a question of generic distinctions (realist foreclosure of contradiction versus modernist opening to contradiction) that is not clearly the case in Kristeva's theory of poetic language. But a more striking problem presents itself when Heath's version of negativity is compared with Kristeva's critique of the transcendental subject. In Kristeva's theory, the notion of "system" is intimately tied to the problem of "meaning," or rather, the subjective relation in the production of meaning. While the formal system of poetic language is characterized by the disorienting imbrication of the drives—whose biological orientation Kristeva insists upon— by a curious reversal, it also seems capable of producing that disorientation or "dis-position" *in* the subject. Kristeva writes that the semiology of signifying practices "is ready to give a hearing to any or all of those efforts which, ever since the *elaboration of a new position for the speaking subject,* have been renewing and reshaping the status of meaning within social exchanges *to a point where the very order of language is being renewed*: Joyce, Burroughs, Sollers. This is a moral gesture, inspired by a concern to make intelligible, and therefore socializable, what rocks the foundations of sociality" (SSS 10).

In a theory that proceeds from a critique of communication as exchange, a fundamental reciprocity between object and subject seems possible. The revolution in poetic language is understood as producing the possibility of a revolutionary subjectivity. In general, neither Wollen nor Heath questions this idea and indeed its centrality is axiomatic in the discourse of political modernism. In Kristeva, however, this potential only arises in virtue of the privileged relation that poetic language holds with the *presence* of the body. I underscore this term to emphasize the criteria of tactile and sensual experience that Kristeva insists upon in her definition of poetic discourse. Poetic language, music, dance, painting, in fact every instance of artistic practice described by Kristeva requires, on one hand, the presence of the subject as the inscriptional force of his hand or body in the construction of the aesthetic object.[8] On the other hand, while Kristeva leaves this practice untheorized from the side of reception, the categories of reading implied by her theory also require the spatial and temporal copresence of object and subject. The question of mechanical reproducibility—the practices of photography or cinema, and in fact any aesthetic practice founded on the criterion of *absence* or the placing of its audience in a relation of alterity or seriality—is addressed in her theory only with difficulty.[9] To use once again Jakobson's model of the communication act for comparison, it is clear that Kristeva questions the self-identity of this model's punctual moments (addresser, addressee) while leaving intact the remainder of the logocentric apparatus: intersubjective reciprocity, dialectic on the model of dialog, and the intrinsic link between signifier and signified in the form of an identity between subject and object. Simply put, the materialist aspect of Kristeva's theory of poetic language is predicated on an immanent relation between phonetically organized sound and a bodily or biological orientation associated with Freud's theory of the drives. Moreover, the concept of heterogeneity is itself doubly circumscribed: by the immanent relation between system and the speaking subject (which is not in the least contradicted by the idea of heterogeneity), and the bounded space of the subject's body in relation to its speech. In Kristeva's phonological orientation, language still derives from an immanent relation to Being, even if that relation is foreclosed from the subject. Therefore, poetic writing (*écriture*) can only be understood as the interested simulacrum of speech (*parole*).

The difficulties of Wollen's version of political modernism, also founded on a phonocentric model, have already been discussed. Does Heath's theory of narrative space confront similar problems? Although sharing Kristeva's insistence on the importance of negativity and the theory of the drives, Heath does not necessarily subscribe to her emphasis on the biophysiological grounding of signification. Moreover, his emphasis on a theory of narrative discourse seems to obviate the problems posed by a phonocentric conception of poetic language. Instead, the expressly psychoanalytic direction of Heath's essay develops a theory of cinematic identification based on the concept of *suture*.

The concept of suture has been so widely debated in contemporary film theory that it would be redundant to provide a gloss here.[10] As introduced to Lacanian psychoanalytic theory by Jacques-Alain Miller to describe the logic of the signifier in its relation to the subject, the concept of suture was meant neither to offer an account of aesthetic discourse nor to be extendable to problems of subjectivity and aesthetic practice.[11] Through a reading of Gottlieb Frege, Miller offers a brilliant and difficult analysis of Lacan's conception of the relation of the subject to the field of its speech, as well as a convincing indictment of empiricist epistemologies and the identity theory of knowledge. However, the silence of Miller's essay on the question of aesthetic uses of language is deafening. Nor does it necessarily offer the terms for identifying the subject's relation to speech with the question of deixis as part of the formal system of discursive acts. Yet, curiously, in a passage that purports to be a direct gloss on Miller's essay, Heath characterizes the work of suture in the following terms: as a relation where "the signifier is the narration of the subject" (NS 98). The question of narrative or narration appears nowhere in Miller's analysis. And indeed Heath's characterization of suture by this term, in its suggestion of an activity of predication of one entity by another, can only be understood as a radical reduction of Miller's intricate and complex critique of causality. However, Heath does not simply misconstrue or misunderstand Miller's arguments. In this respect, it is worth citing Heath's gloss at length.

> In psychoanalysis, "suture" refers to the relation of the individual as subject to the chain of its discourse where it figures missing in the guise of a stand-in; the subject is an effect of the

signifier in which it is represented, stood in for, taken place (the signifier is the narration of the subject). [Here Heath footnotes Miller.] Ideological representation turns on—supports itself from—this "initial" production of the subject in the symbolic order (hence the crucial role of psychoanalysis, as prospective science of the construction of the subject, within historical materialism), directs it as a set of images and fixed positions, metonymy stopped into fictions of coherence. What must be emphasised, however, is that stopping—the functioning of suture in image, frame, narrative, etc.—is exactly a *process*: it counters a productivity, an excess, that it states and restates in the very moment of containing in the interests of coherence. . . . (NS 98-99)

Heath's reading of Miller yields three observations. First, Heath assumes as given the originary status of suture or its "initial" production of the subject in language. What begins in Miller's essay as an analysis of the relation of the subject to *its* speech is rendered, without further argument or comment on its specifically linguistic context, as a general theory of discourse including aesthetic discourse. Perhaps such an extension is possible. But the point is that Heath has already accepted it as given.[12] Second, it is also given that the concept of suture is virtually synonymous with Heath's conception of negativity. Although the coefficients of "zero and lack" in relation to the identity of the subject are fundamental to Miller's notion of suture, it is neither clear nor given that these concepts, which are an intervention in Lacan's "algebra," have any relation to the theory of the drives or a sense of negativity as heterogeneity or excess. Third, the desire to equate suture with a theory of narration leads Heath to identify, on the one hand, the speech of the subject and the linking of shots with the concept of a discursive chain or series. On the other, if in Miller the signifier is understood as a "place-holder" [*tenant-lieu*] for the subject, this idea has already been interpreted by Heath as being coextensive with deictic forms, including point of view structures in film, as "signifiers of subjectivity." All of which is to say that suture, which is invoked by Heath as the a priori foundation for narrative space as a theory of ideology, appears as a concept already worked through by the theory it is supposed to justify.

It is certain that Miller reasserts the Lacanian axiom that the subject is an effect of the signifier. "We must hold together," he writes, "the definitions which make the subject *the effect of the signifier* and the signifier *the representative of the subject*: it is a circular, though non-reciprocal, relation" ("Suture," 34). But with respect to Heath's adaptation of Miller for a theory of narrative space, it is necessary to ask the following questions. What criterion or what desire necessitates the identification of suture with a theory of narration? What is at stake in insisting that "ideological representation *directs* the subject *as* a set of images"? These questions set in place Heath's version of political modernism.

These questions are clarified by Heath's essay "Screen Images, Film Memory,"—a product of the 1976 Edinburgh Film Festival event on "Psychoanalysis/Cinema/Avant-Garde" and a text contemporaneous with "Narrative Space." There is little doubt that the term *suture* is attractive to Heath for its succinct and suggestive description of a discursive "join" between the textual system of a film and the spectator it solicits. It also enables him to shift between a semiotic and a psychoanalytic conception of text where questions of identification, pleasure, and the desire of the subject can be formulated. In "Screen Images, Film Memory," he employs another, equally privileged term to perform similar rhetorical work—*montage*. In the first line of this essay, Heath discovers in Lacan's XIth *Séminaire* a direct invocation of this cinematic term to identify and specify the work of the drives.[13] From here on, the term *montage* accomplishes a peculiar condensation where a semiotic concern with spatial construction in film (e.g., the analysis of deictic structures) and Lacanian psychoanalysis are identified as members of the same theoretical set. In fact, the rhetorical work of "montage" in Heath's essay links inseparably a description of the economy of the drives with an account of cinematic discursive features as "montage constructions"; in short, narrative space.

Having erected a bridge between film semiotics and psychoanalysis—that is, between the problem of cinematic narrative/spatial construction and a theory of the subject—Heath addresses two problems. The first problem describes the relation between the structural activity of cinematic (narrative) discourse and the production of a subject. Here Lacan's reference to the term *montage* allows Heath to reprise Kristeva's physiobiological orientation towards the work of negativity in a less forceful and direct way, and thus to locate a join between system and (bodily) subject, the symbolic and the imaginary. Moreover, if the representation and work of the drives is accomplished by "montage" as a certain psychic work, it seems possible that montage as a work of cinematic signification, in its formulation of the possibilities of identification and of the organization and direction of the spectator's vision, could direct the economy of the drives. This provocative claim rests implicit in Heath's argument. He equates spectatorial activity with its narrative representation in film (above all with acts of seeing and representations of point of view) in a logic that is no longer one of analogy. The narrative process "directs [the subject] as a set of images" in a "perpetual retotalisation of the imaginary" (NS 98 and 99). In this manner, the operations of discourse are transformed within the field of a *look* or a *mise-en-regard* that equates problems of perception and the imaginary as a specific space of libidinal investment. Similarly, Heath characterizes this relation between spectator and text as "a reciprocal process of intelligibility" (SIFM 35). And when discussing larger questions of the relation between ideological representation and the formation of the subject, Heath invokes a familiar analogy with Saussure's metaphor of the relation between signified and signifier as the recto and verso of a sheet of paper. Narrative text and subject, symbolic and imaginary, "montage" as representation and drive: these two sets of activities, then, are indestructibly linked and structurally equivalent; the border between them is undecidable.

The second problem in Heath's argument proposes an understanding of the "dialectical" relation between, on the one hand, the cinemas of Alfred Hitchcock and Max Ophuls, and on the other, the work of Malcolm LeGrice or Ken Jacobs as well as that of Eisenstein, Vertov, Godard-Gorin, Straub-Huillet, and Wollen-Mulvey. His assertion that ideological representation *directs* the subject *as a set of images* thus suggests a generic distinction between two sorts of signifying practice in film. In the concluding paragraphs of "Screen Images, Film Memory," Heath states that

It will have become evident in the course of these notes that "film" has often been used as an abbreviation for "film in its dominant historical development and exploitation." The question is open, in other words, as to alternative practices, other cinemas.
     With regard to that open question, three brief remarks. Firstly, from the perspective of what has been said here, narrative remains a necessary and directly avant-garde concern: to transform narrative and its narration of film is to render problematic the relation established between spectator as subject and work in the images of the novelistic, the memory-spectacle. Secondly, this is not, cannot be some simple "destruction" of narrative, some "emptying" of meaning or whatever; rather, it is an insistence on the production in film of contradictions, including the contradictions of that production. . . . Thirdly, to attempt such a production . . . is to pose film exactly as montage in its multiple possibility of engaging drive, its *critical* potential for pleasure. (SIFM 42)

Here Heath's conception of narrative space is clearly rendered by the discourse of political modernism. His concern is less with the classical, Hollywood cinema ("film in its dominant historical development and exploitation") than with posing the possibility of an oppositional and critical aesthetic practice. What remains to be understood is Heath's conception of the *text* of political modernism and the role for the subject decided therein. As Heath asks in his brief analysis of Peter Wollen and Laura Mulvey's *Penthesilea* (1974) in "Narrative Space": "what is a film that speaks, speaks politically? how is the point to be arrived at from which such a question can be formulated in film?" (NS 108).

The concluding statement of "Screen Images, Film Memory" also repeats Heath's principal criticisms of ontological modernism: that there can be no simple opposition between narrative form and film form as distinct ontological entities; that the identification of narrative with the ideological function of cinematic practice is false insofar as one believes the deconstruction or eschewal of narrative produces a perception free of ideology; and therefore the avant-gardes have failed to recognize the importance of narrative as a terrain for working through, in, and against problems of ideology and representation. Heath wishes to retain the problem of narrative because, in describing a dialectic between narrative deixis and cinematic spatial construction, his account of narrative binds semiology and psychoanalysis together in the attempt to propose a materialist theory weighted toward the cultural production of subjectivity rather than the artistic production of texts. In the debate over what counts as a geniunely materialist film practice that sustains its spectator in a "critical" relation, the most damning charge is that of *formalism*—that is, the desire for the production of a totally immanent object or the production of an autonomous form that escapes or circumvents the determinations of ideology. In "Narrative Space," Heath concludes his critique of the current avant-gardes by asserting that

> the narrative space of film is today not simply a theoretical and practical actuality but is a crucial and political avant-garde problem in a way which offers perspectives on the existing terms of that acutality. Deconstruction is quickly the impasse of formal device, an aesthetics of transgression when the need is an activity of transformation, and a politically consequent materialism in film is not to be expressed as veering contact past internal content in order to proceed with "film as film" but rather as a work on the constructions and relations of meaning and subject in a specific signifying practice in a given sociohistorical situation, a work that is then much less on "codes" than on the operations of narrativisation. At its most effectively critical, moreover, that work may well bear little resemblance to what in the given situation is officially acknowledged and defined as "avant-garde"; in particular, and in the context of the whole account offered here of film and space, it may well involve an action at the limits of narrative within the narrative film, at the limits of its fictions of unity. (NS 108-09)

In Heath's view, this action at the limits of narrative involves the modalization of negativity through montage structures to direct or orient the possibility of subjective relations in film. Further, this modalization is governed by the concept of suture. It is worth repeating that for Heath, negativity is not only the foundation of *every* aesthetic practice, classical or avant-garde, it also defines the classical, narrative cinema through its containment of a force that continually threatens to erode the unity of its forms of spectator address. In "Screen Images, Film Memory," this dynamic is described in the following terms:

> Cinema and film can be posed with reference to their own elaboration of a suturing effect: the apparatus of cinema functions— is perfected to function—on the basis of the reconstitution of continuity from a succession of differences; film with narrative's control lays out the images as an uninterrupted direction of sense, the narrative image. The latter returns us to the organization of space. In its narrative layout, film moves against heterogeneity; the elsewhere of every image, every shot, must be recaptured for the film as the unbroken alignment of desire and subject. (SIFM 38)

Here the classical narrative cinema is understood to obey the order of the Lacanian symbolic in a much different sense than in Wollen's account. Rather than characterizing the symbolic as a semiotic metalanguage that brings speech and therefore theory to the dangerous lure of the image, Heath understands the regulatory effect of the symbolic—in its ordering of discourse, desire, and subjectivity—in a way closer to Kristeva. The symbolic—which is dialectically inseparable from negativity as desire, the imaginary, the drives—functions in the order of discourse to manage the subject's relation to contradiction according to the constraints of the reigning social norms of knowledge and behavior. In formal term it irreversibly directs sense, assures homogeneity, and synchronizes the subject, as it were, to the flow of images.

But what is most important in Heath's argument is that "elsewhere which must be recaptured," or the alternative possibility that must be articulated, in the form of a different relation of subjectivity. Kristeva expresses this demand in the form of an ethics, "a moral gesture, inspired by a concern to make intelligible, and therefore socializable, what rocks the foundations of sociality. . . . [The] subject of the semiotic metalanguage must, however briefly, call himself in question, must emerge from the protective shell of a transcendental ego within a logical system, and so restore his connexion with that negativity—drive-governed, but also social, political and historical—which rends and renews the social code" (SSS 10-11). Heath actually pushes further this tentative and conservative formulation by using the concept of suture to extend Kristeva's concept of negativity in a more radical direction. As Heath presses toward the conclusion of "Narrative Space," he cites Merleau-Ponty's comment in "Le Cinéma et la nouvelle psychologie" that " 'the aspect of the world would be transformed if we succeeded in seeing as *things* the intervals between things'. The formulation can now be recast: the relations of the subject set by film—its vision, its address—would be radically transformed if the intervals of its production were opened in their negativity, if the fictions of the closure of those intervals were discontinued, found in all the contradiction of their activity" (NS 107).

In this passage, Heath represents negativity as if it literally articulated the potential for a revolutionary subjectivity. Suffice it to say that for Heath, suture—in its imaging of the spectatorial relation and in its narration of the subject through the possibilities of montage—is bound to the concept of negativity as the forms in which negativity is modalized in different signifying practices.

What Kristeva expresses as an ethical gesture in the domain of theory now achieves an epistemological value in relation to textual practice in Heath's specific appeal to Freudian theory. Whereas for Kristeva psychoanalytic theory responds to the necessity of reintroducing an account of the drives and the body to semiotic theory, in a striking moment in "Screen Images, Film Memory," Heath extends this appeal in an interesting direction: Freudian interpretive theory becomes a model for the narrative text of political modernism. Heath proposes that Freud's writings reveal two distinct theories of fiction or phantasy that are then associated, in Heath's argument, with two potentialities of narrative in their enunciation of desire. The first theory is linked to Freud's analyses of *Familienroman* or "family romances." Heath describes this set of narrative-phantasies as conservative and normative. Subservient to the reality principle, these are phantasies "in which the subject is staged in modified and corrected relations with its parents; the fictioning production serves to regulate and unify, to hold tight in the imaginary" (SIFM 39). Freud's later work in *Beyond the Pleasure Principle*, however, is read as an alternative theory of fiction that "displaces the aim of simple, coherent mastery" contained in the first. Heath focuses on the example of the "fort/da game" where Freud analyzed his grandson's symbolization of his mother's absence through the repetitive casting away of a spool while crying *"Fort!"* ("Gone!"), then retrieving it with a string exclaiming, *"Da!"* ("There!").

In this unending repetition, where the imaginary and the force of negativity continually return to erode the ego's mastery of loss, Heath discovers the potentiality of political modernism. In this eternal return, he emphasizes, the pleasure of fiction is linked fundamentally to negativity as a dialectic of presence and absence that continually transgresses the limits of the symbolic activity seeking to contain it. More importantly, this repetition presents the ever-renewable possibility of creating a new position for the subject to occupy. In Heath's terms it is an "unsuring" of the subject in the effacement of the limits between imagination and reality: "This effacing of limits is not a correction, the cohesion of a position-image, but a disturbance, a perpetual slide of signified into signifier and, in that process, of the subject's representations. What *Beyond the Pleasure Principle* then does is to pose the process directly in its negativity and thus pleasure itself—as in play, fiction— as an alternating, contradictory force, a *time* that contains its own beyond . . ." (SIFM 39).

According to Heath, how and according to what possibilities can this "alternative, contradictory force" be articulated in film? In the next paragraph, Heath reasserts a link that returns us full circle to the opening gambit of "Screen Images, Film Memory." Montage—as the fundamental structuring principle of film space—is expressly tied to negativity and the force of the drives in an equation that opposes the formal values of unity and heterogeneity in a specific field of action. In Straub, for example, Heath locates that "difficult time" in film in a particular conception of space.

> . . . the space articulated in film is punctuated at every moment
> by the heterogeneity of its process (over framing, camera move-
> ment, sound/image lays, shot joins. . .), of its montage (in the
> widest sense of the term; the sense in which Godard-Gorin could
> talk of montage as "the principal political notion", in which
> Vertov, working for heterogeneity as against the unity of subject
> representation, could talk of a Kino-Eye film as being constantly
> "in montage"). Negation on negativity, phasing on disphasure,
> cinema as fiction-machine knows in its films something of the
> bipolarising tension grasped by Freud in the movement of the
> *fort/da* game: film runs across the subject that runs through the
> film, as the game loses its experience of a central presence in
> a radical excentering. It is this run that narrative is used to hold,
> to suspend in image and representation. (SIFM 39-40)

To unpack the logic at work here, it is necessary to understand the condensation that conjoins the multiple senses of the
term *montage*. Three notions must be indestructibly linked for
Heath's version of political modernism to hold: first, montage
as a figure of cinematic spatial construction, above all in its
relegation of point of view; second, montage as a principle of
"political activity" in aesthetic practice whose decisive measure is the mobilization of the "bipolar tensions" of narrative;
and third, montage as the modalization of negativity that works
either for or against the bolstering of unified subject-positions
against the heterogeneity introduced by the investment of the
drives in narrative representation.

In order to accomplish a political action through aesthetic
practice, this condensation also posits the necessary equiva-
lency of "montage" and "suture." Here the idea of the "narration of the subject" is strictly identified with the formal possibilities of deictic representation in the film text, that is, its
organization of point of view and its threading of the spectator's vision therein. Therefore, categories of subjectivity or
the representation of subjectivity seem to be unilaterally determined by the formal possibilities for the articulation, or
strategic disarticulation, of space. In a brief account of Straub/
Huillet's sound/image montage practice in "Narrative Space,"
Heath states that in their films

> It is the coherence of the *fiction* that falls: the fiction film dis-
> respects space [i.e., fragments and reorients it] in order to con-

struct a unity that will bind spectator and film in its fiction; where a Godard breaks space, fragments and sets up oppositions in the interests of analysis ("analysis with image and sound"), Straub/Huillet film a unity, sound and image, in and off, that will never 'make a scene'; in both cases, the address is complex, in process, no longer the single and central vision but a certain freedom of contradictions. (NS 101)

Similarly, in the concluding section of the essay, he accords to the films of Nagisa Oshima (especially *Death by Hanging*) a privileged status among the narratives of political modernism: "The films have an immediate presence of narrative articulation but that presence in each case *presents the absence of another film* the discourse of which, punctuating this film and its space, finds its determinations, its contradictions, its negativity. Split *in* the narrativisation, the films are thus out of true with—out of 'the truth' of—any single address: the subject divided in complexes of representation and their contradictory relations" (NS 109; first emphasis mine).

Across the the sign of negativity in its relations with montage, narrative film contains within itself the possibility of another practice or another potential articulation of space, and thus if one closely follows Heath's reasoning, a "different" articulation of the subject. Earlier I mentioned that for Heath the concept of suture was tied to negativity through the forms of relations it established in different signifying practices. However, it should now be clear that that "difference" can only be expressed in the formula of "either/or." Strongly characteristic of the discourse of political modernism, this binary logic marks the retention of a certain structuralist, and indeed, formalist bias in arguments that purport to be poststructuralist.

From here, two sets of observations are necessary. One involves problems of textual form and system in Heath; the other concerns Heath's attribution of epistemological values to the narrative forms of Freud's case histories.

In Heath's version of political modernism, the term *negativity* performs a complex rhetorical work: it organizes his theoretical discourse by opening a potential for formal reversibility that is controlled and delimited by a precise set of binary oppositions. Within Heath's writings of this period, this logic of binarism is as striking as it is intricate. This logic, which freely intermixes "montage forms" with "forms of subjectivity," may be summarized in the following tabulation of binary terms— continuity:heterogeneity :: unity:multiplicity :: closed:open :: limit:disturbance :: linearity:freeplay :: binding:breaking :: singular address:multiple address :: fiction:analysis :: "familienroman":"fort/da game" :: correction:criticism :: Truth:contradiction :: regulation:freedom. When Heath writes in "Narrative Space" that "the relations of the subject set by film—its vision, its address—would be radically transformed if the intervals of its production were opened in their negativity," or in "Screen Images, Film Memory" that the radicality of Vertov's montage practice is based on "working for the heterogeneity as against the unity of subject representation," a formalism is exposed as it binds itself to certain values—for example, contradiction, criticism, analysis, freedom. For if the potential of montage as a political practice is to be preserved, and if the goal of that practice is the radical transformation of subjectivity through its representations, *then the subject can be considered in no other way than as identical with its formal representations*, regardless of whether those forms are "closed" or "opened" in their negativity, or whether they are organized according to principles of continuity or heterogeneity, linearity or freeplay, and so on. Heath may have shifted the grounds on which the texts of modernism are privileged from the point of view of a generic definition (e.g., narrative versus nonnarrative), but where the question of the subject is concerned, there is ample reason to demand whether he has achieved a break in the theorization of their forms and effects.

This formal, binary logic also structures Heath's reading of Freud and his epistemological valuation of psychoanalytic theory, above all in relation to the case histories. In "Screen Images, Film Memory," psychoanalytic interpretive practice is granted a privileged formal function. Freud's case histories (e.g., Dora, the Rat Man, and the Wolf Man) are invoked neither as models of reading nor as a specific hermeneutic activity, but rather as specific narrative forms. Indeed they are the preferred form of a narrative, political modernism.[14] In the dif-

ficult relation that links yet differentiates the *Familienroman*
narrative and the case histories in Heath's reading, psychoanalytic theory becomes the measure of an epistemological relation in narrative, but only according to the following condition: that it is a knowledge produced from *within* the narrative
text. The knowledge that is recalcitrant in the "family ro-
mance" as the foundation of the novelistic is reproduced in
the narrational structure of the case histories as critical knowledge. Between the two forms of "stories," a space of reversal
is engendered where psychoanalysis is understood as "the novelistic from the other side, the production *in it* of a critical
knowledge of its terms, its instances, its movements, its reasons. Indeed, what are the Dora, Rat Man or Wolf Man case
histories as Freud writes them but the novel overturned (where
'overturned' indicates a work in and against)?" (SIFM 41). In
the next paragraph, Heath emphasizes that psychoanalysis, in
its privileged relation to the theory of the subject, is "crucial
for any *political* understanding." Thus one last set of binary
terms is presented. The required passage from "fiction" to
"knowledge" is a movement that only occurs from *within* narrative discourse. Narrative must find and articulate, inside its
formal border, the outside, the elsewhere, the negativity engendering it.

The decisiveness of the term *montage* for Heath's version of
political modernism can now be fully elaborated. Although it
contains multiple meanings it is not polysemic; it serves not
to disseminate the threads of Heath's arguments but to knot
them together in a rigorously bounded space. Most importantly, in Heath's analysis the term *montage* binds together the
concepts of narration and negativity, the term *suture* being
one description of this binding. This is the point of the essay
on "narrative space": to define a concept that decides the
forms of subject-address, and the placement of the subject, as
the "dialectical" conversion of narrational and spatial systems
organized according to an economy of regulative, deictic forms.
The problem of the articulation of textual systems, of narrativity in relation to spatial construction and linkage of shots,
and finally the investment of the subject's vision or the scopic/
invocatory drives through the determinations of point of view

all become identified with their formal organization through "montage." This term collects within its semantic boundaries the binary terms generated by Heath's argument and organizes them in an equivocal way. It is no longer possible to decide whether the problem of montage refers to a theory of the text or of the subject, to problems of aesthetic form or of the libidinal investment of the spectator. For the relations between subject and object are fully reciprocal, exchangeable, or transposable within it.

This undecidability does not go unmastered in Heath's analysis. A final accounting must be made of the peculiar Hegelianism introduced to his work through the concept of negativity as adapted from Kristeva. Kristeva unambiguously shows respect for the Hegelian dialectic and the Hegelian origins of her conceptualization of negativity. In Heath, however, Hegel most clearly appears at those symptomal points where a rhetorical appeal is made to the *Aufhebung* of the Hegelian dialectic.[15] Heath's dialectical conception of narrative space and its work for the spectator encompasses a scenography of conversion. The process of narrative space, as an incessant passage from one state (the continual fragmentation of mobile frames) to another (the linkages at the level of the frame and the succession of shots ordered by narrative), is ultimately described by this concept familiar to philosophy: "The need is to cut up and then join together in a kind of spatial *Aufhebung* that decides *a superior unity, the binding of the spectator in the space of the film*, the space it realises" (NS 86; my emphasis).

Explicitly or implicitly, as the case may be, the Hegelian *Aufhebung* resolves the oscillation of Heath's binary logic into a definable hierarchization of terms: the forms of the text, indeed the problem of textual formation or formalization, must foreordain the presence of the subject. The more closely one reads Heath, the more it becomes evident that his dialectic resolves itself in the text-object that must logically precede the presence of any subject. Nor can the subject appear or be considered in its identity as such until the forms of this anteriority have been resolved. Narrative space, in its elaboration of deixis in film, thus becomes the formal design of the subject within the space of the text; indeed it decides the forms in which the subject is "visualized." Whether one is addressing the style of the classical, Hollywood cinema or that of a politically consequent modernism, in Heath's account of narrative space textual systems are defined by particular processes of *narrativization*, that is, the coding of spatial relations as deictic markers that direct the spectator's vision according to the demands of a narrative sense. Since the force of negativity may be mobilized either for the purposes of the continuity or disunity of the deictic system of a film, it may formulate textual, narrative economies that, to varying degrees, either contain or liberate contradiction.

But more importantly, Heath argues that the narrative economy of a given film, and the spatial/spectatorial relations characterizing its textual system, are determined by "the spectator it imagines" (NS 97). A subtle rhetorical strategy is at play here that profoundly characterizes the theory of the subject in the discourse of political modernism. While Heath justifiably criticizes a political modernism defined too reductively through an idea of form or structure, his own notions of system and subject are endowed at another level with their own willful autonomy and identity: the system imagines, acts, in fact, performs a subject. Paradoxically, the idea of "system" here, which is only meant to be a powerful theoretical fiction, is endowed with a body and a will: it formulates itself according to the addressee it imagines. The idea of negativity thus perpetuates a particular utopian space. It inscribes, as the foundation of every narrative system, the possibility of the transformation of its subjective relations. And this possibility is always present in the forms of transgression or negation of the system that must be mobilized to reenact the drama of its unity. Within the constraints of Heath's theory, it is no longer so much a question of the subject's libidinal investment in given signifying practices as the text's imagination, "visualization," or bringing into form of its subject. The term *Aufhebung*, then, appears precisely when Heath must describe a vanishing point where the formal categories of montage and the concept of negativity converge in the idea of suture: that dialectic of presence and absence in which the subject is "introduced" to the textual system of the film as the condition of its meaning.[16]

Therefore, what Heath's account of Freud reveals is the peculiar necessity claimed by the discourse of political modernism in its theorization of the subject. Instead of articulating
that productive difference where theoretical practice engages
the aesthetic text in a critical reading, in the discourse of political modernism the potential "activity" of the subject is effaced, sublimated, and resolved into a higher unity: the system
of the aesthetic text in its specific organization of deictic features. Moreover, this particular *Aufhebung* is differentiated
neither historically nor according to particular genres of narrative discourse. To the extent that the question of the subject—its potential positioning in the form of "transcendental
unity" or of "political understanding"—must be decided
through its identification with the aesthetic text, the forms of
the subject will always be identical to those of the object, no
matter how the latter is differentiated. To the extent that the
destiny of the subject is decided "in the text" it can be none
other than a formal problem. Moreover, any relation outside
of the intimate identity between text and subject is foreclosed
in the immediacy and presence of the seam that joins them in
the unilateral production of the subject by the text. In other
words, the subject can admit to no prior existence other than
the forms designated for it by the text. It is rendered as identical to the forms of an object that destines its meaning. The
subject is resolved into a finite and formal system where, one
might say, both sight and site are ineluctably determined.

In sum, the ghost of an idealist, Hegelian identity theory—
that is, the founding of epistemological judgments on the basis
of the unity of subject and object—seem to permeate even the
most emphatic attempts to promote a materialist film theory.
And this is no less true for the appeals that the discourse of
political modernism makes to psychoanalytic theory and especially Lacan.[17] Heath among others has made productive and
justifiable appeals for the potential, radical use of psychoanalytic theory to concieve the subject according to criteria of
contradiction and nonidentity. But the discourse of political
modernism has obfuscated this potential even as it has recognized and promoted it. In the attempt to locate the subject
in the analysis of its textual/discursive representations, the ver-

sion of political modernism offered by Wollen and Heath is
caught in a specific aporia. To the extent that the question of
a different relation to ideology is restricted to the forms of a
textual system, and in the degree to which an epistemological
valuation is required in the subjective relations established by
that system, an identity theory of knowledge must be presumed by even the most psychoanalytically informed versions
of political modernism.[18]

Perhaps, as Heath asserts, the relation between text and
spectator can be characterized as a "reciprocal process of intelligibility," where the subject participates in the process of
textual meaning no less than the text participates in the creation of meaning for the subject. But to that extent that Heath
insists, on the one hand, on the generic specificity of a political
modernism (a textual work that Godard and Straub can accomplish, and Snow or Burch cannot), and on the other, an
idea of suture as the "signifier's narration of the subject," the
two poles of this activity are ultimately not evenly determined
nor fully reciprocal. Jacques-Alain Miller in fact characterizes
suture not in the form of a reciprocity but as an irrecoverable
alterity or alienation: "it is a circular, though non-reciprocal,
relation" ("Suture," 34). In the relation between subject and
signifier, Miller insists on a fundamental *difference*. In the discourse of political modernism (whether in Kristeva or those
discourses that film theory has adapted from *Tel Quel*) this
relation is subsumed in an *Aufhebung* that incorporates the
subject into a superior unity equivalent to the textual system.
For Miller, suture requires a radical nonidentity—a dispersion
of the unity of the subject and its representations through their
regulated distribution along the signifying chain. Even given
the brevity and density of Miller's remarks, it is difficult to
reconcile his notion of suture with the conception of intersubjectivity offered by Lacanian-influenced film theory. For
here the discourse of political modernism insists on a peculiar
dialectic of position and inversion, of the reversibility of binary
terms, and of epistemological judgments based on the logic of
an identity theory that Miller's essay explicitly refutes.

Clearly, Heath's version of political modernism is both more
complex and less systematic than this reading implies. There

is also much to be said for his sidestepping of a strict opposition between modernism and realism as the potential passage from an idealist to a theoretical or materialist knowing. Neither does Heath insist in the same degree as Wollen, Burch, or others, on the inherent epistemological value of modernism. But as long as the discourse of political modernism is conceived as an aesthetic or textual work based on the "radical transformation of subjectivity" in the form of "political understanding," then it is difficult to reconcile Miller's conception of suture with its reading in contemporary film theory. Indeed, the most radical ambition of Miller's analysis is to describe the logic of the signifier as excluding the subject from the field of truth as the very foundation of signification. It is only by shifting the concept of suture onto the space of narrative, and generating in the concept of narrative deixis a space of formal oppositions that the radical nature of Miller's analysis can be repressed according to political modernism's demand for a critical knowledge communicated by the aesthetic text.

This is the peculiar function of the concept of negativity in Heath's theory of narrative space. With its insistence on the function of the imaginary and the unconscious in relation to the subject's representations, the subject is bound to a field of discourse where it is nevertheless occluded. No doubt this is an exact and appropriate formulation of Lacan's description of the relation of the subject to its unconscious. But what can no longer be treated as self-evident is the gesture that maps the specificity of the intersubjective relation in psychoanalysis (a unique situation between analyst and analysand or between the analysand and the field of its speech) onto the field of discourse in all its extensions, including aesthetic discourse.

This gesture produces two principal difficulties in the psychoanalytic conception of the subject forged in the discourse of political modernism. First, despite numerous nods to history and to a materialist understanding of the subject, this conception only understands the subjective relation as intrinsically and exclusively bound to the singularity of an aesthetic representation. The aesthetic text—which decides in its self-identity the field differentiating between political understanding or ideological regulation—ineluctably sets the parameters of response to which the spectator is bound if he or she is to be taken up in a relation of meaning and pleasure. Paradoxically, and despite the criticisms of the formalism of structural film, it is hard to imagine this conception as fundamentally different from Gidal's desire to construct a "1:1 relation" between film and spectator, especially where the idea of a narrative system seems itself to be based on criteria of presence and self-identity.[19] Second, in psychoanalytic film theory the subject can only be conceived in a dialectic that totalizes it under the signs of negativity, of the unconscious, and the imaginary. (Heath, for example, describes the spectatorial relation with respect to negativity as "a perpetual retotalisation of the imaginary" [NS 99].) I would be among the last to assert that unconscious factors of identification, perception, and reading do not have paramount importance for a theory of spectatorship. But it is not the split subject, divided within itself and in its relation to truth, that is ultimately theorized in the discourse of political modernism. Rather it is a subject conceived as identical with itself and with its forms of representation *within* the term "negativity" as the space of this totalization. Only through such a paradox, and the implicit formalism it supports, could one understand Wollen's argument, for example, that the textual production of "gaps in space" yields "fissures and splits" in the consciousness of the spectator.

However, in Heath's writings on problems of subjectivity and cinematic discourse, the terms of an identity theory of knowledge are neither as forceful nor pervasive as I might have portrayed them. Once Heath's insistence on deciding between types of film practice on the basis of epistemological judgments is displaced—and it is an issue that has long ceased to be a dominant emphasis in his writings—the complexities of Heath's association of narrative semiotics and psychoanalysis with a theory of ideology can be pushed in an alternate direction. As I mentioned earlier, Heath's most important accomplishment remains his gradual shift from questions concerning the production of aesthetic texts to a concentration on problems of the cultural production of subjectivity. In this respect, Heath's renewed emphasis on problems relating the cinematic institution to the production of memory opens a space for a theory of *reading* that does not rely on the singularity of the encounter between text and spectator. Moreover, Heath's subsequent work on problems proposed by feminist theory and the need for a differential account of the spectator, as well as his working through of the uses and abuses of the concept of suture, have in many respects proven Heath to be his own best and most brilliant critic.

Teresa de Lauretis has pushed open and developed Heath's ideas concerning modalities of textual production and interpretation. Through de Lauretis's work, it becomes clear that when Heath writes about the narrative perpetuation of memory, what counts is not the singularity of any film, but the production, proliferation, and constant renewal of narrative modalities that bolster given economies of libidinal investment in narrative, and with them, discursive constraints on the spectator's understanding of its subjective relations and identities, including, crucially, those of sexual difference. Aesthetic production is no longer the singular ground for this circulation of memory and for the rememorization of modalities of subjectivity in a historically specific society. Instead, there is a multiple and complex articulation of different discursive practices:

> The problem is, rather, that meanings are not produced *in* a particular film but "circulate between social formation, spectator and film." The production of meanings, I rephrase, always involves not simply a specific apparatus of representation but several. While each can be described analytically in its matters of expression or its social-economic conditions of production (e.g., the technological or economic modalities of, say, sound cinema), what is at issue is the possibility of accounting for their joint hold on the spectator and, *thus*, the production of meanings for a subject and/or of a subject in meaning across a plurality of discourses. If—to put it bluntly and circuitously—the subject is where meanings are formed and if, at the same time, meanings constitute the subject, then the notion of semiotic productivity must include that of modes of production. So "the question of how semantic values are constructed, read and located in history" becomes a most pertinent question.[20]

In this context, the relation between cultural and historical memory can be defined as the regulated dispersion of forms

of representation and meaning; or, in other words, the interlocking means by which a culture disseminates the different
materials and modalities where relations of subjectivity and
knowledge are figured.

What seems inescapable in the discourse of political modernism is a consideration of *the* text as the privileged field for
possible transformations of subjective relations. Here the text-
subject relation can only be thought in terms of an identity
theory organized according to two principles: first, that the
text must be construed as a formal object or system identical
to itself and divisible in its effects from other kinds of texts;
and second, that this conception of text—which is present in
even the most advanced versions of film poststructuralism—
can only locate, address, or conceive of the subject in the form
of a narcissistic repetition of its own formal system.

A historical materialist theory of the subject, however, is
more productively understood as an account of the multiple
potentialities for difference between subject and text. And at
the same time it would have to recognize "the impasse reached
by a certain notion of political avant-garde, a notion which,
like Godard's cinema, today retains its critical force only to
the extent that we are willing to historicize it and to give it
up as the paragon or absolute model of any radical cinema"
(*Alice Doesn't*, 59). Political modernism, which has construed
the subjective relation as an immanent one interiorized within
the forms of the text, must now recognize how the text is
always already worked upon by its own exteriority—that is, on
one hand, by its encounter with subject-spectators already
multiply and historically determined on the basis of gender,
race, class, and national identity (which yet cannot be considered identical to themselves and thus are open to further transformations); and on the other, by its placement within a specific
discursive formation that establishes the conditions, beyond
the imaginary singularity of any text or subject, according to
which a text is constituted as the object of reading, interpretation, or use.

NOTES

1. The essays most relevant to this project have been reedited and
collected in Heath's book *Questions of Cinema* (Bloomington: Indiana

University Press, 1981). In addition to "Narrative Space," originally published in *Screen* 17.3 (Autumn 1976): 68-112 (cited hereafter as NS), I will also make specific reference to "Screen Images, Film Memory," *Edinburgh Magazine* 1 (1976): 33-42; hereafter cited as SIFM.

For those readers unfamiliar with the terminology of linguistics, *deictics* refer to markers of subjectivity in discourse. Since debates in film theory on the question of suture and other theories of subjectivity are heavily indebted to linguistic research, it may be useful to briefly define this concept. Oswald Ducrot and Tzvetan Todorov describe deictics in the folloing way: " 'Deictics' are expressions whose referent can only be determined with repsect to the interlocutors (R. Jakobson calls them *shifters, embrayeurs*). Thus the pronouns of the first and second persons designate, respectively, the person who is speaking and the person spoken to. . . . E. Benveniste has shown that deictics constitute an irruption of discourse within language, since their very meaning (the method used to find their referent), even though it depends on language, can only be defined by allusion to their use." *Encyclopedic Dictionary of the Sciences of Language*, trans. Catherine Porter (Baltimore: The Johns Hopkins University Press, 1979): 252.

2. Heath's criticisms directly refer to Noel Burch's *Theory of Film Practice*. But it could equally refer to Metz's early attempts to establish *"la grande syntagmatique"* as the principal code of cinematic narrative. Cf. the essays collected in *Film Language*, trans. Michael Taylor (New York and London: Oxford University Press, 1974).

3. Many recent genre studies, especially those of the musical, support Heath's point. See, in particular, Jane Feuer's *The Hollywood Musical* (Bloomington: Indiana University Press, 1982) and Stephen Neale's *Genre* (London: British Film Institute, 1980).

4. Wollen describes precisely his relation to *Tel Quel* thought in general and Kristeva in particular. The work that interests him is footnoted throughout the " 'Ontology' " essay. Paradoxically, the directness of Heath's relation to Kristeva is all the more profound for the almost complete absence of reference to her. Neither the name of Kristeva nor the concept of negativity are indexed in *Questions of Cinema*, for example, although at least the latter is repeatedly invoked in his work. Nevertheless, I hope to demonstrate the pervasiveness of Kristeva's work in relation to Heath's. I will argue, in fact, that Heath draws the main points of his theoretical program from Kristeva's work of the early seventies that culminated in the magisterial *La révolution du langage poétique* (Paris: Editions du Seuil,

1974). These points include: the shift from a formalist and structuralist conception of text to a process-oriented, post-structuralist conception; the insistence on the study of aesthetic discourse from the point of view of a theory of the subject; the centrality of a certain modernist practice that located in the work of negativity the potential for a transformation of subjective relations; and most importantly, the necessity of transforming literary semiotics through the introduction of Lacanian psychoanalytic theory with its insistence on accounting for the unconscious and the work of the drives in relation to language.

One might also add that Heath's work subsequent to "Narrative Space," which focuses more clearly on problems of feminism and sexual difference, has accomplished strategic shifts that are more critical of Kristeva's position.

5. (Lisse: Peter de Ridder Press, 1975), cited as SSS. Published originally in the *Times Literary Supplement* (12 October 1973), this essay is a condensed introduction to her *La révolution du langage poétique*.

6. Julia Kristeva, "The Speaking Subject and Poetical Language," paper delivered at Cambridge University (1975): 11; cited in Steve Burniston and Chris Weedon's "Ideology, Subjectivity and the Artistic Text," *Working Papers in Cultural Studies* 10 (1977): 224.

7. "In the case . . . of a signifying practice such as 'poetic language'," writes Kristeva, "the *semiotic disposition* will be the various deviations from the grammatical rules of the language: articulatory effects which shift the phonemative system back towards its articulatory, phonetic base and consequently towards the drive-governed bases of sound-production; the over-determination of a lexeme by multiple meanings which it does not carry in ordinary usage but which accrue to it as a result of its occurrence in other texts; syntactic irregularities such as ellipses, non-recoverable deletions, indefinite embeddings, etc.; the replacement of the relationship between the protagonists of any enunciation as they function in a locutory act . . . by a system of relations based on fantasy; and so forth" (SSS 6).

I will note now and hold in reserve the particular intimate relation in Kristeva's theory between negativity, the presence of the body, and the articulation of sound. One must decide on this basis whether Kristeva's allegiance to psychoanalysis has actually distanced her from a Hegelian identity theory.

8. I repeat Kristeva's insistent use of the masculine possessive pronoun and will discuss the implications of her work for a specifically feminist aesthetic practice in the next chapter.

9. Kristeva has written on the cinema ("Ellipse sur la frayeur et la séduction speculaire," *Communications* 23 [1975]: 73-78; trans. by Dolores Burdick as "Ellipsis on Dread and the Specular Seduction," *Wide Angle* 3.3 (1979): 42-47), and her work on painting, too, is well known. What is interesting here is how her thoughts on the specular relation pick up directly the romantic and surrealist influences on her thought. The fascination of the specular has a relation of immediacy and immanence with the work of the drives. And its revolutionary aspect, its ability to transgress the unity of the subject, is linked to the presumed power of figurative representation to confound verbalized sense. What is open to criticism, however, is the opposition between the figurative and the linguistic that poses them as ontologically distinct activities aligned with a binary logic that associates the latter with the symbolic, Oedipality, the unity and self-identity of the transcendental subject, the law-of-the-Father, as opposed by the former as the imaginary, the preoedipal, heterogeneity, and so on. I will take up these issues again in the next chapter.

10. For two overviews sympathetic to the notion of suture, see the dossier published in *Screen* 18.4 (Winter 1977/78) and Kaja Silverman's *The Subject of Semiotics* (New York: Oxford University Press, 1983), especially 194-236.

11. "La suture (éléments de la logique du signifiant)," *Cahiers pour l'analyse* 1 (1966); trans. by Jacqueline Rose in *Screen* 18.4 (Winter 1977/78): 24-34 as "Suture (elements of the logic of the signifier)." This *Screen* dossier is fascinating in its documentation of the transformations undergone by the concept of suture in its successive adaptations to film theory and above all in its possible conceptual translations in the discourse of political modernism.

I should also clarify now that although I am critical of the way Miller's essay has been read by film theory and inserted, as it were, in an aesthetic theory that it was not intended to support, I find its brilliant critique of empiricist epistemologies to be indisputable and its importance for any theory of ideology to be fundamental.

12. Heath does attempt this justification, with uneven success, in his essay "Notes on Suture," which is part of the *Screen* dossier (pages 48-76). Also see Kaja Silverman's *The Subject of Semiotics* (New York: Oxford University Press, 1983).

13. "To specify drive (*Trieb, pulsion*), psychoanalysis finds the same term that for cinema renders the process of filmic construction—*montage*: 'if there is something that drive resembles, that something is a montage' " (SIFM 33). The interior citation is from *Les quatres concepts fondamentaux de la psychanalyse* (Paris: Editions du

Seuil, 1973): 154. Heath cites additional references on pages 156 and 160.

14. Of course, independent film practice in the seventies and eighties has itself targeted, if in a difficult way, the case histories as a narrative form. Two of the best examples are the Jay Street Collectives' *Sigmund Freud's Dora: A Case of Mistaken Identity* (1979) or Terrel Seltzer's *The Story of Anna O.: A Study on Hysteria* (1979).

15. This notoriously untranslatable term refers to the tertiary and final movement of the Hegelian dialectic. After the positing and negation of a thesis, Hegel says the terms of the dialectic will be *aufgehoben*. In Alexandre Kojève's commentary, "They are 'overcome,' in the threefold sense of the German word *Aufheben*—that is, 'overcome dialectically.' In the first place, they are *overcome* or annulled with respect to whatever is fragmentary, relative, partial, or one-sided in them. . . . Secondly, they are also *preserved* or safeguarded with respect to whatever is essential or universal in them— that is, with respect to what in each of them reveals one of the manifold aspects of the total and single reality. Finally, they are *sublimated*—that is, raised to a superior level of knowledge and of reality, and therefore of truth; for by completing one another, the thesis and the antithesis get rid of their one-sided and limited or, better, 'subjective' character, and as synthesis they reveal a more comprehensive and hence a more comprehensible aspect of the 'objective' real." (In *Introduction to the Reading of Hegel*, trans. James H. Nichols, Jr. (Ithaca and London: Cornell University Press, 1980): 180-81).

In that the Hegelian dialectic is a property of human thought and discourse that renders the identification of Being with Truth, we will have to decide to what degree Heath uses these terms figuratively or whether they return to haunt his views on form and epistemology.

16. For example, in "Screen Images, Film Memory," Heath writes, "Shots at once replace and, according to the rules, continue one another; the succession destroys and conserves. The critical point of this *Aufhebung* is that of the articulation—the cut, the join, the moment of the montage. A constant phasing out and in, film is the production not just of a negation, the continuous replacement of images, but more crucially again of a negativity, the excessive foundation of the process itself, of the very movement of the subject in the film, which movement is then stopped in the succession, the negation, the phasing" (SIFM 38-39).

17. Teresa de Lauretis, for example, has stated that "the retracing of current semiotic and psychoanalytic discourses on narrative to a

seldom-acknowledged source, the Hegelian paradigm, could be use-
fully pursued toward a critical reevaluation of just how much of the
despised structuralism is still active, however repressed, in the so-
called age of poststructuralism (*Alice Doesn't*, 128).

Similarly, Miriam Hansen has pointed out the role the Hegelian
Aufhebung plays in the dialectic of subjectivity adopted by contemporary film theory from Lacan. She argues, rightly I think, that it is
a totalizing conception where the development of the subject is resolved teleologically and irreversibly into progressive stages, where
earlier stages are always already negated and subsumed into later
ones. Cf. her "Pleasure, Ambivalence, Identification: Valentino and
Female Spectatorship," *Cinema Journal* 25.4 (Summer 1986), especially page 11 passim.

18. In his book *Les Iconoclastes* (Paris: Editions du Seuil, 1978),
Jean-Joseph Goux criticizes the Hegelianism that permeates the aesthetic philosophies of modernist painting. He suggests that an idealist
identity theory informs the strategies of Cubism no less than those
of the nonobjective art exemplified by Kandinsky.

In the context of the historical argument concerning "the two
avant-gardes," which privileges an idea of "narrative modernism"
by critiquing nonfigurative art's attempts at a formal and material
purification of painting, Goux's critique is striking. In both Wollen
and Heath, there is a privileging of the "montage" strategies of Cubism that are read as an attempt to subvert the Cartesian perspective
system through a calculated and nonreconcilable multiplication of
points of view. One could not find a more exact statement to describe
Heath's defense of Oshima. Interestingly, Goux calls this strategy a
"*montage of calculated specularization* of a *cogito*" (*Les Iconoclastes*,
93; my trans.). The coincidental use of the term *montage* here has
a much more direct bearing on Heath's arguments than on Lacan's.
Goux criticizes the invocation of identity theory in nonfigurative
painting in the following terms. By refusing any external reference
for the spectator to identify or identify with, nonobjective art attempts, through a radical interiorization, to forge an identity with
the spiritual/mental state of its subject. Alternatively, Cubism organizes itself as a "previsioning" of the subject—a kind of laying
down of tracks or traces that the subject must follow, or the fabrication of a mould shaping the forms of the subject's vision. Unlike
the argument of the two avant-gardes, which attempts to oppose
then to reconcile dialectically these two positions, Goux argues persuasively that they are linked by the same Hegelian emphasis on the
ordering of the subjective as a "specular idealism," even if Hegel

himself could not have imagined a nonrepresentational art: "Painting, says Hegel, *works for perception.* . . . One could even say that painting arranges [*aménage*] vision. The result is a *prefabricated perception.* Prefabricated in view of what? In view, answers Hegel, of the *place of the subject*; in view of the point, or the fixed point, where the spectator will be placed. . . . Everything is already arranged in the object for-the-subject (*Les Iconoclastes*, 73-74; my trans.).

It is important to note that this "centering" of the subject has ultimately nothing to do per se with either the representational system of so-called realist art or the geometrical conception of space within painting. Rather, it is a reflection on the construction of "painting" as an object of aesthetic discourse.

19. In this respect, does not the symptomatic presence of Hegel and the insistence on the forms of the subject's vision as well as the subject's "visualization" by the text, reveal the force of what is fundamentally a *phenomenological* conception of meaning? In his early critiques of Husserl, Jacques Derrida cogently describes how the insistence on a relation between form and meaning always returns to a metaphysical submission of the subject to a "sight." Heath's theory of narrative space might be rethought in the context of the following comments: "As soon as we use the concept of form—even to criticize *another* concept of form—we must appeal to the evidence of a certain source of sense. And the medium of this evidence can only be the language of metaphysics. For [in] that language we know what "form" means, how the possibility of its variations is ordered, what its limits are, and the field of all conceivable disputes concerning it. The system of oppositions in which something like form can be considered, the formality of form, is a finite system. . . .

"All the concepts by which *eidos* or *morphē* could be translated and determined refer back to the theme of *presence in general.* Form is presence itself. Formality is what is presented, visible, and conceivable of the thing in general. . . .

"Although the privilege of *theōria* is not, in phenomenology, as simple as has sometimes been claimed, although the classical theories are profoundly re-examined therein, the metaphysical domination of the concept of form cannot fail to effectuate a certain subjection to the look. This subjection would always be a subjection of *sense* to seeing, of sense to the sense of sight [*au sens-de-la-vue*], since sense in general is in fact the concept of every phenomenological field. The implications of such a *putting-on-view* [*mise-en-regard*] could be unfolded in many directions and by proceeding from what would appear to be the most diverse places within the text and problems of phenomenology. It could be shown, for example, how this this putting-on-view and this concept of form permit a movement between the project of formal ontology, the description of time or of intersubjectivity, the latent theory of the work of art, etc." ("Form and Meaning: A Note on the Phenomenology of Language" in *Speech and Phenomena, and Other Essays on Husserl's Theory of Signs*, trans. David B. Allison (Evanston: Northwestern University Press, 1973): 108-9). I have included Derrida's text in brackets where I think Allison's translation strays from a meaning relevant to my analysis.

This citation provides another interesting point of contrast between Wollen and Heath. Where Wollen ultimately locates the site of meaning in the presence of speech, Heath's effort to define cinema as a discourse, and thereby to elide a linguistic definition of cinematic meaning, paradoxically leads him to associate the meaning of the subjective relation with the organization of vision, to the "putting-on-view" of this relation in its specular representations.

20. *Alice Doesn't*, 32-33. The first citation is from Heath's *Questions of Cinema*, 107; the second from Paul Willemen's "Notes on Subjectivity," *Screen* 19.1 (Spring 1978): 43.

EIGHT

Sexual Difference

To what does the sphinx refer, this reasoning and devouring
hybrid being, which beats its wings as it talks? Why does this
monster, a woman with the body of a beast, take up her place at
the gates of Thebes?
Does not the encounter with this enigmatic figure of femininity
threaten every subject? Is it not she who is at the root of the ruin
of representation?
—Michèle Montrelay, "Inquiry into Femininity"[1]

In recent cultural theory in general and in film theory in particular, no encounter has been more radical than that of feminism and psychoanalysis. And no theoretical discourse has had
more at stake in the questions posed by the discourse of political modernism than that of feminist theory. In this respect,
one must consider with some degree of irony the desire of
political modernism to transform subjective relations in aesthetic discourse, and to rethink a theory of the subject through
psychoanalysis. For if the efforts to pose the problem of the
subject differently have been haunted by an identity theory
of knowledge, feminist theory has demonstrated a more pointed
criticism of film theory and psychoanalysis; namely, a refusal
to understand the subject in its specific difference(s), as being
traversed by difference, and above all by the question of sexual
difference.[2]
The year 1974 witnessed the publication of several books
that revolutionized feminism's relationship with psychoanal-

ytic theory including Juliet Mitchell's *Psychoanalysis and Feminism* (London: Allen Lane), Julia Kristeva's *La révolution du langage poétique* (Paris: Editions du Seuil), and Luce Irigaray's *Speculum de l'autre femme* (Paris: Les Editions de Minuit). In "A Note on the Distinction between Sexual Division and Sexual Difference," Parveen Adams describes the importance of Mitchell's book, for example, as challenging essentialist theories that posed the political problem of sexual difference as a struggle between two mutually exclusive, jointly exhaustive, and eternally antagonistic social groups.[3] The essentialist view cannot advance the cause of feminism in the study of *ideology*, because it reduces the problem of the domination of women by men to arguments of a *biological* nature. Since biology preexists and predetermines social relations, essentialism renders the problem of sexual antagonism irresolvable. In Adams's reading, Mitchell is equally opposed to the sociological view where the individual is conceived as a *tabula rasa* waiting to receive already constituted capacities of experience, cognition, and purposeful action. Further, sociological arguments usually refer to a "second nature": men are bound to predominate because of their aggressivity; women must overcome their passivity to recover an experience fundamental to femininity.

Essentialist and sociological views are both normative and cannot account for the diversity of sexual experience and identity in a given society. Alternatively, by posing sexual difference as a question of *psychical* reality, Mitchell argues, Freud revolutionized the study of sexual difference by theorizing sexuality as a process of the social construction of subjectivity: the instantiation of sexed positionalities as an effect of representation, or the symbolization of the body through a particular, but variable organization of the drives. Moreover, by characterizing this process as one of repression and of the historical constitution of the unconscious, Freud made it impossible to describe forms of subjectivity as integral, homogeneous, or noncontradictory entities. As Parveen Adams notes, Freudian theory was necessary because it displaced the realm of political struggle from the terrain of biology to that of *ideology*: "that as long as feminist theories of ideology work with a theory of representation within which representation is always a representation of reality, however attenuated a relation that may be, the analysis of sexual difference cannot be advanced because reality is always already apparently structured by sexual division, by an already antagonistic relation between two social groups" ("Sexual Division," 52). Only on this basis can patriarchal domination be challenged on the terrain of culture and representation, a struggle in which feminist aesthetic practices would have a definite and powerful role.

In her influential essay "Visual Pleasure and Narrative Cinema," Laura Mulvey was among the first to argue for the importance of psychoanalysis for a feminist critique of representation. Just as importantly, her critique notes *Screen's* repetition of Freud's own difficulties in articulating the problem of feminine identity in the editorial coordination of their former "Brechtian" emphasis with recent developments in semiology and psychoanalysis. "The paradox of phallocentrism," wrote Mulvey in 1975, "in all its manifestations is that it depends on the image of the castrated woman to give order and meaning to its world. An idea of woman stands as lynch pin to the system: it is her lack that produces the phallus as a symbolic presence, it is her desire to make good the lack that the phallus signifies. Recent writing in *Screen* about psychoanalysis and the cinema has not sufficiently brought out the importance of the representation of the female form in a symbolic order in which, in the last resort, it speaks castration and nothing else."[4]

Heath's "Narrative Space," for example, uses psychoanalytic theory to describe narrative cinema's construction of a unified and coherent subjectivity across the deictic agency of the look. However, in Heath's reading this "subjectivity" is totalized in its imaginary identifications with the system of the aesthetic text. Thus his theory is unable to recognize how this coherence trades on the problem of sexual difference. Mulvey, among others, insisted that the narrative organization of point of view and the processes of pleasurable looking in the cinema were founded on a particular representation of sexual difference and of the female body. It was in fact a question of the mastery of the *masculine* gaze, whose forms of pleasurable looking relied on engaging the feminine body in a system of

intelligibility that disavowed the contradiction it expressed—
that of castration and its signification of sexual difference.

In "Woman's Stake: Filming the Female Body," an essay
surveying the issues with which a psychoanalytically informed
feminist theory must confront the question of radical film practice, Mary Ann Doane accurately summarizes the problem. If
indeed the system of representation determined by the cinematic apparatus is structured on voyeuristic and fetishistic
models of pleasurable seeing, which work at the expense of
women and of the figuration of women's bodies, then how
could one define the place of feminine subjectivity and pleasure, in fact, a feminine *écriture* in the cinema?[5] Doane suggests
that feminist film theory should define a poetic syntax devolving from the female body. And this syntax would represent the
feminine body differently, in a way that confounds the linearity
and univocality of the patriarchal discourse, as well as the system of identification characteristic of classical narrative. Doane
suggests that the innovative uses of temporality and syntactic
organization in films such as Chantal Akerman's *Jeanne Dielman* (1975), Wollen and Mulvey's *Riddles of the Sphinx* (1977),
and Sally Potter's *Thriller* (1979) represent the first attempts
to define the specificity of a feminine, aesthetic discourse in
its critical relation with narrative. The need for a theory to
account for a feminine *écriture* and subjectivity is then all the
more profound in order to assess and expand on the work
begun by these films.

That this question had not yet been foregrounded in the
discourse of political modernism by 1974 is even more ironic
when the historical importance of feminist theory to the institutional foundations of contemporary film theory are acknowledged. Doane's conclusion, which favors the use of semiotics and psychoanalysis to define the specificity of a feminine
écriture, is not a new one. It can in fact be traced back to
Mulvey's "Visual Pleasure and Narrative Cinema" itself, which
appeared contemporaneously with Juliet Mitchell's *Psychoanalysis and Feminism* and the "new French feminisms" of
Luce Irigaray, Michèle Montrelay, Hélène Cixous and others.
All of these writers were determined to use psychoanalysis to
analyze and deconstruct a discursive order that allied patriar-

chy with the *episteme* of Western philosophy, and to demonstrate the rapport of feminine *écriture* with a politically consequent modernism. In "Feminism, Film and the Avant-Garde," Laura Mulvey suggests that the history of feminist culture, heretofore only an undercurrent in patriarchal society, is and has been necessarily allied to avant-garde film, on the one hand, and avant-garde theory (such as *Tel Quel*) on the other.[6] The development of the women's movement in the 1970s was linked from the first to an interest in film and visual culture. (No better example could be found than the cooperation of Mulvey, Juliet Mitchell, and the artist/theorist Mary Kelly in the Women's Liberation Workshop in the early seventies in London.) In the watershed year of 1972 the first two international women's film festivals were held in New York and Edinburgh and the influential magazine *Women and Film* was organized in Los Angeles. Consequently, throughout the seventies film journals addressed issues of feminist politics and theory with greater frequency. The following year Claire Johnston organized a women's film season at the National Film Theatre in London and published the influential manifesto *Notes on Women's Cinema* (London: SEFT, 1975). A crucial result of these events was the discovery of the importance of women filmmakers in the history of the cinematic avant-gardes, including Germaine Dulac, Maya Deren, and Joyce Wieland. Moreover, with the publication of the first issue of *Camera Obscura* in 1976, still the only Anglo-American journal devoted exclusively to feminist film theory, another significant trend was revealed. The growth of feminist theory and cultural politics in the seventies coincided with the institutionalization of film theory across the disciplines of semiology, psychoanalysis, and Marxism, taking its place as a key area of investigation.

When situated historically, it is clear that "Visual Pleasure and Narrative Cinema" was initially meant as a polemic and necessary preface for a theory of a political, avant-garde film practice. Mulvey's essay has been primarily applied to the analysis of mainstream films and of "readings against the grain." However, in both the introductory and concluding sections of the essay, she herself is quite clear that her purpose is to prepare the way theoretically for a "politically and aesthetically avant-garde cinema" (VP 8) as a counterpoint to "the dominant ideological concept of the cinema" (VP 7). In the introductory section of her essay, Mulvey states that in targeting those narrative codes and mechanisms of identification that work for the man as against the woman in the structuring of the scopic drive, her object is nothing less than the "destruction of pleasure as a radical weapon." Asserting that psychoanalysis can and must be used to comprehend and undermine the overdetermination of film forms by patriarchal logic, Mulvey aims to discover new cinematic articulations which, by undercutting the satisfaction and reinforcement of the ego and negating the transparency of narrative, will represent a new language of desire. This will be the task of a radical signifying practice allied to a "politics of the unconscious": "to free the look of the camera into its materiality in time and space and the look of the audience into dialectics, passionate detachment" (VP 18). Composed at the same time as her first film, *Penthesilea* (1974), Mulvey's essay demands to be read as a polemic. And as Teresa de Lauretis points out, by correlating political modernism with feminist film theory this attempt to define an aesthetically avant-garde cinema "could only exist in counterpoint to mainstream film as analysis, subversion, and total negation of Hollywood's pleasurable obsessions and its ideological manipulation of visual pleasure."[7]

How then does Mulvey's argument in "Visual Pleasure and Narrative Cinema" represent the possibility of a "politically and aesthetically avant-garde cinema"? From its first pages, Mulvey's essay is organized by a binary logic that opposes masculinity as active subject of the look to femininity as passive object of looking. Also, within this logic of sexual division, she characterizes a "dominant, ideological concept of the cinema" in opposition to a politically consequent modernism. It is important not to lose sight of this dual trajectory in the development of her argument. For it crucially focuses on and devolves from a certain figuration of the feminine body as the attempt to restore the question of femininity to film theory and to build a theory of alternative cinema from that question.

For Mulvey, and for others working within a psychoanalytically based feminist film theory, what the female figure signifies for patriarchal representation is what the look must disavow—the threat of castration and unpleasure: "Ultimately, the meaning of woman is sexual difference, the absence of the penis as visually ascertainable, the material evidence on which is based the castration complex essential for the organisation of entrance to the symbolic order and the law of the father" (VP 13). As given for the male gaze, the figuration of the female body always threatens to reengage the trauma it originally signified, necessitating forms of seeing that allow the masculine unconscious to escape this anxiety. According to Mulvey, pleasure in seeing therefore distributes itself onto two routes, one sadistic, the other fetishistic. Exemplified by the figuration of women in *film noir*, the sadistic avenue is characterized by a "preoccupation with the re-enactment of the original trauma (investigating the woman, demystifying her mystery), counterbalanced by the devaluation, punishment or saving of the guilty object" (VP 13). Sadism is immediately understood to be aligned with the needs of the classic narrative in its formulation of a linear logic of conflict and suspense, ultimately leading to resolution and mastery. The fetishistic avenue, on the other hand, *opposes* itself to linearity with a freezing of the gaze. Here castration anxiety is disavowed by imaging the female body as spectacle and as a figure that is reassuring rather than disturbing. Represented by the cult of the female star, this second avenue "builds up the physical beauty of the object, transforming it into something satisfying in itself" (VP 14).

In sum, Mulvey asserts that the mastery of contradiction—which is the objective of those codes underwriting diegetic illusionism—is always threatened by the imaging of the female body. Subsequently a partnership between narrative codes and structures of pleasurable looking is required to stabilize the male ego.[8] Therefore, the visual mastery of the feminine body is closely tied to the objectives of realism—transparency, linearity, continuity, in fact the mastery of contradiction in all its forms. But more disturbing is Mulvey's demonstration of how this system of representation works against feminine subjectivity or pleasure since it reifies the female body and converts it into an object to sustain the masculine positionality in narrative.

The cruel paradox, of course, is that from the standpoint of the masculine ego the image of femininity only serves as the phantasmatic memory of castration that must be either elided or disavowed. But at the same moment Mulvey's argument suggests an alternative figuration of femininity-as-negativity— a force that can return to confound the privilege of the masculine ego as the ruin of patriarchal representation. If Mulvey's essay seems, as several critiques suggest, to circumlocute the problem of the female spectator, perhaps another reading of this absence is possible, that is, femininity as the unthought or unnamed in patriarchal culture and its system of representations.[9] In Michèle Montrelay's formulations, femininity becomes the "unconscious" or what patriarchy has repressed to preserve the unity, self-identity, and privilege of masculine subjectivity. The concept of femininity is indeed figured this way in the rhetorical structure of Mulvey's argument. For if in the narrative forms of the Hollywood cinema femininity is made to represent the anxiety and subsequent mastery of castration for the masculine ego, it might also be understood as a force of negation that returns to erode or undermine this narrative system.

Mulvey explicitly refers to Julia Kristeva to support this identification of femininity with negation in its potential for a critical theory of poetic language. I have already discussed the importance of Kristeva's conception of signifying practices as the negotiation of subjectivity through the particular, economic imbrication of symbolic material (signs) and psychical material (the drives). Now some brief attention should be given to the importance of her work for Mulvey in particular and for feminist aesthetic theory in general. According to Mulvey, Kristeva's theory draws a specific relation between the discourses of modernism and femininity. Femininity is understood as what is repressed in patriarchal language to maintain the self-presence, self-identity, and self-consciousness of its constitutive forms of subjectivity. In Kristeva, the irruption of poetic excess in the modernist text involves an effect of *jouiss-*

ance that is feminine and a logic that is necessarily opposed to the repression and continuity endemic to patriarchy, splitting its forms of subjectivity—"For feminists this split, the possibility of foregrounding the signifier, has a triple attraction: aesthetic fascination with discontinuities; pleasure from disrupting the traditional unity of the sign; and theoretical advance from investigating language and the production of meaning" ("Feminism, Film and the Avant-Garde," 8).

Kristeva's work criticizes the Western philosophical tradition founded on the concept of the "thetic subject"—a self-present, self-identical entity constituted by and capable of predicating rational utterances. In Kristeva's theory the thetic subject is instituted in the symbolic dimension of discourse. Structured by the unity of the sign, this dimension is also the realm of sociality, of rational and juridical discourses, and of the subject/object relations of predicative syntax. Kristeva's terminology is also strategically coincident with the Lacanian register of the Symbolic. Fully compatible with Jacques Lacan's conception, Kristeva's symbolic register is founded on the repression necessitated by the Oedipus complex and the resolution of the castration complex that constitutes the thetic subject in relation to the transcendental signifier, the phallus—in Lacan's theory, the authoritative support of cultural and linguistic structures.

Signifying practices are not exhausted by the symbolic, however, which Kristeva associates with a patriarchal order of representation. One must also account for the organization of the drives or, in Kristeva's terms, the semiotic order. The symbolic is organized by its repression of the semiotic, which always threatens to disrupt its unity and continuity. Falling before castration and the resolution of the Oedipus complex through identification with the Father, the semiotic is associated with preoedipality and relations with the maternal body. Moreover, for Kristeva the semiotic order has a special relation to both poetic language and the feminine in its systematic deviations from, and disruptions of, "rational" language. However, a simple opposition does not bind the symbolic and the semiotic together. One order cannot be extricated from the other; both are required for semiosis or what Kristeva terms *signifiance*.

In any discursive activity, the two modalities combine and re-combine dialectically according to the function of negativity, in which semiotic excess erupts and is contained or channeled by given symbolic economies.[10] Since the semiotic order is logically prelinguistic and presymbolic, it cannot rest on the notion of a fixed and unitary subjectivity as the support of the symbolic order. As opposed to the thetic subject—character-ized by rationality and univocality—poetic language overturns relations of structural dominance between the symbolic and the semiotic and supposes a "subject in process" that is ulti-mately irreducible to self-identical meaning or the experience of pleasure ordered by the masculine unconscious. Finally, for Kristeva this relation to femininity also presupposes a *critical* relation as an ongoing challenge to patriarchal social and ep-istemological norms.[11]

The text of Mulvey's argument, and the binary logic orga-nizing it, can now be reformulated in a new context that clar-ifies her precis for a theory of political modernism. The im-aging of woman in patriarchal culture can now be reconsidered in film theory as the foundation for an alternative theoretical and aesthetic practice. This alternative practice should be able to undermine the satisfaction and reinforcement of the unified, masculine ego, "[not] in favour of a reconstructed new plea-sure, which cannot exist in the abstract, nor of intellectualised unpleasure, but to make way *for a total negation of the ease and plenitude of the narrative fiction film*. The alternative is the thrill that comes from leaving the past behind without rejecting it, transcending outworn or oppressive forms, or dar-ing to break with normal pleasurable expectations in order to conceive a new language of desire" (VP 8; emphasis mine). Paradoxically, the figuration of woman as castration from the point of view of the masculine subject becomes the ground for a utopian formulation in Mulvey's essay. It anticipates a force, already inscribed within the forms of patriarchal plea-sure and representation, that returns to dismantle or overturn those forms: "Desire, born with language, allows the possi-bility of transcending the instinctual and the imaginary, but its point of reference continually returns to the traumatic mo-ment of its birth: the castration complex. Hence the look, plea-

surable in form, can be threatening in content, and it is woman
as representation/image that crystallizes this paradox" (VP 11).
   The often criticized binarism of Mulvey's argument can
be read in another way, clarifying both the interest and the
difficulties of her theory of political modernism. If Mulvey's
argument begins by identifying with the subjective activity
of the gaze whose passive object is femininity, this equation
also presents the possibility of resolving differently. This possibility can be tabulated in tue following manner—mas-
culinity:femininity :: activity:passivity :: sadism:masochism ::
voyeurism:fetishism :: Hitchcock:Sternberg :: sequence:
simultaneity :: symbolic:imaginary :: oedipality:preoedipality.
My remarking upon the opposition of Alfred Hitchcock to Joseph von Sternberg in this series is not facetious, for in her
discussion Mulvey opposes the two directors' work on the basis
of specific cinematic possibilities: the linear, sadistic, narrative
drive of Hitchcock's films is contrasted to Sternberg's fetishistic imaging of the female body that "freezes" the look and
disrupts the flow of narrative. Mulvey suggests the possibility
of interpreting the figuration of femininity, even within the
confines of classical narrative, as having a radically other temporality that can derail the linearity and continuity of patriarchal representation. This implicit system of polarities, which
circumvents the question of the feminine subject to avoid its
identification with a fundamental masochism, preserves at the
same time a force of resistance associated with the imaginary,
preoedipality, and the feminine body. In "The Field of Language in Film," Peter Wollen draws a similar association to
describe the work of the image in his and Mulvey's films as
disrupting processes of oedipal identification, as well as the
linearity and continuity of oedipalized narrative structures.[12]
   If the binary logic of Mulvey's argument seems to ignore the
female spectator, it can also be understood as formulating a
particular utopian space where the figure of femininity organizes the following concepts: unpleasure, "alien presence," a
freezing of action, distraction, disunity, staticity, and specifically, antiillusion—"as this essay has argued, the structure of
looking in narrative fiction film contains a contradiction in its
own premises: the female image as a castration threat con-

stantly endangers the unity of the diegesis and bursts through the world of illusion as an intrusive, static, one-dimensional fetish" (VP 18). Devoted to underwriting the spatial constructions of the classic, Hollywood film as well as satisfying the compensatory needs of the masculine ego, the narrative forms of pleasurable looking contain within their negative moments the potentiality of a materialist film practice. And this practice could only come into being as a critique of patriarchal ideology. If Mulvey fails to theorize the place of the feminine subject in relation to the classical, narrative film, it is because from the standpoint of the discourse of political modernism, this subject does not yet exist and will only come into being with the realization of an alternative, feminist representational practice.

In this respect, it is easy to see why Peter Wollen refers to Kristeva in " 'Ontology' and 'Materialism' in Film." She provides a ready-made theory that extends and deepens his and Mulvey's account of the implication of psychical processes with symbolic structures. As Mary Ann Doane points out, the importance of Kristeva's theory of radical signifying practices involves more than a notion of a differential articulation of subjectivity; the acquisition of language and the constraints it exercises on the semiotic are understood as devolving from a particular symbolization of the body, dominated by Lacan's conceptualization of the phallus. Perhaps, then, the specificity of a feminine écriture could be defined in the negotiation of sexual difference on the oedipal stage according to woman's differential access to the symbolic. Similarly, Laura Mulvey argues that the importance of Kristeva's theorization of negativity and of the semiotic disposition is that it opens psychoanalysis to a contradiction with respect to femininity where a "poetic confrontational discourse" becomes possible. What is finally most important is the degree to which a feminine écriture might ally itself to the project of deconstruction in its most global sense. Here the opposition code/deconstruction that underwrites the project of the modernist text finds its most extreme formulation in the opposition of the symbolic and the semiotic. For what the specificity of a feminine écriture and jouissance might then achieve would be not only the "ruin of representation" and a differential articulation of subjectivity, it might also contribute to the dismantling of the Western *episteme*, dominated by patriarchal logic. If Mulvey can be criticized for her lack of reflection on the place of the female spectator, at the same time this absence can be read as the figuration of a utopian formulation preserving in the site of the imaginary and the preoedipal relation to the mother the possibility of a writing adequate to the experience of femininity and the feminine body, as well as the ruin of patriarchal representation.

Of course, the real problem with Mulvey's essay is the absence of this formulation or its theorization as such. The logic of binarism and negation organizing her argument seem less to pose the problem of the specificity of a feminine *écriture* or a feminist cinema than that of a nonmainstream, nonpatriarchal cinema. Mulvey implicitly respects the terms of Kristeva's logic where, according to the terms of Lacanian analysis, "woman cannot be, does not fit into the category of being," because from the standpoint of the symbolic measure of the phallus and its legislation of sexual identity the only terms accepted are "male/non-male."[13] Thus Mulvey follows Kristeva in reserving for feminism an essentially *critical* function where "women's practice can only be negative, in opposition to that which exists." What remains implicit in Mulvey's position is explicit in Kristeva's adherence to Lacan: even if poetic language devolves from the preoedipal relation to the maternal body, in the last instance there is no possibility of formulating a language specific to an experience of the feminine body that is outside the logic of patriarchy. As Mary Ann Doane points out, Mulvey's detailed description of those processes of identification wherein *masculine* subjectivity sustains itself as an interweaving of recognition and miscognition not only excludes the question of the feminine subjectivity, it *"absents"* it: . . . the thrust of Mulvey's argument is that, in patriarchal society, this kind of misrecognition and this kind of identity are, quite simply, not available to the woman. Her discussion deals only with the male spectator (as articulated in the use of the pronoun "he") and, by implication, situates female spectatorship as the locus of an impossibility. . . . Built into the mode of seeing legalized by the classical text is the exclusion of the feminine."[14]

Similarly, de Lauretis describes how the epistemological stakes for the "envisioning" of the spectator inscribe Mulvey's argument within a critique of illusionism whose binarism not only makes difficult the conceptualization of a feminine spectatorial activity, but also an understanding of the potential specificity of feminine pleasure:

> Within the discursive framework that opposes mainstream to avant-garde cinema, "illusion" is associated with the former and charged with negative connotations: naive reflection-theory realism, bourgeois idealism, sexism, and other ideological mystifications are part and parcel of illusionist cinema, as of all narrative and representational forms in general. Hence, in this Brechtian-Godardian program, "the first blow against the monolithic accumulation of traditional film conventions (already undertaken by radical filmmakers) is to free the look of the audience into dialectics, passionate detachment. . . ." Therefore, within the context of the argument, a radical film practice can only constitute itself against the specifications of that cinema, in counterpoint to it, and must set out to destroy the "satisfaction, pleasure and privilege" it affords. The alternative is brutal, especially for women to whom pleasure and satisfaction, in the cinema and elsewhere, are not easily available.[15]

Here one must comprehend the double-edged nature of Mulvey's polemical arguments. On one hand, the incorporation of psychoanalysis by feminist theory reveals how codes of identification and the representation of gendered subjectivity in the cinema are determined by patriarchal structures at even the most primary and unconscious levels. For those dedicated to the tenets of political modernism, Mulvey thus provides a persuasive argument against realist aesthetics and any notion of the ideological neutrality of the cinematic apparatus. In "Feminism, Fiction and the Avant-Garde," she mentions this herself in a critique of early feminist films such as Kate Millett's *Three Lives* (1972). According to Mulvey, these films mistakenly assumed that the presence of a woman behind the camera, combined with the representational accuracy of technology and the good intentions of the operator, would enable the recording of essential truths and shared experiences, thereby creating political unity through identification. On the other hand, the determination of the apparatus by patriarchal ideology seems so profound that even the most devoted adherents of the feminist avant-garde such as Constance Penley are forced to admit that "[any] juxtaposition of an avant-garde practice and an avowedly political practice is, and has been historically, problematic" ("The Avant-Garde and Its Imaginary," 3); while Mary Ann Doane notes that "The simple gesture of directing a camera toward a woman has become equivalent to a terrorist act" (WS 23). This extreme situation leads finally to the radical negativity of Peter Gidal who denies, along with representation and narrative, the possibility of any work on the figuration of the female body at all. In fact, Gidal argues that in the present conjuncture the female body is so overcoded by patriarchal culture that any attempt at deconstructing its imagery is doomed from the start to repeat the ideology it is attempting to negate.[16]

The question revealed by Mulvey in her circumlocution of feminine subjectivity in "Visual Pleasure and Narrative Cinema" is one that psychoanalysis, in its inability to overcome the theoretical difficulties of its encounter with femininity, seemed condemned to repeat: *Was will das Weib?* For avant-garde feminist writers such as Hélène Cixous, the symptomatic importance of this question was the polemical wedge it afforded feminist cultural theory. The silence of psychoanalysis on femininity had to be turned against itself in order to reveal, on that "dark continent" that Freud called woman's sexuality, the place from which women could speak: "For me the question 'What does she want?' that is asked of the woman, a question that the woman indeed asks herself because she is asked it, because exactly there is so little place for her desire in society that she ends up, through not knowing what to do with it, by not knowing where to put it, or even whether she has a desire, overlays the most immediate and urgent question: 'How do I have pleasure? What is female *pleasure*, where does it happen, how is it inscribed on her body, in her unconscious? And then how do we write it?'"[17] For Cixous, women must fill the silence of psychoanalysis with their own voice, their *écriture*, and their desire, a task that might unravel the epistemological foundations of psychoanalysis and other phallocentric logics in its construction of a poetic language adequate to the specificity of the female body.

In "Woman's Stake," Mary Ann Doane notes that feminisms opposed to the idea of a biological essentialism (best represented by the journal *m/f*) have followed Juliet Mitchell in turning to psychoanalysis to describe a necessary gap between the body and the psychical constitution of gendered subjectivity. Sexuality and its representations are thus understood as irreducible to the physical. What is gained by this argument is an account of the historical variability of sexual identity. Sexual difference is understood as constructed, a product of social and symbolic relations that predate the subject and exist in a skewed relation with "biological destiny." The alternative to "essentialism" in standard psychoanalytic theory, however, seems to rely fundamentally on a phallocentric logic that posits only a single, masculine unconscious. What may be lost in the haste to overcome essentialism is precisely the possibility of a feminine language defined in relation to the female body and its syntax. Doane argues that the distance between these two extremes must be mediated if feminist film theory is to overcome an impasse on the question of alternative representational practices.

> Both the proposal of a pure access to a natural female body and the rejection of attempts to conceptualize the female body based on their contamination by ideas of "nature" are inhibiting and misleading. Both positions deny the necessity of posing a complex relation between the body and psychic/signifying processes, of using the body, in effect, as a "prop". . . . It is crucial that feminism move beyond the opposition between essentialism and anti-essentialism. This move will entail the necessary risk taken by theories which attempt to define or construct a feminine specificity (not essence), theories which work to provide the woman with an autonomous symbolic representation. (WS 33)

While rejecting essentialism and any notion of biological destiny, Doane also finds the definitive splitting of the body and the psyche, the penis and the phallus, to be disingenuous. She argues that even if sexuality is fully defined in the symbolic, and even if the phallus is defined as logically prior to the penis, one must accept that while the phallus bestows significance to the penis, the presence or absence of the penis is nonetheless necessary for the symbolization permitted by the phallus. By too hastily dividing the social figure of the phallus from its biological support, Doane suggests that feminism risks losing sight of those elements of psychoanalytic theory that might define a feminine *écriture*, or the specific difference of the feminine with respect to language. In order to hold onto this possibility, Doane argues that "the gap between body and psyche is not absolute; an image or symbolization of the body (which is not necessarily the body of biological science) is fundamental to the construction of the psychoanalytical discourse" (WS 26). The body is still of necessity a "prop" or the "stage" where the symbolization of desire and the drama of the subject must take place. This is the meaning of the psychoanalytic term *anaclisis*: where specific drives such as the oral or the anal become detached from the physical organs that were their first objects and displaced metonymically onto other, symbolic objects. What is important to remember is that the drive is initially focalized on its first objects; it does not originate there.

By what alternative theory, then, could the feminine body specify a different and disordering relation to patriarchal language? Two directions have been outlined in psychoanalytic film theory in the seventies. The first, which might be called mimetic, is best represented by the work of Luce Irigaray. This position assumes that a specifically feminine language will have an isomorphic relation with the anatomical specificity of the female body. The second direction, represented by Michèle Montrelay, describes the specificity of feminine language according to woman's difficult relation to the Oedipus complex and her "negative entry" into the symbolic.

Of the new French feminisms, the most radical challenge to the phallocentrism of psychoanalytic thought came from Luce Irigaray, whose book *Speculum de l'autre femme* earned her expulsion from Lacan's École Freudienne. Having begun with

research on the so-called nonrational languages of schizo-
phrenia and senility, which led her to question the criteria of
rationality and universality marginalizing those discourses, Irigaray began to speculate whether there could be a feminine
language radically other to the logic of patriarchy. Irigaray
argues that the Freudian concept of sexual difference is ultimately determined by a logic of identity and the selfsame characteristic of Western discourse since Plato and Aristotle. Although psychoanalysis recognizes the opposition male/female,
it finally prioritizes and assesses value for only one term, that
of maleness. In this context, feminine specificity can only be
proscribed in terms of a negativity, as nonmale, lack, or absence of penis. Because Western philosophical and scientific
discourse is predicated on an isomorphic relation with the
phallus—the privileged unity of the figure of the one, the self-
identical, the specularizable, all corresponding to the male
erection as "becoming in a form"—Irigaray claims that the
dominance of patriarchal language must be opposed by a "mor-
phology" of the female sex. According to Irigaray, this project
is equivalent to a global deconstruction of Western philosophy.[18] Rendered invisible in this paradigm, feminine discourse
can only be articulated as the "unrepresentable" in phallocentric discourse. Mary Ann Doane, for one, sees this proposition as offering a radical alternative to Mulvey's view of
male-dominated identificatory relations. Since women must, in
a certain sense, fail the mirror phase, lacking the means of
"becoming in a form" or of achieving identity through self-
specularization, then perhaps the structure of identification
with its component of miscognition might be less applicable
to the positioning of women.[19]

Similarly, Irigaray argues against the postulation of a single,
masculine libido, and deems it false to suggest that there is no
feminine desire: "It is a specific social and cultural structure
which deprives women of their desire and of the possibility of
their expressing it, viz., because language and the systems of
representation cannot 'translate' that desire."[20] Moreover,
rather than positing a female unconscious, Irigaray speculates
whether women are not themselves the unconscious; or more
precisely, whether what has been historically constituted as

the unconscious might not be some censored or repressed element of the feminine. The experience of analysis, she claims,
reveals a specific feminine discourse that fulfills the functional
criteria attributed to the unconscious by psychoanalytic theory. Irigaray also claims that this discourse radically undermines the Aristotelian logic of the subject-verb-object form
and any notion of a self-identical subject of enunciation. In
their gloss on Irigaray's work, Diana Adlam and Couze Venn
summarize her thought in the following manner: "This 'other'
language . . . is radically non-unitary, does not obey the laws
of consistency and object-ivity and will admit of no meta-dis-
course. It poses a challenge to dominant forms of discursive
order to such an extent that it may be seen as the unconscious
of those forms. That is, this language is not simply *oppressed*,
not allowed, it is radically *repressed*, impossible where current
forms are possible."[21] Therefore, Irigaray refuses the idea that
language is either universal or neutral with respect to sexual
difference: "In the face of language, constructed and maintained by men only, I raise the question of the specificity of a
feminine language: of a language which would be adequate for
the body, sex and the imagination (imaginary) of the woman"
(WE 62).

What Irigaray wishes to discover, then, is a positive rather
than negative means of figuring the feminine body. In *Ce sexe
qui n'en est pas un* (Paris: Les Editions de Minuit, 1977), Irigaray theorizes the discourse proper to the feminine body by
rejecting phallocentrism and valorizing the female sexual anatomy. Claire Pajaczkowska points out that there is some justification for the argument of isomorphism even in Lacan who
specifies the articulation of the drives across "rimlike" structures such as the anus, mouth, and presumably, the vagina.[22]
Of special significance to Irigaray, though, are the two lips of
the labia that in their mutual caress define femininity as a
fundamental autoeroticism. Being defined by two coequal parts,
feminine subjectivity is posited as a structure of the double:
two equal and ceaselessly interchangeable identities. This doubling at the level of sexual anatomy, Irigaray argues, determines feminine discourse as fundamentally plurivocalic and
polysemic. Moroever, this duality of structure does not mimic

the hierarchic system of Freud's *Witz*, but rather "the fact that at each moment there is always for women, 'at least two' meanings, without one being able to decide which meaning prevails, which is 'on top' or 'underneath,' which 'conscious' or 'repressed' " (WE 65). Without the ability or desire to hierarchize terms through the agency of binary oppositions, feminine discourse dismantles self-identical meaning—"In order for there to be a proper meaning, there must indeed be a unity somewhere. But if feminine language cannot be brought back to any unity, it cannot be simply described or defined: there is no feminine metalanguage" (WE 65).

In sum, Irigaray's designation of a specific feminine discourse devolving from the feminine body is meant to oppose patriarchal determinations of univocality and self-identical meaning with a language whose structure is polyvalent, polysemic, and plural. As Mary Ann Doane points out, even though Irigaray's work is highly speculative, it must be valued for the challenge it presents to phallocentric theories: "Her work is a radical rewriting of psychoanalysis which, while foregrounding the process of mimesis by which language represents the body, simultaneously constructs a distinction between a mimesis which is 'productive' and one which is merely 'reproductive' or 'imitative'—a process of 'adequation' and of 'specularization' " (WS 32).

The risk of essentialism in Irigaray's work is mitigated by Michèle Montrelay in her book *l'Ombre et le nom (sur la féminité)* (Paris: Les Editions de Minuit, 1977). In Montrelay's work, masculinity and femininity are described by reworking rather than refusing the phallocentric logic of Freud and Lacan. Sexual identity is still posed in relation to a third term—the phallus—which represents lack for both sexes according to the drama of the castration complex. According to Montrelay's formula, however, the specific difference of the woman is that she "lacks lack"; that is, the male child possesses the means to dramatize castration while the girl child does not.

Montrelay is ultimately unable to accept the Freudian logic problematizing Mulvey's work, for example, that of positing a single libidinal economy that is masculine and phallic. Renewing the challenge of Karen Horney and Ernest Jones to the

Vienna School on the issue of feminine sexuality, Montrelay posits a "concentric" libidinal economy isomorphic with the vagina, designating a specific, feminine unconscious that co-exists with the masculine. Thus Montrelay presents a radical account of a problem generally recognized by psychoanalytic theory. According to the phallocentric explication, feminine sexual identity and the ordering of female subjectivity in the symbolic is achieved only with difficulty. Typically, Freudian theories pose this problem either as a function of women's "negative" relation to Oedipus or with respect to a privileged relation with narcissism and the imaginary. In each case psychoanalytic theory argues that anatomical difference "permits" a different symbolization of the body. But as Parveen Adams notes, in Montrelay "this recognition is linked to the insistence of the real of the woman's body, that real which is by definition outside of symbolisation, all representation."[23]

Like Irigaray, what interests Montrelay most are the conditions under which representation fails. Phallocentric representation, whose privileged figure is metonymy, begins with the introduction of lack since what is symbolized is the absence of a desired object. While dividing the child from the mother, the paternal prohibition against incest also enables symbolization as the articulation of an object desired but forever lost. Access to the symbolic is thus ordered through the problem of castration and resolution of the Oedipus complex, as the signifier of the phallus must intervene in the child's relation with the maternal body whose undifferentiated plenitude is too immediate, too present.

In order for representation to be possible, something must be at stake. If the paternal prohibition against incest is to open a space between desire and its object, something must be capable of being lost. Here one encounters the Lacanian account of Oedipus in the problem of "being" or "having" the phallus in the symbolic negotiation of sexual difference. Belonging to neither sex, the phallus is important only in its function as a signifier, the third term in relation to which the sexes differentiate themselves. In Lacanian theory, both sexes initially define themselves according to the desire of the Other (the mother) in the mode of "being" the phallus, that which the mother lacks and desires. But on the Oedipal stage, the signifier of the phallus divides sexual difference into two routes. With the dissolution of Oedipus complex, the little boy ascends to the mode of "having" the phallus—since he possesses the means (the penis) to symbolize it—identifying with the authority of the symbolic, the law, and the language of the father. The little girl's transition to the symbolic, however, is incomplete with respect to this symbolization. According to the theory of negative entry into the symbolic, because she lacks the means to dramatize the loss of castration, the little girl continues in the mode of "being" the phallus for an other. In Montrelay's theory, the positing of woman's negative entry into the symbolic results in a surprising and paradoxical assessment of the stakes of woman's psychical oppression: "her different relation to language stems from the fact that she has nothing to lose, nothing at stake. Prohibition [castration], the law of limitation, cannot touch the little girl. For the little boy, on the other hand, there is most definitely something to lose" (WS 29).[24] In repeating or doubling the maternal body with her own, the woman is able to recover the originary "stake" of representation. She evades the possibility of losing the first object of desire since she can, in fact, become it. Without the means to symbolize lack, for women the problem of "having" or "not having" remains in the imaginary, the order of preoedipality and of the dual relation with the mother. As Stephen Heath notes, "Divided up in this order of the double, the woman experiences the symbolic castration from a site elsewhere to the man . . ." ("Difference," 68).

Montrelay argues on this basis that femininity is the "ruin of representation." Femininity is an obstacle to the symbolic in the form of the concentric drives (anal, oral, vaginal) that resist phallic symbolization and cannot be represented by it. Lacking the means to represent lack, the woman experiences the signifier as pure difference—a *jouissance* or plenitude unchecked, too present and too full. Failing with respect to symbolic castration in which she has no stake, she circumvents the surplus of repression that inaugurates the unconscious; falling below the symbolic, she is closer to the imaginary and an experience of the body: "For Montrelay, the woman pulls towards the unrepresentable, towards the ruin of representation, feminine sexuality is 'unexplorable', a dark continent 'outside the circuit of the symbolic economy' which the woman's *jouissance* contains and exceeds as an end of language, 'feminine *jouissance* of which nothing can be said, exceeding all meaning, contains by its very 'madness' the symbolic order'; thus 'to the extent that it does not know repression, femininity is the downfall of interpretation . . .' " ("Difference," 72)[25]

Moreover, Montrelay expressly argues for a comparison between the feminine experience of *jouissance* and that of modernist *écriture*, or more precisely, what Roland Barthes has referred to as *signifiance:* "when the text is read (or written) as a moving play of signifiers, without any possible reference to one or some fixed signifieds, it becomes necessary to distinguish signification . . . and the work of the signifier . . . — this work being called *signifiance. Signifiance* is a process in the course of which the 'subject' of the text, escaping the logic of the *ego-cogito* and engaging in other logics (of the signifier, of contradiction) struggles with meaning and is deconstructed ('lost')."[26] In its most radical formulation, the enunciatory source of *écriture* is the body of the woman. By disassembling Aristotelian logic, patriarchal language, and the self-identical ego, the designation of a specifically feminine positionality in language becomes the expression of the differential articulation of subjectivity sought by the discourse of political modernism.

However, as Parveen Adams points out, this possibility of an "antirepresentation" devolving from the feminine body relies on an irresolvable contradiction. If as psychoanalysis dictates, the symbolic is the order of language or that which makes representation possible, and if the feminine body "fails" the symbolic, how could a feminine discourse articulate the "unrepresentability" of the body? Falling outside the symbolic, how could femininity underwrite an alternative form of representation standing against the phallus as signifier of lack? "How *femininity* can otherwise function as an obstacle to the symbolic process is never elucidated. The co-existence of concentricity and phallocentrism which Montrelay sees as defining of the feminine unconscious remains an untheorised incom-

patibility" ("Representation and Sexuality," 78). Stephen
Heath observes that the danger of this notion is its perfect
synchronization with pregiven patriarchal stereotypes of the
woman figured as the irrational, disorder, the hysterical, or
madness. This is precisely the difficulty of Montrelay's metaphor of the Sphinx—the danger of the eternal feminine confronting Oedipus with the "ruin of representation" and a disordering of subjectivity.

The critical debates over Wollen and Mulvey's film *Riddles
of the Sphinx* have been waged in similar terms, "where the
sphinx is produced as a point of resistance that seems nevertheless to repeat, in its very terms, the relations of women
made within patriarchy, their representation in the conjunction of such elements as motherhood as mystery, the unconscious, a voice that speaks far off from the past through dream
or forgotten language" ("Difference," 73). *Riddles of the
Sphinx*—whose premise is to inquire what a "politics of the
unconscious" would be like—opens itself to the following critique. By engaging pregiven meanings even critically, the project of the film is imperiled by an unconscious surplus of signification where a figure of resistance takes on stereotypical
connotations. Even the best efforts of a feminist, political modernism to regain or restore the feminine body or voice can
veer dangerously close to essentialism. This is the argument
of *Riddles'* critics such as Judith Williamson and Peter Gidal.[27]
For Gidal the figure of woman as signified or as profilmic object
is definitely an impossibility. This is first of all because of his
categorical refutation of the signified, and second because of
his conviction that the given representations of "woman" or
"femininity" are so overdetermined by patriarchal culture that
it is impossible to articulate them otherwise. In fact, Gidal
argues in a manner that Mulvey's own essay on visual pleasure
would bear out. The signified of the feminine, of politics, or
even the politics of feminism in the cinema can only be given
in the space of the look, whose illusion of dominance and authority—in short, the *ego's* mastery of the image—can only
occur from a phallocentric position. However, unless one takes
a position as radical as Gidal's, *Riddles of the Sphinx* could be
exonerated by a reading that focuses not on the equation of

women and the unconscious in their film, but in Wollen/Mulvey's critical efforts to deploy the images and representations of femininity into a nonintegrative, contradictory textual economy whose objective is to problematize and open up that equation to discussion.

But in Gidal's critique another problem is presented as *Riddles'* valorization of women's closeness to the imaginary. In an interview in *Wedge*, Mulvey defends the sequence in the film that has received the most criticism. In the second to last of thirteen 360-degree pans comprising the center of the film, Louise, the central character, reads the transcript of a dream to her friend Maxine. Full of mirrors and excessively decorated with "feminine" accoutrements, Maxine's room has all the markings of a utopian, separate world of feminine sexuality defined by narcissism. Mulvey claims that she "wanted to set up narcissism and a sense of the female as something quite strong in opposition to the Oedipus complex."[28] But even taking this into account, Mulvey can only be referring to the level of *signification* in the film, not that of *identification*, which is precisely Gidal's point. The logic operating here—in a film that is expressly "about" the relations of motherhood under patriarchy—links the feminine specifically to the preoedipal, the mother-child dyad, the mirror stage, and primary narcissism.[29] It is also here, as Stephen Heath notes, that something of the "old cinema" returns.

> To define a difference on the basis of this imaginary, taken as a specific value, with characteristic effects of stressed relations between woman and narcissism, regression, and so on, can seem very quickly to repeat a definition maintained in the existing order, whose own imaginary, and imagery, of the woman is heavily implicated in attributions of defining narcissism. . . . Failing the symbolic, outside of representation, it is difficult then not to reproduce the woman as site of the specular, the enclosed reversibility of specularity, a cinema for the man and for herself; and it is not by chance that Montrelay can refer to the evidence of films. . . . ("Difference," 76-77)[30]

After this discussion, Heath presents another argument that has serious consequences both for *Riddles* and for Wollen's theory of "post-Brechtian materialism." Heath warns that,

strictly speaking, psychoanalytic theory cannot support a simple equivalence between the imaginary and the specular. Nor
should questions of identification and subjectivity be considered as a simple progression or transaction between the imaginary and the symbolic where the former is considered to be
some original, primary moment.[31] This caution has clear implications for Wollen's discussion of the assumed effects of
their representational strategies with respect to identification
and sexual difference. For example, Wollen's essay "The Field
of Language in Film" explicitly states the degree to which the
aesthetic strategies of his and Mulvey's films attempt to problematize identification by complicating the image/sound relation as mapped conceptually onto the relation between the
imaginary and the symbolic. Language, especially verbal language, threatens to "regulate" the spectator, to repeat his or
her placement in the symbolic as the order of Oedipus and of
patriarchy. However, language is also understood as breaking
the excessive lure of the image, of the imaginary and primary
narcissism.[32]

With its emphasis on the voice, not as language or the symbolic but as the specificity of feminine expression or feminine
écriture, Riddles of the Sphinx attempts to transpose the terms
of this opposition. According to Wollen and Mulvey, the complex interactions between Mulvey's direct address, the "voice"
of the Sphinx, and the diegetic speech of the characters are
intended to produce a feminine identification and a dispersal
of subjectivity as opposed to the "language of Oedipus . . .
transparent, assertive, and closed" ("Field of Language," 56).
As Heath points out, the specificity of feminine écriture is often
described by its closeness to the voice as "a trace of the in-
tensity of the attachment to the mother" or as "a voice imagined in the field of the Other as invocation of the mother,
movement through words to the invocatory 'grain of the
voice' " ("Difference," 83). The voice opposes itself to the
look as characterized in Hegel's aesthetics, for example, as
"theoretical" in terms of its acuity, neutrality, and mastery of
objects. Similarly, Irigaray attributes a disembodiment of sexuality or an impoverishment of the body to the domination of
the voice by the look.[33] The bridging of these terms—imagi-

nary:symbolic :: image:sound—is one of the more interesting
strategies of Wollen and Mulvey's film. But this only holds if
one accepts Wollen's simplified schema of the forms of identification thought to correspond to these terms and their necessary effect on the construction of the spectator. Moreover,
if this were the case, any historical understanding of identification processes would be reduced to a teleological system
that proceeds simply from the imaginary to the symbolic and
in which the system of the aesthetic text simply replays the
psychoanalytic constitution of subjectivity. Although meant to
regain the maternal, the preoedipal and the materiality of the
feminine body, Wollen and Mulvey's reformulation of the voice
threatens to collapse into the search for a lost, originary nature.
As Judith Williamson points out, "This use of the Sphinx can
be seen as part of a strategy intended to evoke mystery and
an image of inscrutable womanhood, as a preliminary to their
'deconstruction' with the later role of the Sphinx as a speaking
subject: 'she' is given a voice. But this involves a fundamental
misconception: you don't dispel a myth by trying to make it
speak, or reject an image by giving it a voice with which to
deny itself" ("Two or Three Things," 132). Once again, Wollen and Mulvey's theoretical justifications for their film must
strike a delicate balance between resistance and repression in
the articulation of a social myth.

Despite contradictory formulations, what theories of feminine *écriture* hope to offer to a psychoanalytic and political
consideration of the modernist text is the delineation of three
problem areas: (1) the possible relations between the sexed
body and its symbolization; (2) an account of structures of
identification with respect to sexual difference; and (3) a theory
of the avant-garde text that seeks to claim a special province
for the specificity of feminine identity and pleasure. Regarding
these issues, Stephen Heath has summarized four basic assumptions concerning the specificity of a feminine *écriture*.[34]
   1. *The woman is by nature a writer* because her excessive
jouissance, always in excess at the expense of the phallus and
the signifier, is itself a limit experience and an experience of
écriture: "feminine *jouissance* can be understood as *writing* . . .

this *jouissance* and the literary text (which is also written like an orgasm produced from within discourse), are the effect of the same murder of the signifier" (Montrelay, "Inquiry into Femininity," 99).

2. *The woman's experience of écriture is profound because she is close to the body, less divided from it in the symbolic, and thus closer to the "source" of writing.* Cixous writes that "a feminine textual body can be recognized by the fact that it is always without end, has no finish, which moreover is what makes the feminine text very often difficult to read."[35] Similarly, Irigaray insists that the woman's experience of *écriture*—a syntax of autoaffection, fluid and plural in style, whose source is the two labia—opposes itself to the phallocentric and self-identical "I" of Aristotelian logic.

3. *The woman's position with respect to language falls outside the law, the logic of patriarchy, and the order of the symbolic.* This assumption informs even textual analyses of realist texts. In her assessment of the critical work of Claire Johnston, Janet Bergstrom points out that Johnston was quick to accept—in the account of woman's negative entry into the symbolic and its corollary the repression of the feminine and the preoedipal as a condition of language—the possibility of feminine discourse specific to women filmmakers. In Johnston's work on Dorothy Arzner, for example, Bergstrom explains that "the discourse of the woman, or rather her [Arzner's] attempt to locate it, and to make it heard, is what gives the system of the text its structural coherence, while at the same time rendering the dominant discourse of the male fragmented and incoherent."[36] And when writing on films of the feminist avant-garde, such as those of Chantal Akerman, Johnston takes Kristeva at her word. In Bergstrom's reading, Johnston argues that *Jeanne Dielman*, "by refusing to present us with the security of the reverse shot, opens up an eruption of the semiotic (which in this essay seems to be equated with the drives as well as the 'feminine'), and that the rupture here threatens the fragmentation of the Symbolic order itself through the over-inscription of the repression of sexual difference."[37] The specificity of a "language" of the feminine body is thus linked to a director's "*écriture*" and articulated within the context of film author-

ship. Similarly, the opposition between realism and modernism in the discourse of political modernism is reworked as the opposition between masculine and feminine discourse.

4. *Feminine écriture has no metalanguage*, in fact, it is *antitheoretical.* This is a significant departure from previous conceptualizations in the discourse of political modernism. According to Irigaray, the specificity of feminine language resides in its "jamming of the machinery of theory" and its deconstruction of Aristotelian logic and syntax. Here the reference to Marxism is dropped. The opposition to ideology through a critique of representation is defined in the struggle *against* patriarchy, not *for* theoretical practice.

Within these terms it appears that the theoretical discourse on femininity appears ready-made as a mythology of the avant-garde text. More clearly, in its recourse to the vocabulary of "deconstruction" the discourse *of* femininity maps itself across the opposition of *écriture* to *parole* with startling consequences. Where the conceptualization of the feminine "voice" coincides with a modernist *écriture*, it becomes a discourse of autoaffection; perhaps not one of self-identical consciousness, but certainly one of a repressed, but articulable Being. Paradoxically, by presuming a direct, internal, and determinate relation with the subject of enunciation, this autoaffecting feminine discourse has specific structural correspondences with the assumed autointelligibility of epistemological modernism.

Why insist then on the feminine body as the origin of this "writing"? Beverly Brown and Parveen Adams reason that the attractiveness of this idea devolves from the following principle: "in taking up and standing by the experience of the feminine body, it will be possible to discover simultaneously an authentic definition of the feminine and a politics based upon the liberation of a political force."[38] This assumption centers the diverse theories of a specific feminine practice in language, including essentialist positions as well as the attempts to transcend them. Despite differences in their work, Irigaray, Montrelay, Kristeva, and many of those in film influenced by them stand in the same relation to a theory of the feminine body in representation and politics on the basis of three points.

1. The theory requires that the feminine body be the definite locus of the feminine itself; that is, the body must provide "proper" recognition of feminine sexuality. Moreover, recognition of this body would enable an overthrow of the discursive and social practices that have censored it until now.

2. An appeal to the originary force of the feminine body stands for the experiential over the rational. Opposed to predication by patriarchal discourse, it is the antitheoretical body and stands outside of any "structure, practice or discourse, an externality registered by making the body natural or pre-social; and it is ordered by its capacity to feel, to experience" (FBFP 36).

3. The experience of the body is thought to find expression primarily through speech or voice; or more precisely, that voice that finds expression as an unmediated relation with the rhythms of the body.

However, it is equally necessary to explain the differences between Irigaray, Montrelay, and Kristeva with respect to these issues. This is less a matter of essentialism than of the degree of determination given to the mimetic relation of language to body. On one hand, Irigaray appeals to an anatomical reality mapped onto speech through a structural correspondence, if not mimesis strictly speaking. Kristeva and Montrelay, on the other hand, who are closer to Lacanian theory, submit that "the repression of the feminine is not merely something which a patriarchal discourse does, historically speaking, effect, but that this exclusion is the condition for there to be discourse at all" (FBFP 39).

In her commentary on Freud's analysis of "Dora," Jacqueline Rose suggests that the inherent difficulties of these arguments must be overcome by considering femininity not *as* discourse, but rather *within* discourse as a position to be assumed, refused, or renegotiated within a specific social system of representation.[39] I do not want to reconsider the intricacies of Rose's excellent analysis here, but a summary of some of her conclusions will be helpful.

Rose notes how work on feminine sexuality, especially that which resists or exceeds the genital and reproductive function of the body, stresses the preoedipal attachment between the mother and the girl child. Since the function of the Oedipus complex and its symbolization of the body is to sunder this relation, placing the girl in a circuit of symbolic exchange, theorists assign a radical status to this resistance to positioning: "What seems to happen is that the desire to validate the preoedipal instance as resistance to the Oedipal structure itself leads to a 'materialisation' of the *bodily* relation which underpins it, so that the body of the mother, or more properly the girl's relation to it, is then placed as being somehow outside repression" ("'Dora'," 11). In Montrelay, the maternal body becomes the site of the unrepressed; in Irigaray, that of a primary autoeroticism whose restoration would mean the return of the feminine exile. Kristeva poses the maternal body in relation to different registers of language: the symbolic—a postoedipal linguistic structure marked by the phonologico-syntactic organization of the sentence—is opposed to the semiotic, a preoedipal linguistic register characterized by rhythm and intonation. In this manner, the discourses of the hysteric, the schizophrenic, the ecstatic, and others who have "failed repression" are defined in terms of a poetic, specifically feminine, discourse.

From these arguments, two primary assumptions about the feminine-as-discourse can be described, and both reveal the contradictoriness of posing any strict identity between the body and language. First, according to Rose, the concept of anatomical mimesis is contrary to the linguistic definition of the sign as arbitrarily motivated because an unmediated relation between the body and language is presupposed. Paradoxically, where linguistics assigns value in terms of *difference*, the body achieves an intrinsic relation to language as the essential unity of a signifier to signified or an integral sign identical to being. Second, "the concept of the feminine as outside discourse involves a theory of language in which a non-excentric relation to language would be possible, the subject as control and origin of meaning which is to render meaningless both the concept of the unconscious and that of the subject" ("'Dora'," 14-15). Emphasizing the deconstructive and decentering aspects of plurality and polyvocality, the psychoanalytic justifications of feminine discourse must paradoxically presuppose both a self-identical sign and a self-identical subject of enunciation.

If the project of political modernism stands or falls on its different articulation of the subject, one last criticism of theories of feminine *écriture* is possible. Does not the concept of a modernist "decentering" of identity *presuppose the subject as an already integral entity?* The unity of the subject within itself and in relation to its language is, of course, a hypothesis that psychoanalysis has continued to refute. Further, as Parveen Adams questions, "Is it not the case that in operating with unified entities we are kept busy explaining unities while the effect of practices of representation are *not*, in fact, unified? To say this is to suggest that a series of sexual differences is constructed through practices of representation and in such a way that sexual distinctions set up under different discursive conditions may vary, overlap, be contradictory, etc. ("Sexual Division and Sexual Differences," 56).

These criticisms do not necessarily refute the idea of a feminine aesthetic practice. Instead, they suggest that if this practice is to have consequences for a theory of ideology, then a relation of nonidentity between the body and representation must be presupposed. In a sense, this is what Kristeva and Montrelay suggest when they discuss the texts of Stéphane Mallarmé, Antonin Artaud, Georges Bataille, Alfred Jarry, and so on. Rather than rejecting difference, this position accounts for the variability of identification in relation to enunciative positions and potentialities. By confronting the linearity, closure, and self-identity of patriarchal discourse, the notion of *écriture* still articulates the possibility of a feminine discourse. But here the feminine loosens itself from an anatomical definition, transgressing the lines of biological sex. The association of poetic language with Kristeva's semiotic and preoedipality can be read in another way. In response to Brown and Adams, Mary Ann Doane points out that far from being synonymous with a state of nature, preoedipal sexuality already assumes an organized network of erotogenic zones and object relations, opened up across the infant's body in the desiring relations submitted to it by its parents, especially the mother. It is a pregiven structure of fantasy—organized by, and representing the desire of, the parents—that constructs the infant's sexual identity. Doane cites Jean Laplanche in defense of this observation: "These zones, then, attract the first erotogenic maneuvers from the adult. An even more significant factor, if we introduce the subjectivity of the first 'partner': these zones *focalize parental fantasies* and above all *maternal fantasies,* so that we may say, in what is barely a metaphor, that they are the points through which is *introduced into the child that alien internal entity* which is, properly speaking, the *sexual excitation.*"[40]

In its definition of the maternal relation, preoedipality is an already given scenario to which the infant is submitted. The parents are the agents of sociality in their articulation of a formative desire and a sexual identity on the infant's body, thus displacing any notions of a natural sexuality. As Doane herself notes, without recognition of this anchoring of sexuality in the social, psychoanalysis is condemned to repeat the vicious circle of patriarchy in its theorizations of the body.

In psychoanalytic theory, the difficulty in differentiating between a masculine and feminine unconscious—exactly the problem Mulvey is unable to overcome in her account of cinematic identification—is insurmountable only as long as one refuses to recognize that sexuality is not a content or a component of the body, but a process that fully engages the bisexual disposition of every individual. The unconscious is the fact of the division of the subject in the symbolic. Rather than determining the division of male from female, this ordering of the unconscious establishes difference as a transactional relation between the masculine and feminine positions through which the social and sexual history of the subject is negotiated (and renegotiated) in the symbolic. Jacqueline Rose offers an interesting demonstration of these ideas in a reading of Freud's essay on " 'A Child Is Being Beaten'." In an analysis of what are primarily feminine fantasies, Freud shows that designations of male and female cannot be simply assimilated to qualities of activity and passivity. Further, there is always a split between the sexual object and the sexual aim, or between the object and the subject of desire. In social and cultural terms, what Freud's text reveals is that there is no sexual difference that predates representation. The splitting of subjectivity and the series of identifications accomplished across the states of the beating fantasy demonstrate a process of being held to *a* sexual representation (masculinity *or* femininity). This identity, however, has no immediate or stable referent in terms of either biological or ontological origins. For what Freud's analysis of the fantasy reveals is not the fixing of identity to a body, but rather a shifting structure of symbolization and differentiation as well as the continuing permutation of the fantasy's constituent, imaginary terms.[41]

Ultimately, the theorization of problems of identification and sexual difference in alternative aesthetic practices should not seek to divide or typify "writing" on the basis of anatomical difference. Rather this theory should work through the socially and historically determined positions and relations of meaning that construct and deploy discourses on masculinity and femininity within patriarchal culture. To ask whether a text is "masculine" *or* "feminine" is to posit empirical criteria, physical or metaphysical, against which difference must be measured. Therefore, the necessary question for any psychoanalytically informed theory or practice equating feminism and modernism will be the following: *Will this measure be the body itself or the socially given symbolizations of the body?*

Most essays on the representation of women assume a measure against the "real," just as most essays on the relation of sexual difference to feminine discourse assume a measure against the physical real in the form of presence or absence of the penis in relation to its imaginary operator, the phallus. The former relies on metaphysical and essentialist judgments, the latter on a mechanical materialism. In their fundamental determination by a logic of binarism and opposition, both arrive at the same conclusion with respect to the body's support of these judgments—sexuality divides and distributes beings irrevocably into mutually exclusive and antagonistic groups. Ideology does have a stake in remembering anatomical difference in its hierarchical organization of beings according to largely unconscious relations of power. But one must also understand the profoundly social dimension of representation and the symbolization of the body in a skewed and uneven relation to the real. Where ideology takes effect is in the transactions between masculine and feminine positions assumed consciously or not by individuals. The symbolization organized by ideology does not blossom from the body; the body receives this symbolization. The body is figured and ordered by ideology.

What must be held onto is not the utopia of the "real" of the female body, but the phantasmatic organization of sexual difference and sexuality in and through discursive formations. Teresa de Lauretis emphasizes this point in her account of Kaja Silverman's essay *"Histoire d'O:* The Story of a Disciplined and Punished Body":

> "The structuration of the female subject begins not with her entry into language, or her subordination to a field of cultural desire, but with the organization of her body" by means of a discourse which speaks for her and to which she has no access. The body "is charted, zoned and made to bear meaning, a meaning which proceeds entirely from external relationships, but which is always subsequently apprehended as an internal condition or essence." That internal condition, the essence of femininity, is then a product of discourse.[42]

Identity and identification are not fixed through their analogical coincidence with the body. Rather, the division of the subject in language traverses distinctions of internality or externality, as well as the temporal assignation of origins, in its organization through processes of identification. Furthermore, these processes are always incomplete and must seek continually to inscribe or rememorize sexual difference as positionalities through which the subject articulates its (imaginary) relation to its body, its sexuality, and its relation to others.

Those views considering gendered identity, language, or representation as derived a priori from the biologically sexed body must be opposed to a historical materialist account of how sexual identity is organized, perpetuated, and legislated by different discursive practices, including the medical and legal as well as the aesthetic. As Brown and Adams argue, "If, further, the *sexed* body exists differently for those practices, then the question of identification is made even more problematic. The consequence is that neither the individual, nor

the sum of individuals, can find a primary location within their
bodily definition. Instead, one finds a variety of agents, with
varying rights and forms of recognition, and this cannot simply
be reduced to a totality of individuals, or even a totality of
men and a totality of women" (FBFP 43).

Teresa de Lauretis has also proposed a critique of essentialism and of theories of identification founded on a binary
logic of mutually exclusive subjective categories. Taking Freud
at his word, in *Alice Doesn't* de Lauretis forwards several arguments demonstrating the incompatibility of psychoanalytic
and ontological accounts of sexual difference. First, identification is a *process* of ego formation; it is fundamentally historical, open-ended, ongoing, and it can never be fixed to an
ontological state. In even the most sympathetic analyses, the
place of the female spectator is forgotten by erring on this
point, which subscribes fully to a certain phallocentrism in
Lacan. In Freud, writes de Lauretis,

> The point, however, is made . . . that "femininity" and "mas-
> culinity" are never fully attained or fully relinquished: "in the
> course of some women's lives there is a repeated alternation
> between periods in which femininity or masculinity gain the
> upper hand." The two terms, femininity and masculinity, do not
> refer so much to qualities or states of being inherent in a person,
> as to positions which she occupies in relation to desire. They
> are terms of identification. And the alternation between them,
> Freud seems to suggest, is a specific character of female sub-
> jectivity. . . . The analogy that links identification-with-the-look
> to masculinity [activity, sadism] and identification-with-the-im-
> age to femininity [passivity, narcissism or masochism] breaks
> down precisely when we think of a spectator alternating be-
> tween the two. Neither can be abandoned for the other, even
> for a moment; no image can be identified, or identified with,
> apart from the look that inscribes it as image, and vice versa. If
> the female subject were indeed related to the film in this man-
> ner, its division would be irreparable, unsuturable; no identi-
> fication or meaning would be possible. This difficulty has led
> film theorists, following Lacan and forgetting Freud, practically
> to disregard the problem of sexual differentiation *in the spec-
> tators* and to define cinematic identification as masculine, that
> is to say, as an identification with the gaze, which both histor-

ically and theoretically is the representation of the phallus and
the figure of the male's desire.[43]

Regardless of whether a masculine or a feminine subjectivity
is at stake, whenever one speaks of the *processes* of identification the ego is always *active* in its aims "or at least must
fantasize itself in an active manner" (AD 142). The result, de
Lauretis concludes, is that identification should be understood
not as a singular or simple process, but as a multiple, complex,
and contradictorily determined one, especially in the case of
female spectatorship.[44] Whereas the definition of feminine
écriture in the discourse of political modernism holds onto an
ontological categorization of sexual difference to preserve the
utopian idea of a feminine subject-position as "unsuturable,"
de Lauretis adopts a more pragmatic and precise view. "Femininity" and "masculinity" are detached from reference to ontologically specific categories and defined, in a specifically
Freudian sense, as "positions occupied by the subject in relation to desire, corresponding respectively to the passive and
the active aims of the libido" (AD 143). Language and the
body are irreducible. The forms of subjectivity, multiple and
mobile, that an individual may assume are always received
from the social, from the body's insertion into the symbolic,
and are never interiorized fully. Thus the character of subjectivity and its forms of identification must always be marked
by process, by incompletion, always falling short of the plenitude of self-identical being.

Feminist theory, de Lauretis argues, should no longer concern itself so exclusively with the "forms" of identification—
structures of fetishism or voyeurism—through which the figuration of "femininity" is made to serve the representational
needs of patriarchy. Nor should the equation of femininity with
negation submit itself to this binary logic as the "return of the
repressed" in the attempt to justify forms of an avant-garde
writing as necessarily confounding the unity and hegemony of
patriarchal representation and as forging relations of subjectivity adequate to the feminine body. "For even in the most
overt gesture of opposition," she writes, "in the political remarking of its irreducible difference, the feminist critique is
not pure, absolute negativity but rather historically conscious

negation; the negation of existing cultural values, of current definitions, and of the terms in which theoretical questions are couched." She continues by arguing for the necessity of resisting "the pressure of the binary epistemological model towards coherence, unity, and the production of a fixed self/image, a subject-vision, and to insist instead on the production of contradictory points of identification. . ." (AD 77).

The stakes of this critique are crucial. In its foundation, the ontological justification of feminine *écriture* is idealist and ahistorical; it can only conceive of the female spectator as pure negativity (either a theoretical impossibility from the view of phallocentric accounts, or, in the opposite extreme, as that utopian place standing outside of patriarchal identity or theory) or as a heretofore repressed and degraded, but ultimately recoverable Being. As de Lauretis lucidly reminds us, "film spectators enter the movie theatre as either men or women, which is not to say that they are simply male or female but rather that each person goes to the movies with a semiotic history, personal and social, a series of previous identifications by which she or he has been somehow en-gendered" (AD 145). In their incessant encounters with social discourses, these identifications across sexual difference will be either sustained and rememorized, or challenged in their apparent self-identity. But once again, this discursive "encounter" is neither singular nor simple. It cannot be reduced to an identity theory or to any simple account of subject/object relations. Rather than the encounter of a "subject" with a "text," it is a historical engendering of subjectivity within a multiple, complex, and contradictory intersection of discourses. In Claire Johnston's concise formulation, "feminist film practice can no longer be seen simply in terms of the effectivity of a system of representation, but rather as a production of and by subjects already in social practices which always involve heterogeneous and often contradictory positions in ideologies. In other words, feminist film practice is determined by the conjuncture of discursive, economic and political practices that produce subjects in history."[45]

If a theory of the subject is to be produced in its specific difference(s), that theory can be conceived neither on the basis of the singularity and unity of a text nor that of the identity of a body. The appeal of any text or of any representation is to an individual always already socialized in terms of sexual difference, that difference itself being a function of representation. In their ideological function, texts may either serve to reconfirm and reiterate the already achieved identifications of individuals or they may attempt to challenge them. But note that this discussion remains solely at the level of aesthetic discourse and its assumed subjective effects. I hope to have demonstrated that even the most avant-garde texts can be pulled toward retrogressive readings, and supposedly deconstructive "writing" can simply repeat the terms of a metaphysics, depending upon the theories that they address and that negotiate for them given readings and forms of reception.

This is not to say, however, that the question of a feminist aesthetic practice serves no purpose for the concrete struggles of the feminist movement in its ongoing critique of patriarchal representations and patriarchal power. Quite the contrary, it locates more precisely the effectivity of those practices seeking to shift relations of discourse and power that trade on the assignations of sexual difference in patriarchal culture. On this basis, one may understand the feminist critique of representation to have already been decisive. Toward the end of her chapter on "Imaging" in *Alice Doesn't,* and after having made a strong case for overcoming the exclusivity of a certain formalist conception of political modernism, de Lauretis defines her version of the task of a feminist aesthetic practice. She remarks, as Mulvey well noted, that

> In the frame of reference of men's cinema, narrative, and visual theories, the male is the measure of desire, quite as the phallus is its signifier and the standard of visibility in psychoanalysis. The project of feminist cinema, therefore, is not so much "to make visible the invisible," as the saying goes, or to destroy vision altogether, as to construct another (object of) vision and the conditions of visibility for a different social subject. . . . The present task of theoretical feminism and of feminist film practice alike is to articulate the relations of the female subject to representation, meaning, and vision, and in so doing to construct the terms of another frame of reference, another measure of desire. (AD 67-68)

The potential difficulty of this statement resides in a latent essentialism; the standard equating visibility to knowledge— of the represse ¹, unconscious, or impossible place of feminine desire—has not yet been displaced even as it is being criticized. But there is a distinct shift of emphasis in de Lauretis's work that obviates this criticism. The insistence on defining a feminist aesthetic practice, and the function this problem serves in her work, are not founded on the centrality of the text as a self-identical object fully adequate to a feminine subjectivity. Her emphasis, rather, is *intertextual* in the sense of an interlocking grid of discourses that support and perpetuate given paradigms of meaning and subjectivity in a historically specific culture. In this context, the interrelatedness of feminist theory and practice cannot be ignored. Feminist criticism is understood not only as transforming the conditions of aesthetic production; it also questions the institutional complicities—acknowledged or unacknowledged—between theoretical and critical practices, aesthetic practices, and hegemonic social discourses. Certainly, transformations within the field of aesthetic practice are crucial to this project. But if the ultimate goal is knowledge—creating different relations or possibilities of knowledge, subjectivity, and desire— then this process resides not solely in the formal possibilities of a text. It takes place in the transformations and displacements that must begin (and potentially have begun) to occur in the set of institutional discourses of cinema, and beyond, of the practices of knowledge and the representations of sexual difference.

Therefore, this struggle—which has produced effects as certain as they are fragile—is a conjunctural one. It is defined not through an ontological conception of identity—which determines a teleological movement toward the redemption of a suppressed but articulable Being—nor through an overvaluation of aesthetic *text* as the determining site of subjectivity and of a definitive break with ideology. Rather, this struggle moves forward in multiply and unevenly determined discursive series where aesthetic practices are received, read, and transformed in relation to the institutional practices of theory, criticism, and pedagogy, and to the organized struggle of political movements. Thus de Lauretis concludes that "if the project of feminist cinema—to construct the terms of reference of another measure of desire and the conditions of visibility for a different social subject—seems now more possible and indeed to a certain extent already actual, it is largely due to the work produced in response to that self-discipline and to the knowledge generated from the practice of feminism and film" (AD 155).

What the encounter of psychoanalytic theory with sexual difference demonstrates is that a text is not the same for everyone; its potential meanings and effects engage spectators differently. But this is not to suppose that, conversely, texts are different for everyone or even that they are integrally and essentially different for male or female spectators. This is tantamount to accepting automatically what sexual difference, in its socially given forms, presupposes as the fixity and irreversibility of its opposing term—masculine *or* feminine. It is the potential mobility and multiplicity of identities traversing this polarity that is regulated by the logic of patriarchal and phallocentric representation. Alternatively, to open up this opposition, and to refuse the terms of its fixity could only expand rather than defuse its political impact. As Stephen Heath argues, it would be a profound mistake if feminism were reduced to the "feminine," which is exactly the error of essentialist theory: "feminism, feminist practice and theory, is based on the analysis of the real experience and situation of women, part of which analysis has involved exactly the demonstration and refusal of the fixing of the 'feminine,' 'femininity' " (*The Sexual Fix*, 142). Moreover, the subject addressed by a film, or by any other discourse, is always distinct from the individual who may or may not assume the invited position. And, similarly, individuals may confront films with critical or theoretical contexts that radically challenge the films' modes of address. Any theory of film and ideology hoping to account for problems of spectatorship and of the productivity of meaning must accept that readings are neither necessarily determined nor free, but are given historically in the forms of intelligibility underwriting norms of representation and interpretation. What is needed, then, and what I hope to have begun here, is a more complete account of how theories (articulated or not) subtending the production and reception of films are regulated by an intertextual network of discourses that pose both the possibilities and the limitations of textual interpretations and uses.

NOTES

1. Trans. Parveen Adams, *m/f* 1 (1978): 89.
2. See Jacqueline Rose's "The Cinematic Apparatus: Problems in Current Theory" in *The Cinematic Apparatus*, eds. Teresa de Lauretis and Stephen Heath (New York: St. Martin's Press, 1980): 172-86, and Constance Penley's " 'A Certain Refusal of Difference': Feminism and Film Theory" in *Art After Modernism: Rethinking Representation*, ed. Brian Wallis (Boston: David R. Godine, Publisher, Inc., 1984): 375-89.
3. *m/f* 3 (1979): 51-57.
4. "Visual Pleasure and Narrative Cinema," *Screen* 16.3 (Autumn 1975), 6; hereafter cited as VP. Both the Wollen and Heath essays discussed in the last chapter were published the year *after* Mulvey's essay, interestingly enough. Heath's writing, however, later took a decisive shift in an effort to respond to these questions. See his important essay "Difference," *Screen* 19.3 (Autumn 1978): 50-112.
5. *October* 17 (Summer 1981): 23-36; cited as WS.
6. *Framework* 10 (Spring 1979): 3-10. For other useful synoptic accounts of feminism's encounter with film theory, see Annette Kuhn's *Women's Pictures: Feminism and Cinema* (London: Routledge and Kegan Paul, 1982); Christine Gledhill's "Recent Developments in Feminist Criticism," *Quarterly Review of Film Studies* 3.4 (Fall 1978): 457-93; E. Ann Kaplan's *Women and Film: Both Sides of the Camera* (New York: Methuen, 1983); and Peter Wollen's "Counter-Cinema and Sexual Difference" in Jane Weinstock, ed. *Difference: On Representation and Sexuality* (New York: The New Museum of Contemporary Art, 1985): 35-39.
7. Teresa de Lauretis, *Alice Doesn't* (Bloomington: Indiana University Press, 1984): 58; cited as AD.
8. Mulvey offers the following summary of the dialectic in which the female body ceaselessly threatens and reconfirms the coherence of narrative and spectacle: "the female image as a castration threat constantly endangers the unity of the diegesis and bursts through the world of illusion as an intrusive, static, one-dimensional fetish. Thus the two looks materially present in time and space are obsessively subordinated to the neurotic needs of the male ego. The camera becomes the mechanism for producing an illusion of Renaissance

space, flowing movements compatible with the human eye, an ideology of representation that revolves around the perception of the subject; the camera's look is disavowed in order to create a convincing world in which the spectator's surrogate can perform with verisimilitude. Simultaneously, the look of the audience is denied an intrinsic force: as soon as fetishistic representation of the female image threatens to break the spell of illusion, and the erotic image on the screen appears directly (without mediation) to the spectator, the fact of fetishisation, concealing as it does castration fear, freezes the look, fixates the spectator and prevents him from achieving any distance from the image in front of him" (VP 18).

9. See, for example, my own "Difficulty of Difference," *Wide Angle* 15.1 (Spring 1981): 4-15 and Teresa de Lauretis's *Alice Doesn't*, especially pages 59-60. I would also like to thank Elissa Marder for several of the ideas that follow and for sharing them with me. My analysis of the desire for a theory of political modernism as inscribed within the binary logic of "Visual Pleasure" is fundamentally indebted to her reading of Mulvey's essay.

10. In *La révolution du langage poétique*, Julia Kristeva claims that signifying practices distribute themselves into four topoi, depending on the particular character of the transaction between the symbolic and semiotic registers. This material has been presented in English as "Four Types of Signifying Practices," a paper delivered at Columbia University, September 1973.

This transaction between the two orders or registers of semiosis has also been explained succinctly by Steve Burniston and Chris Weedon: "Drawing on Lacan's theory of the constitution of the subject in language, Kristeva describes the semiotic as what can be hypothetically posited as logically preceding the imposition of the symbolic order on the individual via the mirror phase and the acquisition of language. It is the already-given arrangement of the drives and so-called primary processes which displace and condense energies in the form of facilitations or pathways (*Bahnungen* in Freud) and their return to the symbolic system proper in the form of rhythms, intonations and lexical, syntactical and theoretical transformations. This arrangement of drives, which underpins language and the symbolic order, is termed the *semiotic chora* by Kristeva. It is the site of what she calls *negativity*, the process of semiotic generation whereby the drives constantly challenge and transform the subject in the symbolic order. The semiotic order is heterogenous to meaning, i.e. external to it, meaning being contained within the symbolic order. It is however always either with a view to meaning or in a relation of negation or excess with regard to it. Kristeva stresses that in poetic language, which *is* socially communicable, this semiotic heterogeneity that theory can posit is *inseparable* from the symbolic function of *signifiance.*" ("Ideology, Subjectivity and the Artistic Text," *Working Papers in Cultural Studies* 10 [1977]: 224.)

11. In her essay, "Writing the Body: Toward an Understanding of *L'écriture feminine,*" Ann Rosalind Jones explains Kristeva's identification of femininity with a possible revolutionary subjectivity in the following terms: "How do women fit into this scheme of semiotic liberation? Indirectly, as mothers, because they are the first love objects from which the child is typically separated and turned away in the course of his initiation into society [through the passing of the Oedipus complex]. In fact, Kristeva sees semiotic discourse as an incestuous challenge to the symbolic order, asserting as it does the writer's return to the pleasures of his preverbal identification with his mother and his refusal to identify with his father and the logic of paternal discourse. Women, for Kristeva, also speak and write as 'hysterics,' as outsiders to male-dominated discourse, for two reasons: the predominance in them of drives related to anality and childbirth, and their marginal position vis-à-vis masculine culture. Their semiotic style is likely to involve repetitive, spasmodic separations from the dominating discourse, which, more often, they are forced to imitate.

"Kristeva doubts, however, whether women should aim to work out alternative discourses. She sees certain liberatory potentials in their marginal position, which is (admirably) unlikely to produce a fixed, authority-claiming subject/speaker or language: 'In social, sexual and symbolic experiences, being a woman has always provided a means to another end, to becoming something else: a subject-in-the-making, a subject on trial.' Rather than formulating a new discourse, women should persist in challenging the discourses that stand: 'If women have a role to play, . . . it is only in assuming a *negative* function: reject everything finite, definite, structured, loaded with meaning, in the existing state of society. Such an attitude places women on the side of the explosion of social codes: with revolutionary movements.' In fact, 'woman' to Kristeva represents not so much a sex as an attitude, any resistance to conventional culture and language. . ." *(Feminist Studies* 7.2 [Summer 1981]: 249.) The interior citations are from *New French Feminisms*: 166-67. Also see Kristeva's "Le sujet en procès" in *Polylogue* (Paris: Editions du Seuil, 1977).

12. *October* 17 (Summer 1981): 53-60.

13. In her analysis of Nicholas Roeg's *Bad Timing* (1980), de Lauretis cites Kristeva's definition of negativity: "Believing oneself 'a woman' is almost as absurd and obscurantist as believing oneself 'a man.' I say almost because there are still things to be got for women: freedom of abortion and contraception, childcare facilities, recognition of work, etc. Therefore, 'we are women' should still be kept as a slogan, for demands and publicity. But more fundamentally, women cannot *be*: the category woman is even that which does not fit into *being*. From there, women's practice can only be negative, in opposition to that which exists, to say that 'this is not it' and 'it is not yet.' What I mean by 'woman' is that which is not represented, that which is unspoken, that which is left out of namings and ideologies" (AD 94-95). Kristeva's comments are cited from an interview conducted by Claire Pajaczkowska in *m/f* 5/6 (1981): 166.

14. "Misrecognition and Identity," *Cine-tracts* 11 (Fall 1979): 29. My own essay "The Difficulty of Difference" also criticizes Mulvey on this point and goes on to explain her symptomatic silence in terms of a political reluctance to account for feminine spectatorship on the basis of an economy of masochism. Mulvey has updated her argument in "Afterthoughts on 'Visual Pleasure and Narrative Cinema' Inspired by 'Duel in the Sun'," *Framework* 15/16/17 (Summer 1981): 12-15. Also see Mulvey's essay "Changes," *Discourse* 7 (Spring 1985): 11-30.

15. AD 59-60. De Lauretis attenuates her comments in the following manner: "The importance of Mulvey's essay, marking and summing up an intensely productive phase of feminist work with film, is not to be diminished by the limitations of its theoretical scope. . . . And indeed the program has not been rigorously followed by feminist filmmakers. Which is not meant, again, as a *post-factum* criticism of an ideological analysis that has promoted and sustained the politicization of film practice, and feminist film practice in particular; on the contrary, the point is to assess its historical significance and to locate the usefulness of its lesson in the very limits it has posed and allowed to be tested" (AD 60-61).

There is another point that bears noting here. Mulvey has been criticized by de Lauretis and others for downplaying, even disparaging, the problem of pleasure in relation to a possible feminist aesthetic practice. However, I believe that when Mulvey speaks of the problem of "pleasure," she is not promoting a cinema of "unpleasure." Rather, she implicitly invokes the distinction, often used by both Barthes and Kristeva, between *plaisir* and *jouissance*. In Stephen Heath's gloss, "pleasure" or *plaisir* is "linked to cultural enjoyment and identity, to the cultural enjoyment of identity, to a homogenizing movement of the ego," while *jouissance* is "a radically violent pleasure . . . which shatters—dissipates, loses—that cultural identity, that ego." See his "Translator's Note" to *Image/Music/Text* (Glasgow: Fontana, 1977): 9.

In their anthology, *New French Feminisms* (Amherst: University of Massachusetts Press, 1980), Elaine Marks and Isabelle de Courtivron explain the explicitly feminist connotations of the concept of *jouissance:* "This pleasure, when attributed to a woman, is considered to be of a different order from the pleasure that is represented within the male libidinal economy often described in terms of the capitalist gain and profit motive. Women's *jouissance* carries with it the notion of fluidity, diffusion, duration. It is a kind of potlatch in the world of orgasms, a giving, expending, dispensing of pleasure without concern about ends or closure" ("Introduction III, 36-37, n.8).

16. Gidal states, "The system of identification which ultimately reproduces the dominant codes of meaning and behaviour, of sex position or of other 'values,' is the basic support structure for the telling of the (patriarchal) story, that recurrent search for the origin of truth, the word, the law, power." Cited from his "Some Problems 'Relating to' Andy Warhol's *Still Life* (1976)," *Artforum* (May 1978), in Gidal's "The Anti-Narrative," *Screen* 20.2 (Summer 1979): 82. Gidal's criticisms of Mulvey's film work with Peter Wollen is particularly severe on this account. See his "The Anti-Narrative," 77, 82-83 passim., and "Technology and Ideology in/through/and Avant-Garde Film," in *The Cinematic Apparatus*, eds. Teresa de Lauretis and Stephen Heath (New York: St. Martin's Press, 1980): 169.

17. Hélène Cixous and Catherine Clément, *La jeune née* (Paris: Union Générale d'Editions, 1975): 151, cited in Stephen Heath's translation in *The Sexual Fix* (London: The MacMillan Press, 1982): 111.

18. Carolyn Burke provides a detailed analysis of Irigaray's complex and difficult relation to Derrida's philosophical practice. See her "Irigaray through the Looking Glass," *Feminist Studies* 7.2 (Summer 1981): 288-306.

19. See her "Misrecognition and Identity," especially page 30.

20. "Woman's Exile: Interview with Luce Irigaray," trans. Couze Venn, *Ideology and Consciousness* 1 (May 1977): 71; cited as WE.

21. "Introduction to Irigaray," *Ideology and Consciousness* 1 (May 1977): 60.

22. See her "Introduction to Kristeva," *m/f* 5/6 (1981): 152

23. "Representation and Sexuality," *m/f* 1 (1978): 67.

24. Doane continues by noting the hidden costs that this theory, in its attempt to define the specificity of woman's language, entails: ". . . as Montrelay's work demonstrates, the use of the concepts of the phallus and castration within a semiotically oriented psychoanalysis logically implies that the woman must have a different relation to language from that of the man. And from a semiotic perspective, her relation to language must be deficient since her body does not 'permit' access to what, for the semiotician, is the motor-force of language—the representation of lack. Hence, the greatest masquerade of all is that of the woman speaking (or writing, or filming), appropriating discourse. To take up a discourse for the woman (if not, indeed, by her), that is, the discourse of feminism itself, would thus seem to entail an absolute contradiction. . . .

". . . unless we want to accept a formulation by means of which woman can only mimic man's relation to language, that is, assume a position defined by the penis-phallus as the supreme arbiter of lack, we must try to reconsider the relation between the female body and language, never forgetting that it is a relation between two terms and not two essences. Does woman have a stake in representation or, more appropriately, can we assign one to her? Anatomy is destiny only if the concept of destiny is recognized for what it really is: a concept proper to fiction" (WS 30-31).

25. The interior citations are from Montrelay's "Inquiry into Femininity," 88-90.

26. Cited in Adams's "Representation and Sexuality," 80 from Stephen Heath's trans. in *Image/Music/Text*. Here Barthes has most certainly borrowed the term *signifiance* from Kristeva.

27. See, for example, footnote 15 in this chapter. Williamson's critique appears in her "Two or Three Things We Know About Ourselves: A Critique of *Riddles of the Sphinx* and *Three Women*" [1977] in *Consuming Passions* (New York: Marion Boyars, 1986): 131-43. I would like to thank Peter Gidal for bringing to my attention several of the following points.

28. "Women and Representation: An Interview with Laura Mulvey," *Wedge* 2 (Spring 1978): 51. A thoughtful defense of the film is provided in Jacqueline Suter and Sandy Flitterman's interview/analysis "Textual Riddles: Woman as Enigma or Site of Social Meanings?," *Discourse* 1 (Fall 1979): 86-127.

29. "The film is really 'about' the imaginary—it doesn't go beyond that—that's what it's raising questions about. It's opening out a space within the imaginary and not making a leap into the symbolic. It's all about pre-Oedipal issues" (Mulvey in "Textual Riddles," 122).

The Crisis of Political Modernism

30. In her essay "The Cinematic Apparatus: Problems in Current Theory," Jacqueline Rose criticizes similar positions in feminist aesthetic theory since any challenge to the imaginary—on the basis of the unreality, fictionality, or difference of an image—only takes place within the terms of the imaginary itself. Moreover, one could add that such a challenge assumes a priori the ontological status of a referent (feminine body) as the measure of the falsification or inadequacy of an image. The impetus of such a strategy, says Rose, is clear: "the attempt to place woman somewhere *else,* outside the forms of representation through which she is endlessly constituted as image" ("Cinematic Apparatus," 181). By defining feminine specificity in reference to preoedipality, the imaginary, and as outside the terms of representation or as "pre-representation," the pitfalls of this position are obvious: "Film process is then conceived as something archaic, a lost or repressed content ('continent'), terms to which the feminine can so easily be assimilated, and has been in classical forms of discourse on the feminine as outside language, rationality, and so on." ("Cinematic Apparatus," 181).

31. Thus Heath notes, "If imaginary and specular are taken as equivalent, the conception of the imaginary slides easily towards such a priority, the area to be repossessed, a separate enclosure: where the need is much rather to avoid limiting the imaginary to a biographical evolution of the individual, to grasp that it is a necessary and permanent function of the history of the subject, and, simultaneously, of the subject in history. It can then no longer be a question of 'rediscovering' (nor, conversely, of 'abandoning'), but one of displacing, transforming. It might be said . . . that the play on the equivalence/disextensiveness of specular and imaginary as regards the history of the subject is a major factor in the force of cinema's ideological effects" ("Difference," 77)

32. The following citation betrays the excessive simplicity with which Wollen sometimes confronts psychoanalytic issues in film: "In fact, however, it is precisely the interface between image and word which concerns us. It is here that sexual difference, the subject of our films, takes shape. To restrict ourselves to the imaginary [that is, the image track] would be to restrict ourselves to the (prolonged) pre-Oedipal phase which, even if it could be interpreted as a form of resistance, would involve, in psychoanalytic terms, both a repression and a regression, and, in political terms, a flight from the society in which we are in fact living and from history. To restrict ourselves to the symbolic [the sound track], on the other hand, would involve a denial . . . of the persistence of the pre-Oedipal and of the ima-

ginary within and alongside the symbolic, ceaselessly structured by it yet escaping from it in the form of desire. This would be to deny history in another way, be revoking wish and memory in their full force" ("The Field of Language in Film," 54).

33. Interview in M.-F. Hans and G. Lapouge, eds., *Les femmes, la pornographie, l'érotisme*, cited in "Difference," 84. Once again we find a theory of *écriture*, opposing itself, literally, to the Hegelian thought that Althusser characterizes in the form of empirical knowing.

34. See "Difference," especially pages 78-83, and *The Sexual Fix*, Chapter VIII.

35. "La sexe ou la tête" in *Les Cahiers du GRIF* 13 (octobre 1976): 14. Cited in Heath's *The Sexual Fix*: 116.

36. "Dorothy Arzner: Critical Strategies," in Claire Johnston, ed. *The Work of Dorothy Arzner* (London: BFI, 1975): 4. Bergstrom's illuminating essay is "Rereading the Work of Claire Johnston," *Camera Obscura* 3/4 (Summer 1979): 21-31.

37. "Rereading Johnston," 25. The Johnston essay in question is "Towards a Feminist Film Practice: Some Theses," *Edinburgh Magazine* 1 (1976): 50-59.

In her essay "Aesthetic and Feminist Theory: Rethinking Women's Cinema," Teresa de Lauretis poses an interesting critique of this position: "To ask of these women's films: what formal, stylistic or thematic markers point to a female presence behind the camera?, and hence to generalize and universalize, to say: this is the look and sound of women's cinema, this is its language—finally only means complying, accepting a certain definition of art, cinema and culture, and obligingly showing how women can and do "contribute," pay their tribute, to 'society.' Put another way, to ask whether there is a feminine or female aesthetic, or a specific language of women's cinema, is to remain caught in the master's house and there, as Audre Lorde's suggestive metaphor warns us, to legitimate the hidden agendas of a culture we badly need to change" *(New German Critique* 34 [Winter 1985]: 158.)

38. Beverly Brown and Parveen Adams, "The Feminine Body and Feminist Politics," *m/f* 3 (1979): 35; cited as FBFP.

39. Jacqueline Rose, " 'Dora'—fragment of an analysis," *m/f* 2 (1978): 5-21.

40. *Life and Death in Psychoanalysis*, trans. Jeffrey Mehlman (Baltimore: Johns Hopkins University Press, 1976); cited in WS 32-33.

41. "The Cinematic Apparatus: Problems in Current Theory," 181-82. I have presented similar arguments in reference to this Freud essay in my article "The Difficulty of Difference."

42. AD 149. The internal citations are from Silverman's manuscript, page 6.

43. AD 142-43. The interior citation is from Freud's essay "Femininity" in *The Standard Edition of the Complete Psychological Works of Sigmund Freud*, ed. James Strachey (London: Hogarth Press, 1955), vol. 22, 131.

44. De Lauretis also follows Freud's analysis of female fantasies in his essay " 'A Child is Being Beaten'," *SE*, vol. 17, 177-204. I would like to note that her arguments reprise and confirm the conclusions I have drawn from my own analysis of this essay in "The Difficulty of Difference."

45. Claire Johnston, "The Subject of Feminist Film Theory/Practice," *Screen* 21.2 (Summer 1980): 30.

NINE

The Crisis of Political Modernism

> The statement [is] a specific and paradoxical object, but also . . .
> one of those objects that men produce, manipulate, use,
> transform, exchange, combine, decompose and recompose. . . .
> [The] statement circulates, is used, disappears, allows or prevents
> the realization of a desire, serves or resists various interests,
> participates in challenge and struggle, and becomes a theme of
> appropriation or rivalry.
> —Michel Foucault, *The Archaeology of Knowledge*[1]

The title of this book—*The Crisis of Political Modernism*—is
meant to be provocative. Throughout, I have developed two
distinct fields of reference for understanding the terms of this
crisis. The first is located within the discourse of political modernism itself and comprises those rhetorical strategies that posit
a theory of aesthetic signification as a "crisis of codes." This
theme—whose repetitions, transformations, and dispersions,
constitute the discourse of political modernism—is succinctly
described by Teresa de Lauretis. In her essay "Aesthetic and
Feminist Theory: Rethinking Women's Cinema," she capsu-
lizes a period of film theory where "it was argued that, in order
to counter the aesthetic of realism, which was hopelessly com-
promised with bourgeois ideology, as well as Hollywood cinema, avant-garde and feminist filmmakers must take an oppositional stance against narrative 'illusionism' and in favor of
formalism. This assumption was that 'foregrounding the process itself, privileging the signifier, necessarily disrupts aes-

thetic unity and forces the spectator's attention on the means of the production of meaning.' "[2]

From chapter to chapter this theme has been articulated and rearticulated from diverse points of view: in the rhetoric of the break (between realism and modernism, modernism and semiology, ideological and theoretical practice) and in the epistemological valuation of certain textual practices (named Form in Burch, structure in Gidal, language or text in Wollen, negativity in Heath, and in the experience of feminine écriture). In every case, these ideas were organized according to an agonistic conception of the aesthetic text whose terms were divided and opposed in a binary logic of identity and negation.

I want to conclude, however, by fully exploring the terms of another crisis that appears in my construction of the discourse of political modernism as an object of critical and historical reading. The questions posed by political modernism do not simply define a local, transient problem in film theory; rather, they have determined the institutional foundations of that theory in its currently reigning forms. Moreover, there are larger historical and philosophical issues at stake. For example, by 1972 Michel Foucault and Jacques Derrida's work had charted in an exemplary manner the breakup of the constitutive unities of sign, structure, and subject that were characteristic of a certain era of knowledge.[3] At the same time these unities were being refashioned and recombined in that curious hybrid of structuralism and poststructuralism called contemporary film theory. If there is now a sense of a historical impasse in current theory, and an erosion of the consensus that early on forged a complex, contradictory unity from the fields of literary semiology, Lacanian psychoanalysis, and Althusserian Marxism in the study of film and ideology, how can the equivocations, contradictions, and dissemblances of this complex unity be exposed and overcome?

The sum of these contradictions—their regularity as such rather than the system of knowledge they claim for themselves—has constituted the discourse of political modernism as the object of my critical reading. But until now, this reading has remained implicit and untheorized in my analysis. Standing between the two terms of crisis I have outlined, the activity of this reading can now be clarified by displacing and reconstituting that strange object called "the text." What I wish to trace out now, with respect to a theory of the text where the themes of structure, sign, and subject emerge in the discourse of political modernism, is paradoxically the *absence* of a theory. Make no mistake. I have never opposed myself to the discourse of political modernism. Nor do I presume now to replace it simply with another theory or to speculate on its internal contradictions from the security of an integral outside. "The passage beyond philosophy," Derrida wrote long ago, "does not consist in turning the page of philosophy (which usually amounts to philosophizing badly), but in continuing to read philosophers *in a certain way*."[4] In another context, Derrida simply and elegantly describes this activity of reading: "Doubtless it is more necessary, from within semiology, to transform concepts, to displace them, to turn against their presuppositions, to reinscribe them in other chains, and little by little to modify the terrain of our work and thereby produce new configurations. . . ."[5]

For film theory in particular and theories of cultural representation in general, the decades of the sixties and seventies will deservedly be remembered as a singularly productive era. However, to the extent that particular correlations of "text" and "subject" are the most striking constants in the diverse theoretical formulations of this period, and to the extent that these discourses were defined as a form of "political" inquiry or activity, a curious relation was established between aesthetic practice and aesthetic theory. Each set of theoretical statements that I examined was ultimately founded on a notion of the aesthetic text as an intrinsic, formal system. The text was a bounded space required to accomplish a specific "meaning-effect"—the "deconstruction" of its relation to ideology and a transformation of the positions of meaning offered to the spectator. This thesis produced the following paradox in the discourse of political modernism: *there is no text in theory*. Or more clearly, the discursive and institutional force of theory was reduced or dissembled by the attribution of an epistemological self-validation to the "materialist text."

The ascription of "theoretical practice" as a function of a "materialist" film practice, the differentiation of film form according to criteria of epistemology, identity, and the body, in short, the identification of critical practice and knowledge as a property of these forms, all contributed to marking "theory" as a relation *external* to "the text." Implicitly, the theoretical discourse that articulated these concepts became a supplemental relation: an adjunct to "political/aesthetic" practice but not a part of it; a necessary step toward the accomplishment of a "materialist film practice" that, nevertheless, would be superfluous once the forms of that practice had been decided. For ideally, this "text" would be autodeconstructive of itself and its spectator. No one, of course, ever stated such propositions so baldly. But if the discourse of political modernism is pushed to its logical limits, then its concept of text reduces every exteriority—in the form of its relation to history and the subject—to the identity of its self-actualization.

The forms and relations of this aporia are not difficult to outline. Its regularity is defined by *Tel Quel's* attempts to use Derrida to renovate the vocabulary of dialectical materialism and to justify the division of an avant-garde aesthetic practice from ideological or metaphysical forms of discourse. (Which is not the same, as we shall see, as the attempt to reconcile the practices of deconstruction and Marxist criticism.) Beginning with Sollers and Baudry, I demonstrated how a Derridean-informed notion of *écriture* was adopted to define the "materialism" of an avant-garde stylistics as a political aesthetic. Each of the essays I subsequently discussed drew upon this notion and expanded it, correlating "dialectic" with a textually based structure of aesthetic perception and cognition. In each case, aesthetic cognition was understood as materially determined by the internal dynamics of textual form; significant and strategic alterations of the material character of texts were thought to yield material effects in the forms of subjectivity incumbent upon their reception. Ultimately, those texts inclined toward "idealist" forms of representation (conventional narrative, for example) were described as producing "ideological" forms of cognition. Conversely, the obligation of a "materialist" aesthetic was to negate those forms by engaging

them in a critical relation that could yield traces of the theoretical process in aesthetic cognition.

Insofar as it describes subject/object relations in the discourse of political modernism, this particular use of the term
dialectic is unfortunate. As I argued in Chapter Eight, on concepts of narration and negativity, even the most sophisticated
invocations of this term have raised the ghost of a Hegelian
identity theory. The discourse of political modernism can only
construe the placement of the subject through the unilateral
determinations of the discursive unities (literary or filmic texts,
speech acts, *enoncés* in the strictly linguistic sense) it proposes.
However, this overvaluation of the determining force, adequacy, and efficiency of discursive unities is not simply a property of the discourse of political modernism. It is a statement
of subject/object relations that is reiterated in the most dispersed localities of the reigning theoretical field: in the concept of *parole* and the dialectic of desire in Lacan, in the unity
of the sign and the system of language in Saussure, and in the
Kristevan/*Tel Quel* rereading of Hegelian negativity.

Therefore, is is necessary to question whether the contradictions accruing from the attempt to assimilate Marxism and
"deconstruction" into the field of a semiotically informed modernism were finally resolvable. Derrida's philosophy, like Louis
Althusser's, was adopted by *Tel Quel* to ameliorate theories
defining ideology as a system of mass deception or illusory
consciousness, with their idealization of a falsifiable and thus
ultimately redeemable Being. However, *Tel Quel's* version of
aesthetic deconstruction was ultimately compelled to entertain
rather than criticize those concepts, at least as far as questions
of political aesthetics were concerned. In many respects the
predominance of ideological criticism in the discourse of political modernism engendered, as the very condition of its logic,
a series of oppositions that required the effects of illusion and
falsity as epistemological categories in order to validate the
theoretical project conceived for the filmic avant-gardes. As
the negation of normative or expressive codes, the practice of
écriture took its place in the series of terms opposing modernism to realism, ideological to theoretical practice, idealism
to materialism, and finally the imaginary to the symbolic, where,

in Wollen's essays and often in theories of feminine *écriture*, the relation of *écriture* to "speech" is effectively reversed. Moreover, the dialectic that was thought to energize and direct this series was ultimately resolvable to a simple opposition. All of the theories of deconstructive aesthetic practice I described were tutored by the code/deconstruction opposition. In its attempt to reconcile Althusser and Derrida for a political aesthetic, this opposition served to construct questionable epistemological valuations according to criteria of textual form.

In this context, the risk of reducing Derrida's notions of *écriture* to a formal technique or series of techniques corresponding to the practice of deconstruction is severe. Of course, it is possible to assert that deconstruction is a "technique," at least in the sense of a technical philosophy, whose procedures can be defined and described. In fact, this is often what happens to deconstruction when read through even the most sympathetic glosses. In Derrida's philosophy, however, the concept of *écriture* can neither be said to be a technique nor a practice, even if the activity of deconstruction—when transposing a text to open out suppressed metonymic chains, oppositions, or intertextual liaisons—comes to resemble an avant-garde "writing." *Ecriture* instead names the precondition of language—or more precisely, articulation—whose intelligibility is figured as an effect of spatial and temporal ordering. As Derrida frequently stresses, "writing," whether given in the form of "trace," "différance," or "archi-writing," is the precondition of all "expression" including oral cultures, pictography, nonphonetic scripts, gesticulation, and so on. That Derrida finds Stéphane Mallarmé or Philippe Sollers sensitive to this issue in no way determines avant-garde literatures as having a different epistemological status than other "writings." Nor does it validate the use of this notion of *écriture* to describe a style or stylistics. Alternatively, Gayatri Spivak argues that deconstructive readings have an obvious interest for the practices of criticism in that "problematizing the distinction between philosophy and literature, it would read 'even philosophy' as 'literature.' "[6] But in the examples considered here, far from placing philosophy or literature "under erasure" or untying the opposition that binds them, most proponents of political modernism have instead effected a simple reversal: aesthetic practice *as* philosophy; the avant-garde text *as* theoretical practice.

This cautionary remark suggests three criticisms of the discourse of political modernism. First, despite the recourse to concepts such as "intertextuality," which have a clear function and place in textual semiotics, in order to assert its epistemological status the modernist text requires a degree of autointelligibility (whether in the form of a "dialectical" or reflexive gesture) that is dangerously close to the presence of self-constituting meaning criticized by Derrida as logocentrism. Here a concept like intertextuality is understood only as an "aesthetic" figure, rather than as the acknowledgment by criticism and theory that meaning is not a function of textual interiority, but is constituted in a complex web of different practices and institutions.

Second, *Tel Quel*'s correlation of epistemology and stylistics with deconstruction and *écriture*, and finally with dialectics and materialism, has permeated the discourse of political modernism whether the various theorists acknowledge a filiation with Derrida and *Tel Quel* or not. In the assimilation of Derrida to Marxism and to an avant-garde stylistics, what this correlation suppresses is the element of undecidability that is the motor of deconstructive practice. Undecidability refers to a situation where one may demonstrate, in a logic pretending to formal self-identity, the simultaneous presence of propositions that both do and do not belong to its system. Since such systems usually depend on the criterion of exclusivity as their epistemological foundation, according to Michael Ryan, "For the formal system to be complete . . . it must assume the possibility of a transcendental position that is not simply one item of the formal logic; it must assume an outside to the series that acts as a paradigm."[7]

In the discourse of political modernism, the code/deconstruction opposition precisely describes this paradigm. Here the modernist text is understood as confronting its readers with the epistemological limits imposed by the norms of social intelligibility enforced under capitalism. One should not disregard or underestimate the resistances offered by the avant-garde text in this respect. However, in every case where the discourse of political modernism is regulated by this opposition, what the probing of the paradigm reveals is the assimilation of philosophical concepts that render the required epistemological valuation of the avant-garde text as, precisely, undecidable. As I argued in Chapter Three, in Althusser's epistemology the differential specificity of aesthetic cognition with respect to the ideological was decidable, if debatable, but with respect to theoretical practice, undecidable. For Althusserian critics outside of film studies, theory remained entirely within the province of critical reading. Alternatively, in Derrida the proposition can be demonstrated that deconstruction breaks down the epistemological priority given to philosophy over literature. However, the element of undecidability that achieves this deconstruction resides on the terrain of epistemology itself, not in the opposition of forms or categories of writing. Similarly, Derrida would never conceive of the "science" of grammatology in a manner compatible with Althusser's notions of theoretical practice; for what deconstruction offers is precisely the undecidability of the opposition between ideology and science that is the foundation of that practice.[8]

Finally, Derrida does not prioritize *écriture* in the same manner as, for example, Sollers or Jean-Louis Baudry. This would require the presence of a binary logic when, in fact, concepts such as *écriture* and *parole* are articulated through a differential relation that in no way implies opposition or negation. One necessarily inflects the other, slides beneath it, puts it "under erasure." These criticisms cast doubt on the best efforts of political modernism to define *écriture* as a set of techniques—authorless discourse, intertextuality, acausality, nonrepresentability, deconstruction as dialectic or negation, and so on—and as theoretical practice. No doubt these techniques achieve objectives similar to those of deconstruction such as resistance to closure, open-ended textual productivity, and so on. But wherever there appears a manifesto of political modernism—*Logiques* is one, "Writing/Fiction/Ideology" another, "Propositions" yet another—"deconstruction" is introduced as one side of an opposition that is the center of an epistemology that denies its centers.

Even the best efforts to define a materialist practice in the discourse of political modernism continually reconsider notions of *écriture*, form, structure, and so on, as an essence—hidden by normative language, veiled by logocentrism—and a value, something to be rescued from a hierarchically inferior position. Already in 1971 Derrida criticized the potential missteps of this position as "a purely formalist criticism which would be interested only in the code, the pure play of signifiers, the technical manipulation of the text-object, thereby overlooking the genetic effects or the ("historical," if you will) inscription of the text read *and* of the new text this criticism itself writes."[9]

There will undoubtedly be many objections to this analysis. But despite all the exceptions that could justifiably be named, and without reducing the genuine advances accomplished in the fields of semiology, psychoanalysis, and the theory of the subject, I still hold that the centrality of a certain conception of aesthetic practice, which tends to render theory in a relation of supplemantarity or secondariness, has reduced and even inhibited the possibility of a historical conception of the subject. Simultaneously, this conception misrecognized the advances it enabled in what can be simply called the *theory of reading*. The theoretical wealth of this period, which still submits us to its institutional force, therefore belies itself to varying degrees. It refuses to recognize, materially and historically, precisely what it has accomplished as a genuine, even revolutionary, transformation of an entire discursive field—a set of intertextual relations where texts emerge and are historically constituted along with their possible meanings and uses. It should be clear that what I now call a "text" cannot be identified with the unity of a form or presence. This conception must be contrasted to that of the discourse of political modernism. For in its division and distribution of texts according to semiotically defined epistemological criteria (e.g., the two avant-gardes, the six categories of *Cahiers*, the debates over narrative versus antiillusionism, and the specificity of writing and sexual difference), political modernism can only envision *the* text as the singularity and self-sufficiency of a preconstituted identity.

I have detailed the manner in which the principal oppositions subtending the discourse of political modernism—modernism/realism, theoretical/ ideological practice, and deconstruction/code—finally coincide in the problem of aesthetic cognition and of the subjectivity of the reader/spectator. Within this problematic, the spectator is considered as constructed, determined, or otherwise identical to the internal dynamics of the text, that is, by an immanent relation with the text that brooks no outside. Although attempting to define itself in opposition to the identity theory of a Hegelianized Marxism according to a series of antiimmanent concepts, the "theory" presupposed by the discourse of political modernism is precisely an immanent one. While valorizing concepts such as heterogeneity, discontinuity, intertextuality, and so on, to characterize both the form and the "subject" of the text of *écriture,* the relation between subject and text is nonetheless posed as intrinsic and self-identical. The effort to dismantle the integrity of the text and the spectatorial relations it is thought to determine relies fundamentally on the supposition of an identical subject/object of enunciation. In its most extreme and most compelling form, this position is argued in Kristeva's concept of negativity. Here poetic language is thought to "decenter" the subject according to a dialectic that continuously and simultaneously converts psychical and semiotic material, collapsing the history of the subject (as posed by psychoanalysis) and that of modes of production (as posed by dialectical materialism) into coextensive moments.

But what if one wished to engage another notion of dialectic and history? If the discourse of political modernism is in crisis, it is now possible to rethink theoretical practice in its expressly discursive and political dimensions, to recognize its productive difference, and to understand it as a practice of reading and as an intervention in the institutional formations of knowledge. Curiously, such an alternative is simply and elegantly proposed in the "Introduction" to *Edinburgh Magazine* 1, a publication that helped introduce Kristeva to film theory and that I char-

acterized earlier as marking the emergence of the discourse
of political modernism.

> [T]he politics of film criticism . . . stems from the premise that
> what has to be interrogated is the dialectic constituted by the
> fact that there is a perennial disjuncture between the inscribed
> reader of the text and the social subject who is invited to take
> up this position. Although the social subject always exceeds the
> subject implied by the text, because he/she is also placed by a
> hetereogeneity of other cultural systems and is never co-exten-
> sive with the subject placed by a single fragment (i.e. one film)
> of the overall cultural text, the social subject is also restricted
> by the positionality which the text offers it.[10]

What these critics are suggesting is another "decentered" relation where the subject implied by the aesthetic text is always
irreducible to the individual it hails. Moreover, this relation is
complicated by a network of cultural and institutional discourses whose function is to negotiate and delimit the range
of possible encounters between subject and text. If the crisis
of political modernism is to be overcome, and if semiology and
psychoanalysis are to advance in the areas of political aesthetics
and criticism, further work must be accomplished in two areas:
that of the theory of reading and what might be called the
political economy of film culture.

In "La lecture comme construction," Tzvetan Todorov ded-
icates himself to defining an unexplored domain: the logic of
reading.[11] Todorov isolates two levels of activity in the reader's
encounter with a text—that of signification and that of symbolization. The level of signification refers to the most basic
level of reading as communication through the agency of a
common code. Tony Bennett, though not referring to Todorov,
has suggested another way of explaining this relation with the
text, but with an opposite emphasis: "The text the reader or
critic has in front of him or her is encountered as a resisting
force, constraining the interpretive and analytical options that
may be adopted in relation to it."[12]

Textual semiotics has analyzed more or less precisely the
operations of this level of textual activity and codification.
However, the level of signification constitutes only one dis-

cursive series confronting the reader in his or her encounter
with texts. One must also consider the level of symbolization—
a level of interpretation varying from one reader to the next.
The level of symbolization or interpretation is not arbitrary,
however; the reader is not able to freely apply interpretations
as he or she may. Therefore, two sets of determinations constrain the possibility of any given reading. One devolves from
the given text itself since its particular organization of signs
may either serve to facilitate or resist certain avenues of interpretation. The second series consists of cultural constraints
or conventions regulating modes of textual interpretation and
consumption, or what Bennett calls "reading formations."

Linguistics has served as the authoritative science in the
analysis of these two sets of determinations. And in this respect, it has both enabled and constrained the possibilities for
a theory of reading. Bennett, for one, has noted two principal
linguistic approaches to the question of text-subject relations
that must be overcome before a theory of reading can be inaugurated. The first approach focuses solely on the level of
signification as the text's codification of "reading positions."
In literary theory, this concept is mobilized under the sign of
the "implied," "model," or "preferred reader"; in film theory
it is articulated as the problem of enunciation, subject-positioning, or subject-address. In either case, the effective unity
and self-identity of the text is presupposed through an analysis
that concentrates on the formal syntactic and syntagmatic operations of the text. A pertinent example is Heath's extrapo-
lation, soon revised, of subject-positions from the deictic features of narrative space.[13]

The second approach is characteristic of Umberto Eco's theory of reading. Although this approach attempts to account
for the historical variability of readers and reading, it too is
limited by a linguistic paradigm. Here the distinction between
langue and *parole* holds sway. The text exhibits all the systemic
and structural limits of *"langue"* in its regulation of the variability and contingency of the individual reading or individual
actualization of the text as *"parole."*[14] In spite of the empirical
and common-sensical observation of the eccentricity of readings, the text nonetheless confronts the reader as a structural

and semiotic limit that cannot be overcome. In the last instance, it must tutor and authenticate the individual reading.

> In short, the study of reading occupies the same relation to the
> study of the text as, in linguistics, pragmatics occupies in relation
> to syntactics. It is the area in which the reign of the subject,
> excluded from the analysis of textual structures just as much as
> from the study of *langue*, is triumphantly reinstalled. . . . [This]
> approach construes the text as an object, a structure, a system
> of necessary relations . . . that is pregiven to the reader. Read-
> ings may vary but, when all is said and done, they are all readings
> of the same thing: "the text" as a set of necessary and objective
> relations conceived of as existing in some pure and limiting
> condition of "in-itselfness" that is independent from the reading
> relations that regulate its productive activation in different mo-
> ments of history. (This condition of "in-itselfness," it should be
> added, is not *of* the text, but rather, is a space produced *for* it
> by the specific terms of theorization employed.) Such an ap-
> proach cannot help but be normative; it inevitably ranks and
> assigns readings their place according to their degree of con-
> formity with the reading that analysis of the "text itself" con-
> firms as most correct, most meaningful, most valid, or most ap-
> propriate.[15]

The "text itself," or the ontological definition of the text as
an autonomous, self-identical formal object, must be dismantled before the intertextual force of reading and reading formations can be theorized and understood. Following Pierre
Macherey, Tony Bennett questions the value of understanding
the text, implicitly or explicitly, as a self-identical or self-suf-
ficient object. Instead, he argues, attention should be directed
to "the history of its use, of its perpetual remaking and transformation, in the light of its inscription into a variety of different material, social, institutional and ideological contexts"
(TSP 3). The radical nature of this claim should not be diminished. Bennett is neither arguing for a reception aesthetic
properly speaking, nor is he attempting simply to redeem the
study of literary context. He wishes to rewrite the concept of
text as something that is inconceivable as "independent of the
varying contexts which define the real history of its productive
consumption . . ." (TSP 3).

Similarly, throughout this book one of my main themes, perhaps the main theme, has been to challenge both the idea of
the formal self-identity of the aesthetic text and the subject-
object relations this idea presupposes. By hastening to forge
a definitive break with ideology, and by theorizing this break
within a logic of binary opposition, the discourse of political
modernism was doomed to perpetuate the utilitarian conceptions of language and the identity theory of knowledge it attempted to challenge. Tony Bennett summarizes concisely why
a theory of the subject based on a formal conception of the
text is bound to fail. Following Derrida, Bennett notes that
"the text is totally iterable; that, as a set of material notations,
it may be inscribed within different contexts and that no context—including that in which it originated—can enclose it by
specifying or fixing its meaning or effect for all time and in all
contexts" (TSP 5).[16] This iterability renders undecidable the
attempt to theorize a relation of identity between text and
subject: "the reader's response cannot be deduced from an
analysis of the formal properties of the text; . . . there are
independent determinations bearing on the ideological and
cultural formation of the reader which must be taken account
of in order to analyze the history and social distribution of
varying aesthetic and political responses" (TSP 5). This is particularly true when, in the age of mechanical reproduction,
aesthetic work takes the form of commodities and captialism
organizes historical subjectivity in the sphere of consumption.
Thus Bennett notes the observations of Walter Benjamin and
T. W. Adorno that when the auratic singularity of the artwork
is dispersed through the agency of technical reproducibility,
its conditions of historical and social existence are radically
altered: the potential meaning of the artwork cannot be decided in advance of the contexts in which it might be invoked.
    In many senses, this has been my emphasis from the begin-
ning. By choosing to work through the *discourse* of political
modernism, and by refusing to accept the self-identity of self-
sufficiency of any aesthetic or theoretical work, I have tried
to demonstrate the inadequacy of a certain notion of text and
of the epistemological valuation of the "modernist" text. However, the historical materialist emphasis of my own critique

should not be mistaken for an aesthetic "nihilism" in its dissolution of text, subject, and the possible relations of knowledge into the variable constellation that is a discursive formation. This is not to say, following Bennett, that "texts do not exist,

> nor that a knowledge of them is impossible—although one would want to insist on the plural, on the *knowledges* produced by the rules and procedures of the bodies of theory (Marxism, psychoanalysis, semiology) brought to bear on the study of . . . texts. But to contend that texts can be known only from within specific systems of knowledge is not to posit an unknowable *Ding-an-sich*, a text hidden behind the material surface of the empirically given text, somehow *there* but unreachable. To put the matter this way is to concede the ground to idealist formulations even in the process of contesting them. The point is not that the "text itself" is unknowable, but rather that the very notion of the "text itself" is inconceivable, an impossible object. (TSP 5-6)

To the extent that signification and symbolization together serve to constrain the productivity of meaning, one may say that they are ideological. The level of symbolization is necessarily so since, being discontinuous with respect to the level of signification and irreducible to it, it regulates the variability of meaning or the fact that any given meaning is undecidable. Texts may be endlessly reinterpreted. As Bennett notes, "Meaning is a transitive phenomenon. It is not a *thing* that texts can *have*, but is something that can only be produced, and always differently, within the reading formations that regulate the encounters between texts and readers. To be sure, some readings regularly carry more cultural weight than others . . ." (TRRF 8).

More radically, according to Bennett there is no "text" that preexists its constitution in a historically given reading formation. Similarly, Paul Willemen argues that "films are read unpredictably, they can be pulled into more or less any ideological space, they can be mobilised for diverse and even contradictory critical projects."[17] However, this neither means that a given text is open to any number of readings, nor that the text will be slaved to the interpretive frames negotiating its readings: "the activity of the text must be thought in terms of which set of discourses it encounters in any particular set of circumstances and how this encounter may re-structure both the productivity of the text *and* the discourses with which it combines to form an inter-textual field which is always in ideology, in history. Some texts can be more or less recalcitrant if pulled into a particular field, while others can be fitted comfortably into it" (NOS 55).

Because the relation between the levels of signification and symbolization is undecidable, texts will always be productive of contradiction. A critical understanding of the ideological work of reading conjunctures or reading formations can be founded only on this principle. Thus Bennett notes that

> What most needs to be stressed . . . is that, whatever the material form or the social context in which the text reaches the reader, is does so only as already covered by a pre-existing horizon of interpretative options, options which are encountered as limits, as a force that has to be reckoned with. As Fredric Jameson has argued, "texts come before us as the always-already-read; we apprehend them through the sedimented layers of previous interpretations, or—if the text is brand-new—through the sedimented reading habits and categories developed by those inherited interpretive traditions". It is not some shadowy ideal text, a text hidden within the materiality of the text, but the text in its specific material form as inscribed within a definite set of social relations and as already covered by an accumulated history of readings that, in the present, exerts a determinacy over the modes of its consumption. It is the readings already produced in relation to a text, and not some notional "text itself," which bear upon and limit present and possible readings of a text. It is for these historical, and not at all for essentialist reasons, that texts are encountered as a resistance. (TSP 6)[18]

Codified representational norms certainly constrain meaning at the level of signification. But to the extent that texts are productive of contradiction, it is necessary for political criticism to recognize the way these contradictions may be contained or dissimulated by modes of consumption or interpretation extrinsic to the text. Texts may be inserted into reading conjunctures that either complete their meanings and rationalize their contradictions, or that identify, analyze, and challenge those contradictions. This is precisely the terrain on which a political criticism will operate as an activity of reading.

Two conclusions may be drawn from this critique in the context of my discussion of the crisis of political modernism. First, once the structural integrity and self-sufficiency of the text are questioned, once the text is no longer conceived under the philosophemes of identity and presence, any notion of the text's unilateral determination of subjectivity is proven inadequate. Despite the insistence within the discourse of political modernism on the centrality of a theory of the subject, it is the centrality of questions of the aesthetic text and of aesthetic form that have predominated. Moreover, having made the question of aesthetic form decisive for the study of ideology, the discourse of political modernism produces a notion of text that sublates the question of the subject, rendering it as the specular simulacrum of the text's own image.

Second, political modernism's particular delimitation of the text as a site of "political" activity can now be understood as naive. Once the criteria devolving from the formal self-identity of the text are challenged, the required epistemological judgment—which decides between ideological and theoretical or illusionist/idealist and materialist films—is rendered inconclusive. As Francis Mulhern argues, what a text may demonstrate of its mode of production is of incontestable importance; but with respect to theoretical or critical knowing, the effect of such a demonstration is not decisive. A text is not an event but a function, determined by its historical placement within a mode of consumption or interpretation: "its condition of *production* can have no special priority in analysis over its subsequent and variable conditions of *existence and activity*."[19]

Cahiers du cinéma's axiom that "all films are political" should therefore be rewritten as "all films are ideological." Indeed, I would assert even against Althusser that aesthetic practice is indistinguishable by any criterion of judgment, epistemological or not, from the area of the ideological. This is not to displace or diminish the necessity of textual analysis, ideological criticism, or the political activity of artists and intellectuals. Nor is it to claim that the discursive practices of artists and intellectuals do not intervene decisively in the formations of discourse, the practices of knowledge, and the transformation of social identity and desire. Instead, I wish to challenge the impasse of structuralist and even so-called poststructuralist concepts in the discourse of political modernism and to transform our understanding of the relation between criticism and ideology, subject and text. For the efforts to locate theoretical knowledge within the text, and to circumscribe the process of knowledge within the formal borders and self-sufficency of the aesthetic work have dissembled the concrete accomplishments of the intense and productive theoretical activity of the past twenty years.

Yet there is a difficulty in Bennett's analysis that must be pointed out. His emphasis on *reading* formations and on the reader's "productive activation" of the text seems continually, if only implicitly, to return to the presence and punctuality of the subject even as the subject is being questioned. The idea of the reading formation is productively and critically compared to the Foucaldian theory of discursive formations. Bennett has thoroughly and unquestionably placed into doubt the self-evidence of the text's unity, as well as the sublation of the subject into the forms of the text's identity. But even in its historical variability, the idea of a reading formation threatens to return as a principal of unification of discourse and subject, the brevity of this encounter and its mobility in time notwithstanding. I do not dispute the importance of the idea of reading formations, of the analysis of their institutional foundations, or even their empirical existence. But to the extent that "reading" is construed as the productive activation of a text by the subject according to the constraints of a reading formation, one must still assume the singularity of an encounter, even a historically contingent one, where the unitary presence of a subject is sustained by the regularity of the discourses it mobilizes. The reading formation, which now happily occupies the field of discursive identity that the text had to relinquish, looks not so very different from the (historical) reading pragmatics that Bennett criticizes. While the identity of the text only emerges in the reading formation that mobilizes it, at the same moment this notion of reading threatens to restore meaning as the meaningfulness of *a* subject, who attains a specific relation to knowledge in his/her activation, actualization, or use of the formation.

This criticism is an important one. For while Bennett productively emphasizes the contradictions occurring *between* reading formations, and politicizes the activity of criticism and historical analysis in the struggle for meaning in the conflict *of* reading formations, this level of contradiction is pertinent neither to a theory nor a critique of the category of the subject. In fact, Bennett potentially reconsiders the self-identity of the subject in the regularity of its "use" of the reading formation. One is then left in the position of construing the subject as either a presence anterior to the regulated, discursive unity of the reading formation, or else as an identity emerging within that unity as its mirror image. In either case, Bennett's theory only displaces the terms of the linguistic approaches he criticizes ("reading formation" for "text"), while leaving their problematic relation to the subject intact. Alternatively, Foucault is careful to emphasize the multiplicity of sites through which the subject encounters an instance of discourse. In Bennett, the unity of the subject becomes an implicit criterion for the theorization of reading formations; in *The Archaeology of Knowledge*, Foucault demonstrates that any "reading" is traversed by multiple and contradictory discursive series that can be resolved neither to the unity of a subject nor to the intergral identity of a reading formation. Reading—which may suggest a self-conscious activity where the subject realizes or authenticates itself in a relation of knowledge—is productively contrasted to Foucault's idea of "enunciative modalities" that regulate the institutional sites, situations, and authorizations for the production of discourse. "[I]nstead of referring back to *the* synthesis or *the* unifying function of *a* subject," writes Foucault,

> the various enunciative modalities manifest his dispersion. To the various statuses, the various sites, the various positions that he can occupy or be given when making a discourse. To the discontinuity of the planes from which he speaks. And if these planes are linked by a system of relations, this system is not established by the synthetic activity of a consciousness identical

with itself . . . but by the specificity of a discursive practice. . . .
Thus conceived, discourse is not the majestically unfolding manifestation of a thinking, knowing, speaking [reading] subject,
but, on the contrary, a totality, in which the dispersion of the
subject and his discontinuity with himself may be determined.
It is a space of exteriority in which a network of distinct sites
is deployed. (AK 54-55)[20]

The potential danger in Bennett (and I am not sure that it is
an actual one) is that in its identity with the reading formation,
the subject will be construed as actualizing the "text," when
in fact it is only through the multiple, contradictory, and intertextual correlations of discourse that either text or subject
may appear.

Once its unity is questioned, and the self-sufficiency of its
meaning is displaced according to an ineluctable iterability,
the question of *the* text as the authoritative guarantor of knowledge or even a relation of knowledge is dissolved into a complex series of critical, discursive relations. Therefore, another
important emphasis of my choice to study the discourse of
political modernism is to displace along with the notion of text
a certain emphasis on the concept of "production," focusing
instead on relations of consumption. What I call the political
economy of film culture is conceived in this context. While
attempting to theorize the subjective relation in its formal
identity with the aesthetic text, the discourse of political modernism blinded itself to its power as a specific discursive formation. Even though it enabled a new conception of aesthetic
practice, and transformed fundamentally the way films were
discussed, analyzed, understood, and taught, the discourse of
political modernism was unable to assess adequately the power
of its own critical theory, its role as an oppositional practice,
and its transformations of the sphere of aesthetic consumption.

Criticism and discussion of this problem have been linked
historically with positions developed in the institutional context of the Independent Film-makers' Association (IFA) in Britain, a loose national union of not only filmmakers, but also
educators, theorists, and critics. A short account of the history
of the IFA (now the Independent Film and Videomakers Association) provides a practical model of what I speculatively

refer to as work on the political economy of film culture. Sparked by protest over a BBC program on "independent cinema" broadcast in 1974, the IFA began as a solidarity group organized to question the lack of coherent policy on the part of the government and its institutions (such as the BBC and the British Film Institute) with respect to the funding and support of independent filmmaking. Early on, the IFA recognized the necessity of including critics and educators in its membership and of theorizing the question of an alternative or oppositional cinema as one of "integrated practice": the regulation and reinforcement of patterns of aesthetic consumption and the production of meaning in relation to the institutional network where films are produced, distributed, and exhibited.

In "Independent Film-making in the 70's," a discussion paper drafted for the May 1976 organizational conference of the IFA, the failures of previous independent film movements were attributed to a tendency to concentrate analysis and struggle on only one sector of film culture, that of production. In "Notes on the Idea of Independent Cinema," Claire Johnston details this argument.[21] She states that the problem with defining independence solely in economic terms is that dependence is understood in relation to productive forces alone, leaving others areas of film culture untheorized and open to humanist ideologies of self-expression and creative freedom. Here one assumes that a viable, alternative film culture will blossom, and that one will be able to produce freely, within the agency of an adequate state patronage. Neither can one concentrate simply on the use of films in alternative distribution and exhibition for the purposes of organization, agitation, or consciousness raising. This position ignores questions of signification and mistakenly assumes the ideological neutrality of representational norms and of the cinematographic apparatus. Moreover, it also tends to overestimate cinema's rhetorical potency and underestimate the diversity and heterogeneity of audiences. Finally, neither can independence be defined solely by questions of aesthetic form and cognition: "Representation is a political question—but it cannot answer political questions. The breaking of the position of the spectator cannot of itself constitute [a] political goal. The development of an institutional space

around production/ distribution/ exhibition founded on a process of meaning production must think its audience in its specificity if any cultural intervention is to be effected . . ." ("Independent Cinema," 3-4).

In "Notes Towards a Social Practice of Production/Distri-
bution/ Exhibition/Criticism," a position paper developed by
a group of feminists at the first Annual General Meeting and
Conference of the IFA in February 1977, one of the fundamental objectives of the IFA was described as building such
an institutional space as a problem of social or "integrated
practice." In their report on the conference published in *Screen*,
Jonathan Curling and Fran McClean also speculate on the necessity of filmmakers' engagement with theoretical discourse
and with the activity of film theorists and educators in their
midst.[22] What the presence of theoretical activity within the
IFA entails, they argue, is a recognition that the potential for
meaning does not lie purely and integrally in the level of textual production. Aesthetic texts determine neither their audiences nor the contexts of their reception. Rather, audiences
are constituted by social and historical determinations independent of aesthetic texts: patterns of consumption and use
determined at the levels of distribution and exhibition that
produce their own discourses on the "proper" meanings and
forms of social intelligibility of cinema attendance.[23]

The importation of theory to independent practice is necessary, for it contributes both to the criticism of normative
patterns of consumption and to the creation of new audiences
and contexts for the production, reception, and interpretation
of films. To argue the necessity of film's engagement with theoretical practice need no longer be necessarily understood as
the production of "theoretical films" or films that inculcate
positions of nonideological knowing on the part of their presumed spectators. Instead, theoretical practice is concerned
with comprehending the various discursive sites where the
intelligibility of film and film viewing is formulated, worked
through, and renegotiated according to a continuing process
of ideological and institutional struggle.

By concentrating on the discourse of political modernism as
an intertextual system of intelligibility, my intention has not

been to refute its project. Rather, I wish to extend its significance for political aesthetics. To criticize and dismantle the
opposition that divides the "modernist" from the "realist" text
on the basis of the forms of aesthetic cognition they presuppose
is neither to condemn the former nor redeem the latter. Credibility can be given to a theory of the avant-garde text that
stresses its resistances to interpretation or normative readings.
Obviously, this is work at the level of signification about which
certain claims can justifiably be made. But the danger of arguments defending the "unreadability" of the avant-garde text
is that, rather than posing absolute resistances to ideological
readings, these texts are more freely mobilized at the level of
symbolization or interpretation because of their ambiguity at
the level of signification.

Here the importance of theory must be confronted as one
of the key issues of political modernism in its comprehension
of the role of intellectuals in the political economy of film
culture. Only on this basis will the political stakes of theory
be clarified—first, in its productivity at the level of possible
readings and interpretations of texts, and second in its challenges to the present intelligibility of representational and interpretive norms. As Willemen notes, "In this sense, the accuracy, the precision of a reading is always conditional upon
a recognition of its place and effects within a given (fragment
of the) socio-historical conjuncture. The production of readings, and hence of criticism and theory, is always a more or
less well calculated intervention in the 'battle of ideas,' in the
ideological formation which provides the 'battleground' " (NOS
57).

If the discourse of political modernism has failed to define
for aesthetic practice the effects of a politically consequent
modernism, perhaps its real achievements may be accounted
for in another area of textual activity—that of a poltically consequent theory and criticism. To the extent that a concept like
intertextuality is used to define a protocol for the modernist
as opposed to the realist text, it can only return on the basis
of the opposition it presupposes to define an immanent relation
and a self-identical, if "dialectical," object. Conversely, to dismantle the integrity of the text, to open it up to the intertextual

network that negotiates its social intelligibility, and to articulate the contradictions that may accrue therein, is precisely
to engage the text in a politics of reading.

Nowhere in the discourse of political modernism has the
political practice of theory been more striking than in the contribution of feminism. In the short history of political modernism, the lessons of feminist theory and criticism have in fact
set the standard (if sometimes with difficultly and contradictorily) for the role of oppositional intellectuals in their challenge to the norms of knowledge and power in the reigning
discursive formations. This role of the oppositional intellectual—who works on the terrain of criticism and theory, transforming the dominant discursive formations by the displacement she or he can effect within it—is admirably described by
Teresa de Lauretis. In *Alice Doesn't*, she writes that

> Strategies of writing *and* of reading are forms of cultural resis-
> tance. Not only can they work to turn dominant discourses in-
> side out (and show that it can be done), to undercut their enun-
> ciation and address, to unearth the archaeological stratifications
> on which they are built; but in affirming the historical existence
> of irreducible contradictions for women in discourse, they also
> challenge theory in its own terms, the terms of a semiotic space
> constructed in language, its power based on social validation
> and well-established modes of enunciation and address. So well-
> established that, paradoxically, the only way to position oneself
> outside of that discourse is to displace oneself within it—to re-
> fuse the question as formulated, or to answer deviously (though
> in its words), even to quote (but against the grain). (AD 7)

This practice is both a material and pragmatic one. For if
the historical formations of discourse serve as the effective
limit of what can be thought, said, conceived, visualized, or
questioned in a culture, then intellectuals (who after all must
work in institutions that preserve and perpetuate these formations) have a unique and powerful responsibility. They may
either respect and reproduce dominant discursive paradigms,
or they can facilitate the emergence of new and unforeseen
possibilities. "In this manner," writes de Lauretis, "a new text,
a different interpretation of a text—any new practice of discourse—sets up a different configuration of content, introduces

other cultural meanings that in turn transform the codes and rearrange the semantic universe of the society that produces it" (AD 34).

Just as importantly, feminist cultural theory demonstrates, on the level of a political economy of film culture, a possibility that the discourse of political modernism formulated and even accomplished without being able to adequately theorize that accomplishment; namely, a utopian conception of the emergence of new categories and modalities of subjectivity. This statement is paradoxical only if the unities of sign, structure, and subject have not yet been relinquished along with the relations of identity that binds them. To understand the possibilities for either the perpetuation or renovation of subjectivity in a given discursive formation, recourse to the unity of a transcendental subject or of a psychological subjectivity must be given up. Similarly, even if the subject is constrained by discourse, the unity of a subject can never be conflated with the *regularity* of a discursive formation in its contradictions and its multiple determinations. Rather, work on the political economy of film culture devolves from recognition of the "multiple planes" from which the subject speaks, repeats, or produces statements; or what Foucault calls the enunciative modalities that empower discourse by according rights to its use, and by enabling or disabling particular relations of practical knowledge. Enunciative modalities refer neither to the self-identity of a subject nor to the discursive unities of the statement, book, film, or *oeuvre.* They are correlative sets of institutional relations that enable as well as constrain the production of discourse and "speaking subjects."[24] These modalities are defined by: the sanctioning of the use of discourse as well as the rights and status of the speaker (in teaching, in criticism, and in aesthetic production); the constraints of the institutional sites from which discourse is produced (the university, the academic press or journal, the economic and technological apparatus of filmmaking); and finally the regularity of a theoretical field that correlates "subject-positions" with groups of objects, concepts, questions, definitions—in short, the practices and possibilities of knowledge. By confronting the establishment and functioning of enunciative modalities with the question of sexual difference (a question Foucault failed to address adequately and that still poses certain limits in his work, we can delineate within the discourse of political modernism not only the emergence of a new set of problems, but also, and more importantly, the possibility of a "new" social subject. Thus Teresa de Lauretis observes that "As a form of political critique or critical politics, and through the specific consciousness that women have developed to analyze the subject's relations to sociohistorical reality, feminism has not only invented new strategies or created new texts, but more importantly it has conceived a new social subject, women: as speakers, writers, readers, spectators, users and makers of cultural forms, shapers of cultural processes" (AFT 162-63).

On this basis, the emergence of a previously unrecognized and untheorized utopian dimension in the discourse of political modernism—in both theoretical and aesthetic practice—can be marked as both the possibility of new enunciative positions and the accordance of the social and legal rights of subjects (across lines of gender, race, and class) to occupy them. In this respect, my critique of the concept of feminine *écriture* was not meant to disparage the attempts to theorize an autonomous feminine aesthetic practice. Nor should my critique be understood as undermining the importance of posing the question of recovering a feminine subjectivity from patriarchy or as a critique of patriarchy. Both theoretical and aesthetic practice have already produced "effects" in this regard in the form of specific displacements of, and points of resistance to, patriarchal ideology in the discourses of reception (criticism and pedagogy) as well as production. But the measure of these displacements can be indexed neither to the singularity of a body nor to that of the formal system of a text. Rather, as Gertrud Koch points out, in aesthetic practice and reception the political force of feminist theory will be measured by criteria other than those of an identity theory or of an ontologically specific subjectivity.

> The aesthetically most advanced films resist any facile reading, not only because they operate with complex aesthetic codes but also because they anticipate an expanded and radicalized notion of subjectivity. What is achieved in a number of these films is

a type of subjectivity that transcends any abstract subject-object dichotomy; what is at stake is no longer the redemption of woman as subject over against the male conception of woman as object. What is at stake is less—and at the same time more—than the most general sense of the concept of subject: in the sense that Marx could speak of the working class as the subject of the revolution, in the sense that the women's movement could be the subject of the transformation of sexual politics. The most advanced aesthetic products represent a utopian anticipation of a yet to be fulfilled program of emancipated subjectivity: neither of a class nor of a movement or a collective, but as individuals, as concrete subjects [as] they attempt to insist on their authentic experience.[25]

Nonetheless, one would want to insist on the concrete, semiotic, and discursive foundations of this experience. And by the same token, to insist that it will be the discursive transformations undertaken by critical and theoretical practice, in the politics of reading and teaching, for example, that will render manifest this utopian potentiality.

In conclusion, what I envision as a political economy of film culture resembles what Terry Eagleton refers to as a "revolutionary criticism" that deconstructs the ruling unities of discourse and intervenes in the institutional sites of the production of knowledge. Such a criticism strives to dismantle the self-identity of the aesthetic and place it in relation to the total field of cultural practices. At the same time, this criticism works to transform the apparatuses of cultural production themselves and conceives of reading as a specific kind of political intervention. It would deconstruct hierarchies of aesthetic value "and transvaluate received judgments and assumptions; engage with the language and 'unconscious' of . . . texts, to reveal their role in the ideological construction of the subject; and mobilize such texts, if necessary by hermeneutic 'violence', in a struggle to transform those subjects within a wider political context." [26]

But ultimately, what a political criticism must hold onto is the recognition that textual determinations on the "placement" of the subject are both undecidable and unpredictable. The contribution of psychoanalysis to twentieth-century thought is that meaning is always in excess of the signifier, and that similarly, the subject is always in excess of meaning. This recognition dooms an immanent theory of reading; that is, one that poses an intrinsic relation between reader and text. If what the study of ideology finally reveals is the maintenance of social power through the production, circulation, and perpetuation of meaning in the historical specificity of discursive formations, what a political criticism must concentrate on are the inter-textual networks of discursive practices as they function to restrain contradiction by posing limits to the productivity of meaning as well as the possibilities of subjectivity. The discourse of political modernism, and the crisis it represents, is but a local manifestation of that long and arduous transformation in the foundations of philosophy and the human sciences that is our inheritance from Marx, Nietzsche, and Freud. And to the extent that this discourse participates in the announcement of "the end of man" in the era of late capitalism, it also celebrates difference in the multiplication of sites of resistance and possibilities of subjectivity heretofore unimagined and unimaginable.

NOTES

1. Trans. A.M. Sheridan Smith (New York: Harper Torchbooks, 1972): 105; cited as AK.
2. *New German Critique* 34 (Winter 1985): 155; cited as AFT. The interior citation is from Laura Mulvey's "Feminism, Film and the Avant-Garde," *Framework* 10 (Spring 1979): 6.
3. In particular, I am thinking of the work culminating in Foucault's *L'archéologie du savoir* (Paris: Editions du Seuil, 1969) and in Derrida's *La dissémination* (Paris: Editions du Seuil, 1972).
4. Jacques Derrida, "Structure, Sign, and Play in the Discourse of the Human Sciences" in *Writing and Difference*, trans. Alan Bass (Chicago: University of Chicago Press, 1978): 288.
5. Jacques Derrida, "Semiology and Grammatology: Interview with Julia Kristeva," trans. Alan Bass in *Positions* (Chicago: University of Chicago Press, 1981): 24. First published in *Information sur les sciences sociales* 7 (3 juin 1968).
6. See Spivak's "Preface" to Derrida's *Of Grammatology* (Baltimore: Johns Hopkins University Press, 1976): lxxii.

7. Michael Ryan, *Marxism and Deconstruction* (Baltimore: Johns Hopkins University Press, 1982): 16.

8. For Althusser's own critique of his opposition between ideological and scientific knowing, see his *Essays in Self-Criticism*, trans. Graham Locke (Thetford: New Left Books, 1976).

9. Jacques Derrida, "Positions: Interview with Jean-Louis Houdebine and Guy Scarpetta" in *Positions*, 47. This interview was first published in *Promesse* 30/31 (Autumn/Winter 1971).

In light of my comments concerning the relationship of Derrida to *Tel Quel*, as well as *Tel Quel*'s on the rhetorical strategies of political modernism, it is interesting to reproduce the following translator's note: "On 12 September 1969 *L'Humanité*, the newspaper of the French Communist Party, published an article by Jean Pierre Faye entitled *'Le Camarade Mallarmé'* (Comrade Mallarmé). Faye had been one of the editors of *Tel Quel*, until ideological differences led him to found his own journal, *Change*. Further, *Tel Quel* at the time was openly supporting the French Communist Party. Without mentioning names, Faye attacked *Tel Quel*, alleging, among other things, that 'a language, derived from Germany's extreme-right [in the period between the wars], has been *displaced*, unknown to all, and has been introduced into the Parisian left.' A week later, Philippe Sollers, for *Tel Quel*, and Claude Prevost, a party intellectual, responded to Faye's attack, in letters published both in *L'Humanité* and *Tel Quel*. Both letters attacked Faye for confusing Heidegger with his Nazi interpreters, and accused him of defaming Derrida. Faye insisted upon a counter-response, published in *Tel Quel* 40, which was again counter-attacked, this time by the entire editorial board of *Tel Quel*.

"The ironic sequel to these events is that in June 1971, *Tel Quel* broke with the Communist Party and declared itself Maoist. Eventually Sollers and *Tel Quel* attacked, and broke with, Derrida on political-theoretical grounds. June 1971 is also the date of this interview with Houdebine and Scarpetta, and the date might explain why Houbedine seems to press Derrida more and more, as the interview continues, on the question of Marxism. Houbedine seems to want Derrida to take a yes-or-no *position* on the compatibility of his work with dialectical materialism. Derrida always insists, as he says in the postscript of his letter to Houbedine which concludes this text, on the metaphysical nature of taking a yes-or-no position, preferring the ambiguity of positions, whence the title of this interview.

"This is not the place to pursue further the political history of Sollers and *Tel Quel*. Suffice it to say that neither is any longer Maoist or Communist" (*Positions*, 103-4). Subsequently, *Tel Quel* was dissolved in 1982 and a new journal, *L'Infini*, was launched.

10. Phil Hardy, Claire Johnston, and Paul Willemen, *Edinburgh Magazine* 1 (1976): 5.

11. *Poétique* 24 (1975): 417-25.

12. Tony Bennett, "Text and Social Process: The Case of James Bond," *Screen Education* 41 (Winter/Spring 1982): 6; hereafter refered to as TSP.

13. For example, in "Difference," published two years after "Narrative Space," Heath writes the following: "It is possible with regard to a film or group of films to analyse a discursive organisation, a system of address, a placing—a construction—of the spectator. . . . This is not to say, however, that any and every spectator—and for instance, man or woman, of this class or that—will be completely and equally in the given construction, completely and equally there in the film; and nor then is it to say that the discursive organisation and its production can exhaust—be taken as equivalent to—the effectivity, the potential effects, of a film" (*Screen* 19.3 [Autumn 1978]: 105-6).

14. Bennett's critique of Eco is interestingly compared to that of Teresa de Lauretis. See, for example, *Alice Doesn't*, chapters one and six, and especially, pages 168-82.

15. Tony Bennett, "Texts, Readers, Reading Formations," *Publication of the Midwestern Modern Language Association* 16.1 (Spring 1983): 9-10; hereafter cited as TRRF.

Teresa de Lauretis offers a similar but more succinct critique. In the last chapter of *Alice Doesn't* she writes, "More pointedly than 'the subject of semiotics,' Eco's Model Reader is presented as a *locus* of logical moves, impervious to the heterogeneity of historical process, to difference or contradiction. For the Reader is already contemplated by the text, is in fact an element of its interpretation. Like the Author, the Reader is a textual strategy, a set of specific competences and felicitous conditions established by the text, which must be met if the text is to be 'fully actualized' in it potential content" (176).

16. In "Semiology and Grammatology," Derrida puts his argument in the following terms: "In the extent to which what is called 'meaning' (to be 'expressed') is already, and thoroughly, constituted by a a tissue of differences, in the extent to which there is already a *text*, a network of textual referrals to *other* texts, a textual transformation in which each allegedly 'simple term' is marked by the trace of another term, the presumed interiority of meaning is already worked

upon by its own exteriority. It is always already carried outside itself. It already differs (from itself) before any act of expression. And only on this condition can it constitute a syntagm or text. Only on this condition can it 'signify' " (*Positions*, 33).

17. Paul Willemen, "Notes on Subjectivity," *Screen* 19.1 (Spring 1978): 55; cited hereafter as NOS.

18. The interior citation is from Jameson's *The Political Unconscious* (Methuen: London, 1981), n.p.

19. "Marxism in Literary Criticism," *New Left Review* 108 (March/ April 1978): 82. For the arguments which follow, I am especially indebted to Thomas E. Lewis's "Aesthetic Effect/Ideological Effect," *Enclitic* 7.2 (Fall 1983): 4-16. Also see the last section of Tony Bennett's *Formalism and Marxism* (London: Methuen, 1979).

20. Even Foucault, however, has implicit recourse to a unification of the subject of knowledge. This unification takes place symptomatically across the paradigm of sexual difference as revealed by his incessant use of the masculine, possessive pronoun, but also, and more importantly, by developing the anthropological problematic and critique of the subject across the idea of "man." As Teresa de Lauretis notes, "There is indeed reason to question the theoretical paradigm of a subject-object dialectic, whether Hegelian or Lacanian, that subtends both the aesthetic and the scientific discourses of Western culture; for what that paradigm contains, what those discourses rest on, is the unacknowledged assumption of sexual difference: that the human subject, Man, is the male" (AFT 157). There is a definite sense in which Foucault, while challenging this problem, is himself not exempt from it.

21. British Film Institute, n.d. Also see her "The Subject of Feminist Film Theory/Practice," *Screen* 21.2 (Summer 1980): 27-34.

22. "The Independent Film-makers' Association—Annual General Meeting and Conference," *Screen* 18.1 (Spring 1977): 107-17.

23. Barbara Klinger has thoroughly and brilliantly demonstrated the determinations of context on cinematic meaning. See her *Cinema and Social Process: A Contextual Theory of the Cinema and its Spectators*, dissertation, The University of Iowa, 1986.

24. In my use of terms such as *statement, discourse*, and *speaking subject*, which in the current *episteme* are as inescapable as they are problematic, I follow both Foucault, and in a different way, Teresa de Lauretis in positing "a non-linear semantic space constructed not by one system—language—but by the multilevel interaction of many heterogeneous sign-vehicles and cultural units, the codes being the networks of their correlations *across* the planes of content and

expression. In other words, signification involves several systems or discourses intersecting, superimposed, or juxtaposed to one another, with the codes mapping out paths and positions in a virtual (vertical) semantic space which is discursively, textually and contextually, constituted in each signifying act" (AD 35).

25. Gertrud Koch, "Ex-Changing the Gaze: Re-Visioning Feminist Film Theory," *New German Critique* 34 (Winter 1985): 151-52.

26. *Walter Benjamin, or Towards a Revolutionary Criticism* (London: Verso Editions, 1981): 98.

Index

Index

Note on the Author

D. N. Rodowick is associate professor of American Studies and Comparative Literature, and Director of Undergraduate Studies in film at Yale University, in New Haven, Connecticut.